American Constitu
Powers and Libertı‿s

MW00761389

Third Edition

2011 Supplement

2011 Supplement

American Constitutional Law: Powers and Liberties

Third Edition

Calvin R. Massey
Professor of Law
University of California
Hastings College of Law

Wolters Kluwer
Law & Business

Copyright © 2011 CCH Incorporated.

Published by Wolters Kluwer Law & Business in New York.

Wolters Kluwer Law & Business serves customers worldwide with CCH, Aspen Publishers, and Kluwer Law International products. (www.wolterskluwerlb.com)

To contact Customer Service, e-mail customer.service@wolterskluwer.com, call 1-800-234-1660, fax 1-800-901-9075, or mail correspondence to:

Wolters Kluwer Law & Business
Attn: Order Department
PO Box 990
Frederick, MD 21705

Printed in the United States of America.

1 2 3 4 5 6 7 8 9 0

ISBN 978-0-7355-0736-4

Library of Congress Cataloging-in-Publication Data

Massey, Calvin R.

    American constitutional law : powers and liberties/Calvin Massey. — 3rd ed.
      p. cm.
    Includes index.
    ISBN 978-0-7355-7856-2 (casebook)
    ISBN 978-0-7355-0736-4 (supplement)
1. Constitutional law — United States — Cases. I. Title.

KF4549.M318 2005
342.73 — dc22

                                   2005000972

About Wolters Kluwer Law & Business

Wolters Kluwer Law & Business is a leading global provider of intelligent information and digital solutions for legal and business professionals in key specialty areas, and respected educational resources for professors and law students. Wolters Kluwer Law & Business connects legal and business professionals as well as those in the education market with timely, specialized authoritative content and information-enabled solutions to support success through productivity, accuracy and mobility.

Serving customers worldwide, Wolters Kluwer Law & Business products include those under the Aspen Publishers, CCH, Kluwer Law International, Loislaw, Best Case, ftwilliam.com and MediRegs family of products.

CCH products have been a trusted resource since 1913, and are highly regarded resources for legal, securities, antitrust and trade regulation, government contracting, banking, pension, payroll, employment and labor, and healthcare reimbursement and compliance professionals.

Aspen Publishers products provide essential information to attorneys, business professionals and law students. Written by preeminent authorities, the product line offers analytical and practical information in a range of specialty practice areas from securities law and intellectual property to mergers and acquisitions and pension/benefits. Aspen's trusted legal education resources provide professors and students with high-quality, up-to-date and effective resources for successful instruction and study in all areas of the law.

Kluwer Law International products provide the global business community with reliable international legal information in English. Legal practitioners, corporate counsel and business executives around the world rely on Kluwer Law journals, looseleafs, books, and electronic products for comprehensive information in many areas of international legal practice.

Loislaw is a comprehensive online legal research product providing legal content to law firm practitioners of various specializations. Loislaw provides attorneys with the ability to quickly and efficiently find the necessary legal information they need, when and where they need it, by facilitating access to primary law as well as state-specific law, records, forms and treatises.

Best Case Solutions is the leading bankruptcy software product to the bankruptcy industry. It provides software and workflow tools to flawlessly streamline petition preparation and the electronic filing process, while timely incorporating ever-changing court requirements.

ftwilliam.com offers employee benefits professionals the highest quality plan documents (retirement, welfare and non-qualified) and government forms (5500/PBGC, 1099 and IRS) software at highly competitive prices.

MediRegs products provide integrated health care compliance content and software solutions for professionals in healthcare, higher education and life sciences, including professionals in accounting, law and consulting.

Wolters Kluwer Law & Business, a division of Wolters Kluwer, is headquartered in New York. Wolters Kluwer is a market-leading global information services company focused on professionals.

Contents

Table of Cases

American Constitutional Law: Powers and Liberties

Third Edition

2011 Supplement

Chapter 2
Doctrines Limiting the Scope of Judicial Review

C. Justiciability: The Proper Role of the Federal Courts

2. Standing to Sue

a. The Constitutional Core of Standing

Page 77: Insert at the end of note 1a:

In Summers v. Earth Island Institute, 555 U.S. 488 (2009), the Court reiterated the necessity of establishing personal immediate injury in fact. Earth Island and other environmental interest groups challenged the validity of the Forest Service's regulations that exempt small fire-rehabilitation and timber salvage projects from notice, comment, and appeal processes that generally apply to Forest Service land use regulations. One member of the plaintiff organizations successfully established that he had a personal injury in fact with respect to an exempt project to be undertaken in a discrete area known as Burnt Ridge. After the Burnt Ridge controversy had been settled and was no longer at issue the plaintiffs continued to assert that they had standing "to challenge the regulations in the absence of a live dispute over a concrete application of those regulations." The Ninth Circuit upheld a district court's nationwide injunction of the regulations that had been at issue in the Burnt Ridge project. The Supreme Court reversed.

The regulations "neither require nor forbid any action on the part of respondents [but] govern only the conduct of Forest Service officials engaged in project planning." To establish injury in fact the plaintiffs were required to show that "application of the regulations by the Government will affect *them*." They were unable to do so because they could not point to any interest of any of their members that would be immediately threatened by the regulations. The mere statistical probability that some unknown number of the plaintiff organizations' members would suffer personalized injury in some unknown place at some unknown future time was insufficient.

Nor was there a sufficient procedural injury. The fact that the plaintiff organizations had lost the ability to comment on small fire-rehabilitation and

1

timber salvage projects was irrelevant because "deprivation of a procedural right without some concrete interest that is affected by the deprivation — a procedural right *in vacuo* — is insufficient to create Article III standing." While Congress can "can loosen the strictures of the redressability prong of our standing inquiry — so that standing existed with regard to the Burnt Ridge Project, for example, despite the possibility that Earth Island's allegedly guaranteed right to comment would not be successful in persuading the Forest Service to avoid impairment of Earth Island's concrete interests [—] the requirement of injury in fact is a hard floor of Article III jurisdiction that cannot be removed by statute."

Page 94: Insert at the end of note 4:

ARIZONA CHRISTIAN SCHOOL TUITION ORGANIZATION v. WINN
131 S. Ct. 1436 (2011)

JUSTICE KENNEDY delivered the opinion of the Court.

Arizona provides tax credits for contributions to school tuition organizations, or STOs. STOs use these contributions to provide scholarships to students attending private schools, many of which are religious. Respondents are a group of Arizona taxpayers who challenge the STO tax credit as a violation of Establishment Clause principles under the First and Fourteenth Amendments. . . .

To obtain a determination on the merits in federal court, parties seeking relief must show that they have standing under Article III of the Constitution. Standing in Establishment Clause cases may be shown in various ways. Some plaintiffs may demonstrate standing based on the direct harm of what is claimed to be an establishment of religion, such as a mandatory prayer in a public school classroom. School Dist. of Abington Township v. Schempp. Other plaintiffs may demonstrate standing on the ground that they have incurred a cost or been denied a benefit on account of their religion. Those costs and benefits can result from alleged discrimination in the tax code, such as when the availability of a tax exemption is conditioned on religious affiliation. Texas Monthly, Inc. v. Bullock (plurality opinion).

For their part, respondents contend that they have standing to challenge Arizona's STO tax credit for one and only one reason: because they are Arizona taxpayers. But the mere fact that a plaintiff is a taxpayer is not generally deemed sufficient to establish standing in federal court. To overcome that rule, respondents must rely on an exception created in Flast v. Cohen. For the reasons discussed below, respondents cannot take advantage of *Flast*'s narrow exception to the general rule against taxpayer standing. As a consequence, respondents lacked standing to commence this action, and their suit must be dismissed for want of jurisdiction.

I. Respondents challenged § 43-1089, a provision of the Arizona Tax Code [that] allows Arizona taxpayers to obtain dollar-for-dollar tax credits of up to $500 per person and $1,000 per married couple for contributions to STOs. If the credit exceeds an individual's tax liability, the credit's unused portion can be carried forward up to five years. [A] charitable organization could be deemed an STO only upon certain conditions. The organization was required to be exempt from federal taxation under § 501(c)(3) of the Internal Revenue Code of 1986. It could not limit its scholarships to students attending only one school. And it had to allocate "at least ninety per cent of its annual revenue for educational scholarships or tuition grants" to children attending qualified schools. A "qualified school," in turn, was defined in part as a private school in Arizona that did not discriminate on the basis of race, color, handicap, familial status, or national origin.

In an earlier lawsuit filed in state court, Arizona taxpayers challenged § 43-1089, invoking both the United States Constitution and the Arizona Constitution. The Arizona Supreme Court rejected the taxpayers' claims on the merits. Kotterman v. Killian, 193 Ariz. 273, 972 P.2d 606 (1999). This Court denied certiorari. Rhodes v. Killian, 528 U.S. 810 (1999); Kotterman v. Killian, 528 U.S. 921 (1999).

The present action was filed in the United States District Court for the District of Arizona. It named the Director of the Arizona Department of Revenue as defendant. The Arizona taxpayers who brought the suit claimed that § 43-1089 violates the Establishment Clause of the First Amendment, as incorporated against the States by the Fourteenth Amendment. Respondents alleged that § 43-1089 allows STOs "to use State income-tax revenues to pay tuition for students at religious schools," some of which "discriminate on the basis of religion in selecting students."

Respondents requested . . . an injunction against the issuance of § 43-1089 tax credits for contributions to religious STOs. The . . . Arizona Christian School Tuition Organization and other interested parties intervened. The District Court . . . dismissed respondents' suit . . . for failure to state a claim. [The] Court of Appeals reversed, [holding] that respondents had standing under *Flast*. Reaching the merits, the Court of Appeals ruled that respondents had stated a claim that § 43-1089 violated the Establishment Clause of the First Amendment. . . . This Court granted certiorari.

II. . . . Under Article III, the Federal Judiciary is vested with the "Power to resolve not questions and issues but "Cases" or "Controversies." This language restricts the federal judicial power "to the traditional role of the Anglo-American courts." Summers v. Earth Island Institute, 555 U.S. 483 (2009). . . . By rules consistent with the longstanding practices of Anglo-American courts a plaintiff who seeks to invoke the federal judicial power must assert more than just the "generalized interest of all citizens in constitutional governance." Schlesinger v. Reservists Comm. to Stop the War, 418 U.S. 208 (1974). Continued adherence to the case-or-controversy requirement of Article III maintains the public's confidence in an unelected but restrained Federal Judiciary. If the judicial power were "extended to every *question* under the constitution," Chief Justice Marshall once explained, federal courts might take possession of "almost every subject proper for legislative discussion and decision." 4 Papers of John Marshall 95 (C. Cullen ed. 1984) (quoted in DaimlerChrysler Corp. v. Cuno, 547 U.S. 332, 341

(2006)). . . . For the federal courts to decide questions of law arising outside of cases and controversies would be inimical to the Constitution's democratic character. And the resulting conflict between the judicial and the political branches would not, "in the long run, be beneficial to either." United States v. Richardson, 418 U.S. 166, 188-189 (1974) (Powell, J., concurring). . . .

III. To state a case or controversy under Article III, a plaintiff must establish standing. The minimum constitutional requirements for standing were explained in Lujan v. Defenders of Wildlife.

> First, the plaintiff must have suffered an "injury in fact" — an invasion of a legally protected interest which is (a) concrete and particularized, and (b) "actual or imminent," not "conjectural" or "hypothetical." Second, there must be a causal connection between the injury and the conduct complained of — the injury has to be "fairly . . . trace[able] to the challenged action of the defendant, and not . . . th[e] result [of] the independent action of some third party not before the court." Third, it must be "likely," as opposed to merely "speculative," that the injury will be "redressed by a favorable decision."

In requiring a particular injury, the Court meant "that the injury must affect the plaintiff in a personal and individual way." . . .

A. Respondents suggest that their status as Arizona taxpayers provides them with standing to challenge the STO tax credit. Absent special circumstances, however, standing cannot be based on a plaintiff's mere status as a taxpayer. This Court has rejected the general proposition that an individual who has paid taxes has a "continuing, legally cognizable interest in ensuring that those funds are not *used* by the Government in a way that violates the Constitution." Hein v. Freedom From Religion Foundation, Inc., 551 U.S. 587, 599 (2007) (plurality opinion). . . . The doctrinal basis for the rule was discussed in Massachusetts v. Mellon, 262 U.S. 447 (1923). There, a taxpayer-plaintiff had alleged that certain federal expenditures were in excess of congressional authority under the Constitution. The plaintiff argued that she had standing to raise her claim because she had an interest in the Government Treasury and because the allegedly unconstitutional expenditure of Government funds would affect her personal tax liability. The Court rejected those arguments. The "effect upon future taxation, of any payment out of funds," was too "remote, fluctuating and uncertain" to give rise to a case or controversy. And the taxpayer-plaintiff's "interest in the moneys of the Treasury," the Court recognized, was necessarily "shared with millions of others." As a consequence, *Frothingham* held that the taxpayer-plaintiff had not presented a "judicial controversy" appropriate for resolution in federal court but rather a "matter of public . . . concern" that could be pursued only through the political process.

In . . . Doremus v. Board of Ed. of Hawthorne, 342 U.S. 429 (1952), the Court considered *Frothingham*'s prohibition on taxpayer standing in connection with an alleged Establishment Clause violation. A New Jersey statute had provided that public school teachers would read Bible verses to their students at the start of each school day. A plaintiff sought to have the law enjoined, asserting standing based on her status as a taxpayer. Writing for the Court, Justice Jackson reiterated the foundational role that Article III standing plays in our separation of powers. "'The party who invokes the power [of the federal courts] must be able to show not only that the statute is invalid, but that he has sustained or is immediately in danger of sustaining some direct injury as a result of its enforcement, and not merely that he suffers in some indefinite way in common with people generally.'"

The plaintiff in *Doremus* lacked any direct and particular financial interest in the suit, and, as a result, a decision on the merits would have been merely advisory." It followed that the plaintiff's allegations did not give rise to a case or controversy subject to judicial resolution under Article III. Cf. *Schempp* (finding standing where state laws required Bible readings or prayer in public schools, not because plaintiffs were state taxpayers but because their children were enrolled in public schools and so were "directly affected" by the challenged laws). . . .

[Recent] decisions have explained that claims of taxpayer standing rest on unjustifiable economic and political speculation. When a government expends resources or declines to impose a tax, its budget does not necessarily suffer. On the contrary, the purpose of many governmental expenditures and tax benefits is "to spur economic activity, which in turn *increases* government revenues." *DaimlerChrysler*. Difficulties persist even if one assumes that an expenditure or tax benefit depletes the government's coffers. To find injury, a court must speculate "that elected officials will increase a taxpayer-plaintiff's tax bill to make up a deficit." And to find redressability, a court must assume that, were the remedy the taxpayers seek to be allowed, "legislators will pass along the supposed increased revenue in the form of tax reductions." It would be "pure speculation" to conclude that an injunction against a government expenditure or tax benefit "would result in any actual tax relief" for a taxpayer-plaintiff.

These well-established principles apply to the present cases. Respondents may be right that Arizona's STO tax credits have an estimated annual value of over $50 million. The education of its young people is, of course, one of the State's principal missions and responsibilities; and the consequent costs will make up a significant portion of the state budget. That, however, is just the beginning of the analysis. By helping students obtain scholarships to private schools, both religious and secular, the STO program might relieve the burden placed on Arizona's public schools. The result could be an immediate and permanent cost savings for the State. Underscoring the potential financial benefits of the STO program, the average value of an STO scholarship may be far less than the average cost of educating an Arizona public school student. Because it encourages scholarships for attendance at private schools, the STO tax credit may not cause the State to incur any financial loss.

Even assuming the STO tax credit has an adverse effect on Arizona's annual budget, problems would remain. To conclude there is a particular injury in fact would require speculation that Arizona lawmakers react to revenue shortfalls by increasing respondents' tax liability. A finding of causation would depend on the additional determination that any tax increase would be traceable to the STO tax credits, as distinct from other governmental expenditures or other tax benefits. Respondents have not established that an injunction against application of the STO tax credit would prompt Arizona legislators to "pass along the supposed increased revenue in the form of tax reductions." Those matters, too, are conjectural.

Each of the inferential steps to show causation and redressability depends on premises as to which there remains considerable doubt. The taxpayers have not shown that any interest they have in protecting the State Treasury would be advanced. Even were they to show some closer link, that interest is still of a general character, not particular to certain persons. Nor have the taxpayers shown that higher taxes will result from the tuition credit scheme. The rule against taxpayer standing, a rule designed both to avoid speculation and to insist on particular injury, applies to respondents' lawsuit. The taxpayers, then, must rely on an exception to the rule, an exception next to be considered.

B. The primary contention of respondents . . . is that . . . their suit falls within the exception established by *Flast*. . . . At issue in *Flast* was the standing of federal taxpayers to object, on First Amendment grounds, to a congressional statute that allowed expenditures of federal funds from the General Treasury to support, among other programs, "instruction in reading, arithmetic, and other subjects in religious schools, and to purchase textbooks and other instructional materials for use in such schools." *Flast* held that taxpayers have standing when two conditions are met.

The first condition is that there must be a "logical link" between the plaintiff's taxpayer status "and the type of legislative enactment attacked." This condition was not satisfied in *Doremus* because the statute challenged in that case — providing for the recitation of Bible passages in public schools — involved at most an "incidental expenditure of tax funds." In *Flast*, by contrast, the allegation was that the Federal Government violated the Establishment Clause in the exercise of its legislative authority both to collect and spend tax dollars. In the decades since *Flast*, the Court has been careful to enforce this requirement. *Hein* (no standing under *Flast* to challenge federal executive actions funded by general appropriations); *Valley Forge* (no standing under *Flast* to challenge an agency's decision to transfer a parcel of federal property pursuant to the Property Clause).

The second condition for standing under *Flast* is that there must be "a nexus" between the plaintiff's taxpayer status and "the precise nature of the constitutional infringement alleged." This condition was deemed satisfied in *Flast* based on the allegation that Government funds had been spent on an outlay for religion in contravention of the Establishment Clause. In *Frothingham*, by contrast, the claim was that Congress had exceeded its constitutional authority without regard to any specific prohibition. Confirming that *Flast* turned on the unique features of Establishment Clause violations, this Court has "declined to lower the taxpayer standing bar in suits alleging violations of any constitutional provision apart from the Establishment Clause." *Hein* (plurality opinion); see also

Richardson (Statement and Account Clause); *Schlesinger* (Incompatibility Clause).

After stating the two conditions for taxpayer standing, *Flast* considered them together, explaining that individuals suffer a particular injury for standing purposes when, in violation of the Establishment Clause and by means of "the taxing and spending power," their property is transferred through the Government's Treasury to a sectarian entity. As *Flast* put it: "The taxpayer's allegation in such cases would be that his tax money is being extracted and spent in violation of specific constitutional protections against such abuses of legislative power." *Flast* thus "understood the 'injury' alleged in Establishment Clause challenges to federal spending to be the very 'extract[ion] and spen[ding]' of 'tax money' in aid of religion alleged by a plaintiff." *DaimlerChrysler* (quoting *Flast*). "Such an injury," *Flast* continued, is unlike "generalized grievances about the conduct of government" and so is "appropriate for judicial redress."

Flast found support for its finding of personal injury in "the history of the Establishment Clause," particularly James Madison's Memorial and Remonstrance Against Religious Assessments. In 1785, the General Assembly of the Commonwealth of Virginia considered a "tax levy to support teachers of the Christian religion." Under the proposed assessment bill, taxpayers would direct their payments to Christian societies of their choosing. If a taxpayer made no such choice, the General Assembly was to divert his funds to "seminaries of learning," at least some of which "undoubtedly would have been religious in character." However the "seminaries" provision might have functioned in practice, critics took the position that the proposed bill threatened compulsory religious contributions. In the Memorial and Remonstrance, Madison objected to the proposed assessment on the ground that it would coerce a form of religious devotion in violation of conscience. In Madison's view, government should not "force a citizen to contribute three pence only of his property for the support of any one establishment." This Madisonian prohibition does not depend on the amount of property conscripted for sectarian ends. Any such taking, even one amounting to "three pence only," violates conscience. The proposed bill ultimately died in committee; and the General Assembly instead enacted legislation forbidding "compelled" support of religion. Madison himself went on to become, as *Flast* put it, "the leading architect of the religion clauses of the First Amendment." *Flast* was thus informed by "the specific evils" identified in the public arguments of "those who drafted the Establishment Clause and fought for its adoption." Respondents contend that these principles demonstrate their standing to challenge the STO tax credit. In their view the tax credit is, for *Flast* purposes, best understood as a governmental expenditure. That is incorrect.

It is easy to see that tax credits and governmental expenditures can have similar economic consequences, at least for beneficiaries whose tax liability is sufficiently large to take full advantage of the credit. Yet tax credits and governmental expenditures do not both implicate individual taxpayers in sectarian activities. A dissenter whose tax dollars are "extracted and spent" knows that he has in some small measure been made to contribute to an establishment in violation of conscience. In that instance the taxpayer's direct and particular connection with the establishment does not depend on economic speculation or political conjecture. The connection would exist even if the conscientious dissenter's tax liability were unaffected or reduced. When the government declines to impose a tax, by contrast, there is no such connection between dissenting taxpayer and alleged establishment. Any financial injury remains speculative. And awarding some citizens a tax credit allows other citizens to retain control over their own funds in accordance with their own consciences.

The distinction between governmental expenditures and tax credits refutes respondents' assertion of standing. When Arizona taxpayers choose to contribute to STOs, they spend their own money, not money the State has collected from respondents or from other taxpayers. Arizona's § 43-1089 does not "extrac[t] and spen[d]" a conscientious dissenter's funds in service of an establishment, or "'force a citizen to contribute three pence only of his property'" to a sectarian organization. On the contrary, respondents and other Arizona taxpayers remain free to pay their own tax bills, without contributing to an STO. Respondents are likewise able to contribute to an STO of their choice, either religious or secular. And respondents also have the option of contributing to other charitable organizations, in which case respondents may become eligible for a tax deduction or a different tax credit. The STO tax credit is not tantamount to a religious tax or to a tithe and does not visit the injury identified in *Flast*. It follows that respondents have neither alleged an injury for standing purposes under general rules nor met the *Flast* exception. Finding standing under these circumstances would be . . . a departure from *Flast*'s stated rationale.

Furthermore, respondents cannot satisfy the requirements of causation and redressability. When the government collects and spends taxpayer money, governmental choices are responsible for the transfer of wealth. In that case a resulting subsidy of religious activity is, for purposes of *Flast*, traceable to the government's expenditures. And an injunction against those expenditures would address the objections of conscience raised by taxpayer-plaintiffs. Here, by contrast, contributions result from the decisions of private taxpayers regarding their own funds. Private citizens create private STOs; STOs choose beneficiary schools; and taxpayers then contribute to STOs. While the State, at the outset, affords the opportunity to create and contribute to an STO, the tax credit system is implemented by private action and with no state intervention. Objecting taxpayers know that their fellow citizens, not the State, decide to contribute and in fact make the contribution. These considerations prevent any injury the objectors may suffer from being fairly traceable to the government. And while an injunction against application of the tax credit most likely would reduce contributions to STOs, that remedy would not affect non-contributing taxpayers or their tax payments. As a result, any injury suffered by respondents would not be remedied by an injunction limiting the tax credit's operation.

[Respondents] suggest that Arizonans who benefit from § 43-1089 tax credits in effect are paying their state income tax to STOs. In respondents' view, tax credits give rise to standing even if tax deductions do not, since only the former yield a dollar-for-dollar reduction in final tax liability. But what matters under *Flast* is whether sectarian STOs receive government funds drawn from general tax revenues, so that moneys have been extracted from a citizen and handed to a religious institution in violation of the citizen's conscience. Under that inquiry, respondents' argument fails. Like contributions that lead to charitable tax deductions, contributions yielding STO tax credits are not owed to the State and, in fact, pass directly from taxpayers to private organizations. Respondents' contrary position assumes that income should be treated as if it were government property even if it has not come into the tax collector's hands. That premise finds no basis in standing jurisprudence. Private bank accounts cannot be equated with the Arizona State Treasury. . . . [Reversed.]

JUSTICE SCALIA, with whom JUSTICE THOMAS joins, concurring.

Taxpayers ordinarily do not have standing to challenge federal or state expenditures that allegedly violate the Constitution. In *Flast*, we created a narrow exception for taxpayers raising Establishment Clause challenges to government expenditures. Today's majority and dissent struggle with whether respondents' challenge to the Arizona tuition tax credit falls within that narrow exception. Under a principled reading of Article III, their struggles are unnecessary. *Flast* is an anomaly in our jurisprudence, irreconcilable with the Article III restrictions on federal judicial power that our opinions have established. I would repudiate that misguided decision and enforce the Constitution. I nevertheless join the Court's opinion because it finds respondents lack standing by applying *Flast* rather than distinguishing it away on unprincipled grounds. Cf. *Hein*.

JUSTICE KAGAN, with whom JUSTICE GINSBURG, JUSTICE BREYER, and JUSTICE SOTOMAYOR join, dissenting.

Since its inception, the Arizona private-school-tuition tax credit has cost the State, by its own estimate, nearly $350 million in diverted tax revenue. The Arizona taxpayers who instituted this suit (collectively, Plaintiffs) allege that the use of these funds to subsidize school tuition organizations (STOs) breaches the Establishment Clause. . . . Many of these STOs, the Plaintiffs claim, discriminate on the basis of a child's religion when awarding scholarships. . . . Today, the Court [holds that these] litigants lack standing . . . because the funding of religion they challenge comes from a tax credit, rather than an appropriation. . . . Cash grants and targeted tax breaks are means of accomplishing the same government objective — to provide financial support to select individuals or organizations. Taxpayers who oppose state aid of religion have equal reason to protest whether that aid flows from the one form of subsidy or the other. Either way, the government has financed the religious activity. And so either way, taxpayers should be able to challenge the subsidy.

Still worse, the Court's arbitrary distinction threatens to eliminate *all* occasions for a taxpayer to contest the government's monetary support of religion. Precisely because appropriations and tax breaks can achieve identical objectives, the government can easily substitute one for the other. Today's opinion thus enables the government to end-run *Flast*'s guarantee of access to the Judiciary. From now on, the government need follow just one simple rule — subsidize through the tax system — to preclude taxpayer challenges to state funding of religion. And that result — the effective demise of taxpayer standing — will diminish the Establishment Clause's force and meaning. . . .

Plaintiffs . . . attack a provision of the Arizona tax code that the legislature enacted pursuant to the State Constitution's taxing and spending clause (*Flast* nexus, part 1). And they allege that this provision violates the Establishment Clause (*Flast* nexus, part 2). By satisfying both of *Flast*'s conditions, the Plaintiffs have demonstrated their "stake as taxpayers" in enforcing constitutional restraints on the provision of aid to STOs. . . .

The majority reaches a contrary decision by distinguishing between two methods of financing religion: A taxpayer has standing to challenge state subsidies to religion, the Court announces, when the mechanism used is an appropriation, but not when the mechanism is a targeted tax break, otherwise called a "tax expenditure." In the former case, but not in the latter, the Court declares, the taxpayer suffers cognizable injury.

But this distinction finds no support in case law, and just as little in reason. In the decades since *Flast*, no court . . . has differentiated between appropriations and tax expenditures in deciding whether litigants have standing. Over and over again, courts (including this one) have faced Establishment Clause challenges to tax credits, deductions, and exemptions; over and over again, these courts have reached the merits of these claims. And that is for a simple reason: Taxpayers experience the same injury for standing purposes whether government subsidization of religion takes the form of a cash grant or a tax measure. The only rationale the majority offers for its newfound distinction — that grants, but not tax expenditures, somehow come from a complaining taxpayer's own wallet — cannot bear the weight the Court places on it. If *Flast* is still good law — and the majority today says nothing to the contrary — then the Plaintiffs should be able to pursue their claim on the merits. . . .

Our taxpayer standing cases have declined to distinguish between appropriations and tax expenditures for a simple reason: . . . the distinction is one in search of a difference. To begin to see why, consider an example far afield from *Flast* and, indeed, from religion. Imagine that the Federal Government decides it should pay hundreds of billions of dollars to insolvent banks in the midst of a financial crisis. Suppose, too, that many millions of taxpayers oppose this bailout on the ground (whether right or wrong is immaterial) that it uses their hard-earned money to reward irresponsible business behavior. In the face of this hostility, some Members of Congress make the following proposal: Rather than give the money to banks via appropriations, the Government will allow banks to subtract the exact same amount from the tax bill they would otherwise have to pay to the U.S. Treasury. Would this proposal calm the furor? Or would most taxpayers respond by saying that a subsidy is a subsidy (or a bailout is a bailout), whether accomplished by the one means or by the other? Surely the latter; indeed, we would think the less of our countrymen if they failed to see through this cynical proposal.

And what ordinary people would appreciate, this Court's case law also recognizes — that targeted tax breaks are often "economically and functionally indistinguishable from a direct monetary subsidy." Rosenberger v. Rector and Visitors of Univ. of Va. (Thomas, J., concurring). Tax credits, deductions, and exemptions provided to an individual or organization have "much the same effect as a cash grant to the [recipient] of the amount of tax it would have to pay" absent the tax break. Regan v. Taxation With Representation of Wash. "Our opinions," therefore, "have long recognized . . . the reality that [tax expenditures] are a form of subsidy that is administered through the tax system." Arkansas Writers' Project, Inc. v. Ragland, 481 U.S. 221, 236 (1987) (Scalia, J., dissenting). . . .

And because these financing mechanisms result in the same bottom line, taxpayers challenging them can allege the same harm. . . . Whenever taxpayers have standing under *Flast* to challenge an appropriation, they should also have standing to contest a tax expenditure. Their access to the federal courts should not depend on which type of financial subsidy the State has offered.

Consider some further examples of the point, but this time concerning state funding of religion. Suppose a State desires to reward Jews — by, say, $500 per year — for their religious devotion. Should the nature of taxpayers' concern vary if the State allows Jews to claim the aid on their tax returns, in lieu of receiving an annual stipend? Or assume a State wishes to subsidize the ownership of crucifixes. It could purchase the religious symbols in bulk and distribute them to all takers. Or it could mail a reimbursement check to any individual who buys her own and submits a receipt for the purchase. Or it could authorize that person to claim a tax credit equal to the price she paid. Now, really — do taxpayers have less reason to complain if the State selects the last of these three options? The Court today says they do, but that is wrong. The effect of each form of subsidy is the same, on the public fisc and on those who contribute to it. Regardless of which mechanism the State uses, taxpayers have an identical stake in ensuring that the State's exercise of its taxing and spending power complies with the Constitution.[7]

Here, the mechanism Arizona has selected is a dollar-for-dollar tax credit to aid school tuition organizations. Each year come April 15, the State tells Arizonans: Either pay the full amount of your tax liability to the State, or subtract up to $500 from your tax bill by contributing that sum to an STO. To claim the credit, an individual makes a notation on her tax return and splits her tax payment into two checks, one made out to the State and the other to the STO. [The] STO payment is therefore "costless" to the individual; it comes out of what she otherwise would be legally obligated to pay the State — hence, out of public resources. And STOs capitalize on this aspect of the tax credit for all it is worth — which is quite a lot. To drum up support, STOs highlight that "donations" are made not with an individual's own, but with . . . taxpayers' money. One STO advertises that

---

7. The majority indicates that some persons could challenge these hypothetical government actions based on individualized injury, separate and apart from taxpayer status. . . . That is quite right; indeed, some parents or children likely have standing to challenge the Arizona tax credit on such grounds. But this possibility does not detract from the point made here. The purpose of these illustrations is to show that *if* taxpayer status is the thing alleged to confer standing, it should do so irrespective of the form of the government subsidy.

"[w]ith Arizona's scholarship tax credit, you can send children to our community's [religious] day schools and it won't cost you a dime!" Another urges potential donors to "imagine giving [to charity] with someone else's money . . . . Stop Imagining, thanks to Arizona tax laws you can!" And so Arizonans do just that: It is, after all, good fun to spend other people's money. . . .

The majority offers just one reason to distinguish appropriations and tax expenditures: A taxpayer experiences injury, the Court asserts, only when the government "extracts and spends" her very own tax dollars to aid religion. In other words, a taxpayer suffers legally cognizable harm if but only if her particular tax dollars wind up in a religious organization's coffers. . . .

The majority purports to rely on *Flast* to support this new "extraction" requirement. . . . [Here] is how *Flast* primarily justified its holding: "[O]ne of the specific evils feared by those who drafted the Establishment Clause and fought for its adoption was that the taxing and spending power would be used to favor one religion over another or to support religion in general." That evil arises even if the specific dollars that the government uses do not come from citizens who object to the preference. . . .

And something still deeper is wrong with the majority's "extract and spend" requirement: It does not measure what matters under the Establishment Clause. . . . [C]onsider the following example: Imagine the Internal Revenue Service places a checkbox on tax returns asking filers if they object to the government using their taxes to aid religion. If the government keeps "yes" money separate from "no" money and subsidizes religious activities only from the nonobjectors' account, the majority's analysis suggests that no taxpayer would have standing to allege a violation of the Establishment Clause. The funds used, after all, would not have been "extracted from a citizen and handed to a religious institution in violation of the citizen's conscience." But this Court has never indicated that States may insulate subsidies to religious organizations from legal challenge by eliciting the consent of some taxpayers. . . . Taxpayers incur the same harm, and should have the same ability to bring suit, whether the government stores tax funds in one bank account or two. . . .

As the majority notes, Madison's Memorial and Remonstrance criticized a tax levy proposed in Virginia to aid teachers of the Christian religion. But Madison's passionate opposition to that proposal informs this case in a manner different than the majority suggests. The Virginia tax in fact would not have extracted any monies (not even "three pence") from unwilling citizens, as the Court now requires. The plan allowed conscientious objectors to opt out of subsidizing religion by contributing their assessment to an alternative fund for the construction and maintenance of county schools. Indeed, the Virginia Assessment was specifically "designed to avoid any charges of coercion of dissenters to pay taxes to support religious teachings with which they disagreed." Feldman, Intellectual Origins of the Establishment Clause, 77 N.Y.U.L. Rev. 346, 383 (2002). In this respect, the Virginia Assessment is just like the Arizona tax credit. Although both funnel tax funds to religious organizations (and so saddle *all* taxpayers with the cost), neither forces any given taxpayer to pay for the subsidy out of her pocket.

Madison thought that feature of the Assessment insufficient to save it. By relying on the selfsame aspect of the Arizona scheme to deny the Plaintiffs' claim of injury, the majority betrays Madison's vision. . . .

Today's decision devastates taxpayer standing in Establishment Clause cases. The government, after all, often uses tax expenditures to subsidize favored persons and activities. Still more, the government almost *always* has this option. Appropriations and tax subsidies are readily interchangeable; what is a cash grant today can be a tax break tomorrow. The Court's opinion thus offers a roadmap — more truly, just a one-step instruction — to any government that wishes to insulate its financing of religious activity from legal challenge. Structure the funding as a tax expenditure, and *Flast* will not stand in the way. No taxpayer will have standing to object. However blatantly the government may violate the Establishment Clause, taxpayers cannot gain access to the federal courts. . . .

I respectfully dissent.

c. *Organizational Standing*

Page 96: Insert at the end of the section:

In Summers v. Earth Island Institute, 555 U.S. 488 (2009), the Court repeated the requirement that organizations must "make specific allegations establishing that at least one identified member had suffered or would suffer harm." The dissent proposed that "a statistical probability that some of those members are threatened with concrete injury" should suffice, a contention that the majority said would "replace the requirement of 'imminent' harm . . . with the require-ment of 'a *realistic* threat that reoccurrence of the challenged activity would cause [the plaintiff] harm in the reasonably near future.' "

Chapter 3

The Limits of Federal Legislative Power: Judicially or Politically Enforceable Federalism?

A. Implementing Enumerated Powers and "Default" Rules

1. Implementing Enumerated Powers: The "Necessary and Proper Clause"

Page 141: Insert at the end of section 1, following note 3:

UNITED STATES v. COMSTOCK
130 S. Ct. 1949 (2010)

JUSTICE BREYER delivered the opinion of the Court.

[Federal law permits a district court to order the civil commitment of federal prisoners, even after they have completed their prison sentence, if they have "engaged or attempted to engage in sexually violent conduct or child molestation," currently "suffer[] from a serious mental illness, abnormality, or disorder," and are "sexually dangerous to others." To obtain a civil commitment order, the U.S. Government must prove these facts by clear and convincing evidence. When a civil commitment order is entered, the Attorney General must make "all reasonable efforts" to cause the state of the prisoner's domicile or where he was tried to "assume responsibility for his custody, care, and treatment." Should those efforts fail, the Attorney General is commanded to "place the person for treatment in a suitable [federal] facility" until either the prisoner is deemed no longer to be dangerous or a state assumes responsibility for his custody, in which case the prisoner is to be transferred to the custody of that state. 18 U.S.C. § 4248.]

. . . We have previously examined similar statutes enacted under state law to determine whether they violate the Due Process Clause. See Kansas v. Hendricks, 521 U.S. 346, 356-358 (1997); Kansas v. Crane, 534 U.S. 407 (2002). But this case presents a different question. Here we ask whether the Federal Government has the authority under Article I of the Constitution to enact this federal civil-commitment program or whether its doing so falls beyond the reach of a government "of enumerated powers." [*McCulloch.*] We conclude that the

15

Constitution grants Congress the authority to enact § 4248 as "necessary and proper for carrying into Execution" the powers "vested by" the "Constitution in the Government of the United States." Art. I, § 8, cl.18.

[Among other claims, respondent prisoners contended that Congress, by enacting § 4248 (which authorized their civil commitment),] exceeded the powers granted to it by Art. I, § 8 of the Constitution, including those granted by the Commerce Clause and the Necessary and Proper Clause. The District Court . . . agreed that . . . Congress exceeded its Article I legislative powers. On appeal, . . . the Fourth Circuit [affirmed on this ground.]

II. The question presented is whether the Necessary and Proper Clause . . . grants Congress authority sufficient to enact the statute before us. In resolving that question, we assume, but we do not decide, that other provisions of the Constitution — such as the Due Process Clause — do not prohibit civil commitment in these circumstances. . . . On that assumption, we conclude that the Constitution grants Congress legislative power sufficient to enact § 4248. We base this conclusion on five considerations, taken together.

First, the Necessary and Proper Clause grants Congress broad authority to enact federal legislation. Nearly 200 years ago, this Court stated that the Federal "[G]overnment is acknowledged by all to be one of enumerated powers," [*McCulloch*], which means that "[e]very law enacted by Congress must be based on one or more of" those powers. But, at the same time, "a government, entrusted with such" powers "must also be entrusted with ample means for their execution." [*McCulloch*.] Accordingly, the Necessary and Proper Clause makes clear that the Constitution's grants of specific federal legislative authority are accompanied by broad power to enact laws that are "convenient, or useful" or "conducive" to the authority's "beneficial exercise." [In] determining whether the Necessary and Proper Clause grants Congress the legislative authority to enact a particular federal statute, we look to see whether the statute constitutes a means that is rationally related to the implementation of a constitutionally enumerated power. Sabri v. United States, 541 U.S. 600, 605 (2004). [The] relevant inquiry is simply "whether the means chosen are 'reasonably adapted' to the attainment of a legitimate end under the commerce power" or under other powers that the Constitution grants Congress the authority to implement. We have also recognized that the Constitution . . . "leaves to Congress a large discretion as to the means that may be employed in executing a given power."

Thus, the Constitution, which nowhere speaks explicitly about the creation of federal crimes beyond those related to "counterfeiting," "treason," or "Piracies and Felonies committed on the high Seas" or "against the Law of Nations," nonetheless grants Congress broad authority to create such crimes. And Congress routinely exercises its authority to enact criminal laws in furtherance of, for example, its enumerated powers to regulate interstate and foreign commerce, to enforce civil rights, to spend funds for the general welfare, to establish federal courts, to establish post offices, to regulate bankruptcy, to regulate naturalization, and so forth.

Similarly, Congress, in order to help ensure the enforcement of federal criminal laws enacted in furtherance of its enumerated powers, "can cause a prison to be erected at any place within the jurisdiction of the United States, and direct that all persons sentenced to imprisonment under the laws of the United States shall be confined there." Ex parte Karstendick, 93 U.S. 396, 400 (1876). Moreover, Congress, having established a prison system, can enact laws that seek to ensure that system's safe and responsible administration by, for example, requiring prisoners to receive medical care and educational training, and can also ensure the safety of the prisoners, prison workers and visitors, and those in surrounding communities by, for example, creating further criminal laws governing entry, exit, and smuggling, and by employing prison guards to ensure discipline and security. Neither Congress'[s] power to criminalize conduct, nor its power to imprison individuals who engage in that conduct, nor its power to enact laws governing prisons and prisoners, is explicitly mentioned in the Constitution. But Congress nonetheless possesses broad authority to do each of those things in the course of "carrying into Execution" the enumerated powers "vested by" the "Constitution in the Government of the United States" — authority granted by the Necessary and Proper Clause.

Second, the civil-commitment statute before us constitutes a modest addition to a set of federal prison-related mental-health statutes that have existed for many decades. We recognize that even a longstanding history of related federal action does not demonstrate a statute's constitutionality. A history of involvement, however, can nonetheless be "helpful in reviewing the substance of a congressional statutory scheme," and, in particular, the reasonableness of the relation between the new statute and pre-existing federal interests.

Here, Congress has long been involved in the delivery of mental health care to federal prisoners, and has long provided for their civil commitment. [Between 1855 and 1882] Congress created a national, federal civil-commitment program under which any person who was either charged with or convicted of any federal offense in any federal court could be confined in a federal mental institution. These statutes did not raise the question presented here, for they all provided that commitment in a federal hospital would end upon the completion of the relevant "terms" of federal "imprisonment" as set forth in the underlying criminal sentence or statute. But in the mid-1940's that proviso was eliminated [and in 1949 indefinite civil commitment was authorized if the person was proven to be a danger to the public and no state would assume custody of the person.] In 1984, Congress modified these basic statutes [by, among other things,] directing the Attorney General to seek alternative placement in state facilities, [but retaining the authorization of indefinite civil commitment if no state was willing to assume custody.] In 2006, Congress enacted the particular statute before us, [which] differs from earlier statutes in that it focuses directly upon persons who, due to a mental illness, are sexually dangerous. . . . Aside from its specific focus on sexually dangerous persons, § 4248 is similar to the provisions first enacted in 1949. [It] is a modest addition to a longstanding federal statutory framework, which has been in place since 1855.

Third, Congress reasonably extended its longstanding civil-commitment system to cover mentally ill and sexually dangerous persons who are already in federal custody, even if doing so detains them beyond the termination of their criminal sentence. [Because] the Federal Government is the custodian of its prisoners, . . . it has the constitutional power to act in order to protect nearby (and other) communities from the danger federal prisoners may pose. . . . If a federal prisoner is infected with a communicable disease that threatens others, surely it would be "necessary and proper" for the Federal Government . . . to refuse (at least until the threat diminishes) to release that individual among the general public, where he might infect others (even if not threatening an interstate epidemic). And if confinement of such an individual is a "necessary and proper" thing to do, then how could it not be similarly "necessary and proper" to confine an individual whose mental illness threatens others to the same degree?

Moreover, § 4248 is "reasonably adapted" to Congress'[s] power to act as a responsible federal custodian (a power that rests, in turn, upon federal criminal statutes that legitimately seek to implement constitutionally enumerated authority). Congress could have reasonably concluded that federal inmates who suffer from a mental illness that causes them to "have serious difficulty in refraining from sexually violent conduct" would pose an especially high danger to the public if released. And Congress could also have reasonably concluded . . . that a reasonable number of such individuals would likely *not* be detained by the States if released from federal custody, in part because the Federal Government itself severed their claim to "legal residence in any State" by incarcerating them in remote federal prisons. [This] supports the conclusion that § 4248 satisfies . . . the Constitution's insistence that a federal statute represent a rational means for implementing a constitutional grant of legislative authority.

Fourth, the statute properly accounts for state interests. [The statute does not] invade state sovereignty or otherwise improperly limit the scope of "powers that remain with the States." To the contrary, it requires *accommodation* of state interests: The Attorney General must inform the State in which the federal prisoner "is domiciled or was tried" that he is detaining someone with respect to whom those States may wish to assert their authority, and he must encourage those States to assume custody of the individual. He must also immediately "release" that person "to the appropriate official of" either State "if such State will assume [such] responsibility." And either State has the right, at any time, to assert its authority over the individual, which will prompt the individual's immediate transfer to State custody.

Fifth, the links between § 4248 and an enumerated Article I power are not too attenuated. Neither is the statutory provision too sweeping in its scope. Invoking the cautionary instruction that we may not "pile inference upon inference" in order to sustain congressional action under Article I, [*Lopez*], respondents argue that, when legislating pursuant to the Necessary and Proper Clause, Congress'[s] authority can be no more than one step removed from a specifically enumerated power. But this argument is irreconcilable with our precedents. . . .

For example, in *Sabri* we observed that "Congress has authority under the Spending Clause to appropriate federal moneys" and that it therefore "has corresponding authority under the Necessary and Proper Clause to see to it that taxpayer dollars" are not "siphoned off" by "corrupt public officers." We then further held that, in aid of that implied power to criminalize graft of "taxpayer dollars," Congress has the *additional* prophylactic power to criminalize bribes or kickbacks even when the stolen funds have not been "traceably skimmed from specific federal payments." . . .

Congress has the implied power to criminalize any conduct that might interfere with the exercise of an enumerated power, and also the additional power to imprison people who violate those (inferentially authorized) laws, and the additional power to provide for the safe and reasonable management of those prisons, and the additional power to regulate the prisoners' behavior even after their release. Of course, each of those powers . . . is ultimately "derived from" an enumerated power. [While] every . . . statute must . . . be legitimately predicated on an enumerated power[,] the same enumerated power that justifies the creation of a federal criminal statute, and that justifies . . . additional implied federal powers . . . , justifies civil commitment under § 4248 as well. Thus, we . . . reject [the] argument that the Necessary and Proper Clause permits no more than a single step between an enumerated power and an Act of Congress. . . .

* * *

We take these five considerations together. They include: (1) the breadth of the Necessary and Proper Clause, (2) the long history of federal involvement in this arena, (3) the sound reasons for the statute's enactment in light of the Government's custodial interest in safeguarding the public from dangers posed by those in federal custody, (4) the statute's accommodation of state interests, and (5) the statute's narrow scope. Taken together, these considerations lead us to conclude that the statute is a "necessary and proper" means of exercising the federal authority that permits Congress to create federal criminal laws, to punish their violation, to imprison violators, to provide appropriately for those imprisoned, and to maintain the security of those who are not imprisoned but who may be affected by the federal imprisonment of others. The Constitution consequently authorizes Congress to enact the statute.

JUSTICE KENNEDY, concurring in the judgment.
. . . Respondents argue that congressional authority under the Necessary and Proper Clause can be no more than one step removed from an enumerated power. This is incorrect. When the inquiry is whether a federal law has sufficient links to an enumerated power to be within the scope of federal authority, the analysis depends not on the number of links in the congressional-power chain but on the strength of the chain. [But this] is merely the beginning, not the end, of the constitutional inquiry. The inferences must be controlled by some limitations lest, as Thomas Jefferson warned, congressional powers become completely unbounded by linking one power to another *ad infinitum* in a veritable game of

"'this is the house that Jack built.'" Letter from Thomas Jefferson to Edward Livingston (Apr. 30, 1800), 31 The Papers of Thomas Jefferson 547 (B. Oberg ed. 2004). . . .

The Court concludes that, when determining whether Congress has the authority to enact a specific law under the Necessary and Proper Clause, we look "to see whether the statute constitutes a means that is rationally related to the implementation of a constitutionally enumerated power." The terms "rationally related" and "rational basis" must be employed with care, particularly if either is to be used as a stand-alone test. The phrase "rational basis" most often is employed to describe the standard for determining whether legislation that does not proscribe fundamental liberties nonetheless violates the Due Process Clause. Referring to this due process inquiry, and in what must be one of the most deferential formulations of the standard for reviewing legislation in all the Court's precedents, the Court has said: "But the law need not be in every respect logically consistent with its aims to be constitutional. It is enough that there is an evil at hand for correction, and that it might be thought that the particular legislative measure was a rational way to correct it." Williamson v. Lee Optical of Okla., Inc., 348 U.S. 483, 487-488 (1955). This formulation was in a case presenting a due process challenge and a challenge to a State's exercise of its own powers, powers not confined by the principles that control the limited nature of our National Government. The phrase, then, should not be extended uncritically to the issue before us.

The operative constitutional provision in this case is the Necessary and Proper Clause. This Court has not held that the *Lee Optical* test . . . is the proper test in this context. Rather, under the Necessary and Proper Clause, application of a "rational basis" test should be at least as exacting as it has been in the Commerce Clause cases, if not more so. . . . There is an important difference between the two questions, but the Court does not make this distinction clear. [The Commerce Clause] precedents require a tangible link to commerce, not a mere conceivable rational relation, as in *Lee Optical*. The rational basis referred to in the Commerce Clause context is a demonstrated link in fact, based on empirical demonstration. [While the] Court relies on *Sabri* for its conclusion that a "means-ends rationality" is all that is required for a power to come within the Necessary and Proper Clause's reach[,] *Sabri* . . . certainly did not import the *Lee Optical* rational-basis test into this arena . . . .

A separate concern stems from the Court's explanation of the Tenth Amendment. . . . It is correct in one sense to say that if the National Government has the power to act under the Necessary and Proper Clause then that power is not one reserved to the States. But the precepts of federalism embodied in the Constitution inform which powers are properly exercised by the National Government in the first place. It is of fundamental importance to consider whether essential attributes of state sovereignty are compromised by the assertion of federal power under the Necessary and Proper Clause; if so, that is a factor suggesting that the power is not one properly within the reach of federal power.

The opinion of the Court should not be interpreted to hold that the only, or even the principal, constraints on the exercise of congressional power are the Constitution's express prohibitions. The Court's discussion of the Tenth Amendment invites the inference that restrictions flowing from the federal system are of no import when defining the limits of the National Government's power, as it proceeds by first asking whether the power is within the National Government's reach, and if so it discards federalism concerns entirely.

JUSTICE ALITO, concurring in the judgment.

The Necessary and Proper Clause does not give Congress *carte blanche*. Although the term "necessary" does not mean "absolutely necessary" or indispensable, the term requires an "appropriate" link between a power conferred by the Constitution and the law enacted by Congress. And it is an obligation of this Court to enforce compliance with that limitation. The law in question here satisfies that requirement. This is not a case in which it is merely possible for a court to think of a rational basis on which Congress might have perceived an attenuated link between the powers underlying the federal criminal statutes and the challenged civil commitment provision. Here, there is a substantial link to Congress'[s] constitutional powers.

JUSTICE THOMAS, with whom JUSTICE SCALIA joins, dissenting.

. . . The Necessary and Proper Clause empowers Congress to enact only those laws that "carr[y] into Execution" one or more of the federal powers enumerated in the Constitution. Because § 4248 "Execut[es]" no enumerated power, I must respectfully dissent. . . .

I. In our system, the Federal Government's powers are enumerated, and hence limited. Thus, Congress has no power to act unless the Constitution authorizes it to do so. This constitutional structure establishes different default rules for Congress and the States: Congress'[s] powers are "few and defined," while those that belong to the States "remain . . . numerous and indefinite." The Federalist No. 45, p. 328 (B. Wright ed. 1961) (J. Madison). . . .

Chief Justice Marshall famously summarized Congress'[s] authority under the Necessary and Proper Clause in *McCulloch* . . . : "Let the end be legitimate, let it be within the scope of the constitution, and all means which are appropriate, which are plainly adapted to that end, which are not prohibited, but consist with the letter and spirit of the constitution, are constitutional." *McCulloch*'s summation is descriptive of the Clause itself, providing that federal legislation is a valid exercise of Congress'[s] authority under the Clause if it satisfies a two-part test: First, the law must be directed toward a "legitimate" end, which *McCulloch* defines as one "within the scope of the [C]onstitution" — that is, the powers expressly delegated to the Federal Government by some provision in the Constitution. Second, there must be a necessary and proper fit between the "means" (the federal law) and the "end" (the enumerated power or powers) it is designed to serve. *McCulloch* accords Congress a certain amount of discretion in assessing means-end fit under this second inquiry. The means Congress selects will be deemed "necessary" if they are "appropriate" and "plainly adapted" to the exercise of an enumerated power, and "proper" if they are not otherwise "prohibited" by the Constitution and not "[in]consistent" with its "letter and spirit." Critically, however, *McCulloch* underscores the linear relationship the Clause establishes between the two inquiries: Unless the end itself is "legitimate," the fit between means and end is irrelevant. In other words, no matter how "necessary" or "proper" an Act of Congress may be to its objective, Congress lacks authority to legislate if the objective is anything other than "carrying into Execution" one or more of the Federal Government's enumerated powers.

This limitation was of utmost importance to the Framers. During the State ratification debates, Anti-Federalists expressed concern that the Necessary and Proper Clause would give Congress virtually unlimited power. Federalist supporters of the Constitution swiftly refuted that charge, explaining that the Clause did not grant Congress any freestanding authority, but instead made explicit what was already implicit in the grant of each enumerated power. . . . Roughly 30 years after the Constitution's ratification, *McCulloch* firmly established this understanding in our constitutional jurisprudence. Since then, our precedents uniformly have maintained that the Necessary and Proper Clause is not an independent fount of congressional authority, but rather "a *caveat* that Congress possesses all the means necessary to carry out the specifically granted 'foregoing' powers of [Art. I,] § 8 and all other Powers vested by this Constitution.'". . .

II. No enumerated power in Article I, § 8, expressly delegates to Congress the power to enact a civil-commitment regime for sexually dangerous persons, nor does any other provision in the Constitution vest Congress or the other branches of the Federal Government with such a power. Accordingly, § 4248 can be a valid exercise of congressional authority only if it is "necessary and proper for carrying into Execution" one or more of those federal powers actually enumerated in the Constitution. Section 4248 does not fall within any of those powers. The Government identifies no specific enumerated power or powers as a constitutional predicate for § 4248, and none are readily discernable. Indeed, not even the Commerce Clause — the enumerated power this Court has interpreted most expansively — can justify federal civil detention of sex offenders. Under the Court's precedents, Congress may not regulate noneconomic activity (such as sexual violence) based solely on the effect such activity may have, in individual cases or in the aggregate, on interstate commerce. [*Morrison.*] That limitation forecloses any claim that § 4248 carries into execution Congress'[s] Commerce Clause power, and the Government has never argued otherwise.

This Court, moreover, consistently has recognized that the power to care for the mentally ill and, where necessary, the power "to protect the community from the dangerous tendencies of some" mentally ill persons, are among the numerous powers that remain with the States. As a consequence, we have held that States may "take measures to restrict the freedom of the dangerously mentally ill" — including those who are sexually dangerous — provided that such commitments satisfy due process and other constitutional requirements. Kansas v. Hendricks, 521 U.S. 346, 363 (1997). Section 4248 closely resembles the involuntary civil-commitment laws that States have enacted under their *parens patriae* and general police powers. Indeed, it is clear, on the face of the Act and in the Government's arguments urging its constitutionality, that § 4248 is aimed at protecting society from acts of sexual violence, not toward "carrying into Execution" any enumerated power or powers of the Federal Government. To be sure, protecting society from violent sexual offenders is certainly an important end. Sexual abuse is a despicable act with untold consequences for the victim personally and society generally. But the Constitution does not vest in Congress the authority to protect society from every bad act that might befall it. In my view, this should decide the question. Section 4248 runs afoul of our settled understanding of Congress'[s] power under the Necessary and Proper Clause. Congress may act under that Clause only when its legislation "carr[ies] into Execution" one of the Federal Government's enumerated powers. Section 4248 does not execute *any* enumerated power. Section 4248 is therefore unconstitutional.

III. The Court perfunctorily genuflects to *McCulloch*'s framework for assessing Congress'[s] Necessary and Proper Clause authority, and to the principle of dual sovereignty it helps to maintain, then promptly abandons both in favor of a novel five-factor test supporting its conclusion that § 4248 is a "'necessary and proper'" adjunct to a jumble of *unenumerated* "authorit[ies]." The Court's newly minted test cannot be reconciled with the Clause's plain text or with two centuries of our precedents interpreting it. It also raises more questions than it answers. Must each of the five considerations exist before the Court sustains future federal legislation as proper exercises of Congress'[s] Necessary and Proper Clause authority? What if the facts of a given case support a finding of only four considerations? Or three? And if three or four will suffice, *which* three or four are imperative? At a minimum, this shift from the two-step *McCulloch* framework to this five-consideration approach warrants an explanation as to why *McCulloch* is no longer good enough and which of the five considerations will bear the most weight in future cases, assuming some number less than five suffices. (Or, if not, why all five are required.) The Court provides no answers to these questions. . . .

After focusing on the relationship between § 4248 and several of Congress'[s] implied powers, the Court finally concludes that the civil detention of a "sexually dangerous person" under § 4248 carries into execution the enumerated power that justified that person's arrest or conviction in the first place. In other words, the Court analogizes § 4248 to federal laws that authorize prison officials to care for federal inmates while they serve sentences or await trial. But while those laws help to "carr[y] into Execution" the enumerated power that justifies the imposition of criminal sanctions on the inmate, § 4248 does not bear that essential characteristic for three reasons.

First, the statute's definition of a "sexually dangerous person" contains no element relating to the subject's crime. It thus does not require a federal court to find any connection between the reasons supporting civil commitment and the enumerated power with which that person's criminal conduct interfered. As a consequence, § 4248 allows a court to civilly commit an individual without finding that he was ever charged with or convicted of a federal crime involving sexual violence. That possibility is not merely hypothetical: The Government concedes that nearly 20% of individuals against whom § 4248 proceedings have been brought fit this description.

Second, § 4248 permits the term of federal civil commitment to continue beyond the date on which a convicted prisoner's sentence expires or the date on which the statute of limitations on an untried defendant's crime has run. The statute therefore authorizes federal custody over a person at a time when the Government would lack jurisdiction to detain him for violating a criminal law that executes an enumerated power. The statute this Court upheld in *Greenwood v. United States*, 350 U.S. 366 (1956), provides a useful contrast. That statute authorized the Federal Government to exercise civil custody over a federal defendant declared mentally unfit to stand trial only "'until the accused shall be mentally competent to stand trial or until the pending charges against him are disposed of according to law.'" Thus, that statute's "end" reasonably could be interpreted as preserving the Government's power to enforce a criminal law against the accused. Section 4248, however, authorizes federal detention of a person even *after* the Government loses the authority to prosecute him for a federal crime.

Third, the definition of a "sexually dangerous person" relevant to § 4248 does not require the court to find that the person is likely to violate a law executing an enumerated power in the future. Although the Federal Government has no express power to regulate sexual violence generally, Congress has passed a number of laws proscribing such conduct in special circumstances. All of these statutes contain jurisdictional elements that require a connection to one of Congress'[s] enumerated powers — such as interstate commerce — or that limit the statute's coverage to jurisdictions in which Congress has plenary authority. Section 4248, by contrast, authorizes civil commitment upon a showing that the person is "sexually dangerous," and presents a risk "to others." It requires no evidence that this sexually dangerous condition will manifest itself in a way that interferes with a federal law that executes an enumerated power or in a geographic location over which Congress has plenary authority. . . . In sum, the enumerated powers that justify a criminal defendant's arrest or conviction cannot justify his subsequent civil detention under § 4248.

The remaining "considerations" in the Court's five-part inquiry do not alter this conclusion. First, . . . the Court [says] that the Federal Government has a "custodial interest" in its prisoners and, thus, a broad "constitutional power to act in order to protect nearby (and other) communities" from the dangers they may pose. . . . Once the Federal Government's criminal jurisdiction over a prisoner ends, so does any "special relation[ship]" between the Government and the former prisoner. . . . Second, the Court describes § 4248 as a "modest" expansion on a statutory framework with a long historical pedigree. Yet even if the antiquity of a practice could serve as a substitute for its constitutionality — and the Court admits that it cannot—the Court overstates the relevant history. [Federal laws enacted prior to 1949] did not authorize federal custody beyond the completion of the "term" of federal "imprisonment," and thus shed no light on the question presented here. In 1949, Congress enacted a more comprehensive regime, authorizing the civil commitment of mentally ill persons . . . . This Court addressed that regime in *Greenwood*, but never endorsed the proposition that the Federal Government could rely on that statute to detain a person in the absence of a pending criminal charge or ongoing criminal sentence.

Finally, the Court offers two arguments regarding § 4248's impact on the relationship between the Federal Government and the States. First, the Court and both concurrences suggest that Congress must have had the power to enact § 4248 because a long period of federal incarceration might "seve[r]" a sexually dangerous prisoner's "claim to 'legal residence'" in any particular State, thus leaving the prisoner without any "home State to take charge" of him upon release. [But] States plainly have the constitutional authority to "take charge" of a federal prisoner released within their jurisdiction. In addition, the assumption that a State knowingly would fail to exercise that authority is, in my view, implausible. . . . In light of the plethora of state laws enacted in recent decades to protect communities from sex offenders, the likelihood of such an occurrence seems quite remote. But even in the event a State made such a decision, the Constitution assigns the responsibility for that decision, and its consequences, to the state government alone.

Next, the Court submits that § 4248 does not upset the balance of federalism or invade the States' reserved powers because it "requires accommodation of state interests" by instructing the Attorney General to release a committed person to the State in which he was domiciled or tried if that State wishes to "'assume . . . responsibility'" for him. This right of first refusal is mere window dressing. For once it is determined that Congress has the authority to provide for the civil detention of sexually dangerous persons, Congress "is acting within the powers granted it under the Constitution," and "may impose its will on the States." Section 4248's right of first refusal is thus not a matter of constitutional necessity, but an act of legislative grace. . . .

Absent congressional action that is in accordance with, or necessary and proper to, an enumerated power, the duty to protect citizens from violent crime, including acts of sexual violence, belongs solely to the States.

* * *

Not long ago, this Court described the Necessary and Proper Clause as "the last, best hope of those who defend ultra vires congressional action." [*Printz.*] Regrettably, today's opinion breathes new life into that Clause, and—the Court's protestations to the contrary notwithstanding—comes perilously close to transforming the Necessary and Proper Clause into a basis for the federal police power that "we *always* have rejected." [*Lopez.*] In so doing, the Court endorses the precise abuse of power Article I is designed to prevent—the use of a limited grant of authority as a "pretext . . . for the accomplishment of objects not intrusted to the government." *McCulloch.*

I respectfully dissent.

NOTES

1. The Means-Ends Connection. What was the enumerated power that 18 U.S.C. § 4248 appropriately implemented? The Court rejected the idea that the means chosen by Congress to execute an enumerated power can be no more than "one step removed" from the enumerated power. Does this indicate that Congress has power to enact measures to implement or supplement other laws it has already enacted (which are themselves "necessary and proper" means of executing an enumerated power)? Justice Kennedy, concurring, stated that "the analysis depends not on the number of links in the congressional-power chain but on the strength of the chain." How does one assess the strength of the chain between a constitutionally enumerated federal power, on the one hand, and a series of laws enacted to implement that power, ending with a law that is enacted to bolster the federal power created by the prior laws?

2. The Relevance of *McCulloch*. The Court used a five factor test to conclude that § 4248 was an appropriate means to execute some enumerated power. Does this displace *McCulloch*'s emphasis on means that are "plainly adapted" to a "legitimate" end? Recall the famous quotation from *McCulloch*: "Let the end be legitimate, let it be within the scope of the constitution, and all means which are appropriate, which are plainly adapted to that end, which are not prohibited, but consist with the letter and spirit of the constitution, are constitutional." Is the Court's five factor test a replacement of the *McCulloch* approach, or is it a device to determine which congressionally chosen means are within the "letter and spirit" of the Constitution? Finally, under what circumstances would (should) the Court find a congressionally chosen means to be a "pretext . . . for the accomplishment of objects not intrusted to the government"?

2. Implying "Default" Rules for Federal and State Power

Page 145: Insert at the end of Note 2:

In North Dakota v. United States, 495 U.S. 423, 435 (1990), the Court declared that a state or local law is void "only if it regulates the United States directly or discriminates against the Federal Government or those with whom it deals." In United States v. City of Arcata, 629 F.3d 986 (2010), the Ninth Circuit applied these principles to invalidate two city ordinances that made it a civil offense for the federal government and its employees to "recruit, initiate contact with for the purpose of recruiting, or promote the future enlistment of any person under the age of eighteen into any branch of the United States Armed Forces." The ordinances exempted "individuals who are not employed by or agents of the U.S. government" from "encouraging people under the age of eighteen to join the military." The ordinances were intended to and did in fact regulate the federal government directly and, because of the exemption, also discriminated against the federal government.

Problem: San Francisco law provides: "No department, agency, commission, officer or employee of the City and County of San Francisco shall use any City funds or resources to assist in the enforcement of federal immigration law. . . . " Is this valid?

B. Commerce

4. Limits Imposed by Principles of State Autonomy

b. Procedural Immunity

Page 226: Substitute the following for the last paragraph of Note 2:

In Bond v. United States, 2011 U.S. Lexis 4558, the Supreme Court unanimously concluded that a litigant who has otherwise satisfied the Article III and prudential standing requirements does not lack standing because she asserts that the law that is the cause of her injury violates federalism principles by invalidly infringing upon state autonomy. Carol Bond was prosecuted and convicted under a federal law making it a crime to possess certain chemicals for other than peaceful purposes. She was sentenced to a prison term that she alleged was treble the punishment that would have been meted out for her conduct under state law. The lower courts ruled that she had not standing to assert that the federal law was beyond the powers of Congress, and thus an infringement of state autonomy, because the state was not a party to the prosecution. The Court noted that "[f]ederalism secures the freedom of the individual" as well as preserving "the integrity, dignity, and residual sovereignty of the States." Accordingly, Bond was held to have standing to assert that the law was *ultra vires*.

C. Taxation

Page 231: Insert after existing Note following Kahriger:

Not Quite Dead. CF & I Steel Corporation failed to make a $12.4 million contribution to its pension plans, as required by the Employee Retirement Income Security Act of 1974 (ERISA). Then it filed for bankruptcy protection. Because it had failed to make the required pension contribution, it became

subject to a "tax" of 10% of any "accumulated funding deficiency," imposed by
26 U.S.C. § 4971(a). The federal government sought priority for its claim in the
bankruptcy proceeding, because it was founded on an unpaid tax liability of
$1.24 million. The bankruptcy court ruled that the "tax" was actually a penalty
not entitled to priority. In United States v. Reorganized CF & I Steel Fabricators
of Utah, Inc., 518 U.S. 213 (1996), the Supreme Court affirmed:

> "A tax is an enforced contribution to provide for the support of government; a
> penalty . . . is an exaction imposed by statute as punishment for an unlawful act."
> United States v. La Franca, 282 U.S. 568, 572 (1931). We take *La Franca*'s
> statement of the distinction to be sufficient for the decision of this case; if the
> concept of penalty means anything, it means punishment for an unlawful act or
> omission, and a punishment for an unlawful omission is what this exaction is.

Id. at 224.

The penal character of the "tax" was demonstrated by the fact that failure to
pay it promptly after notice that it was due subjected the entity to a further "tax"
of 100 percent of the accumulated funding deficiency and a separate claim for
100% of that amount by the Pension Benefit Guaranty Corporation.

In Department of Revenue of Montana v. Kurth Ranch, 511 U.S. 767 (1994),
the Court found that a "tax" imposed on possession of marijuana was a penalty
for purposes of the double jeopardy clause. Although unlawful activities may be
taxed, this tax was conditioned on *commission* of a crime. The tax was eight
times the value of the property, and even though "neither a high rate of taxation
nor an obvious deterrent purpose automatically marks this tax as a form of
punishment," those factors "lend support to the characterization of the drug tax
as punishment." Finally, though the tax was styled a property tax, it was "levied
on goods that the taxpayer neither owns nor possesses when the tax is imposed."

Chapter 4
Limiting the Scope of State Power over Interstate Commerce

A. The Dormant Commerce Clause

4. Facially Neutral Regulations with Discriminatory Effects on Interstate Commerce

b. Assessing Discriminatory Purposes

Page 300: Insert at the end of the section:

FAMILY WINEMAKERS OF CALIFORNIA v. JENKINS
592 F.3d 1 (1st Cir. 2010)

LYNCH, Chief Judge.

Massachusetts officials appeal from an injunction against a 2006 Massachusetts statute establishing differential methods by which wineries distribute wines in Massachusetts, Mass. Gen. Laws ch. 138, § 19F. The district court enjoined enforcement of § 19F on the ground that the law discriminates against interstate commerce in violation of the Commerce Clause of the United States Constitution.

Section 19F only allows "small" wineries, defined by Massachusetts as those producing 30,000 gallons or less of grape wine a year, to obtain a "small winery shipping license." This license allows them to sell their wines in Massachusetts in three ways: by shipping directly to consumers, through wholesaler distribution, and through retail distribution. All of Massachusetts's wineries are "small" wineries. Some out-of-state wineries also meet this definition. Wines from "small" Massachusetts wineries compete with wines from "large" wineries, which Massachusetts has defined as those producing more than 30,000 gallons of grape wine annually. These "large" wineries must choose between relying upon wholesalers to distribute their wines in-state or applying for a "large winery shipping license" to sell directly to Massachusetts consumers. They cannot, by law, use both methods to sell their wines in Massachusetts, and they cannot sell wines directly to retailers under either option. No "large" wineries are located inside Massachusetts.

Plaintiffs, a group of California winemakers and Massachusetts residents, assert § 19F was designed with the purpose, and has the effect, of advantaging Massachusetts wineries to the detriment of those wineries that produce 98 percent of the country's wine, in violation of the Commerce Clause. Massachusetts defends § 19F on the basis that its law has neither a discriminatory purpose nor a discriminatory effect. Massachusetts has not argued . . . that there are no legitimate alternative methods of regulation to serve § 19F's asserted purposes. . . .

It is clear that § 2 of the Twenty-first Amendment does not protect state alcohol laws that explicitly favor in-state over out-of-state interests from invalidation under the Commerce Clause. Granholm v. Heald. But § 19F is neutral on its face; it does not, by its terms, allow only Massachusetts wineries to distribute their wines through a combination of direct shipping, wholesaler distribution, and retail sales. Section 19F instead uses a very particular gallonage cap to confer this benefit upon "small" as opposed to "large" wineries.

We hold that § 19F violates the Commerce Clause because the effect of its particular gallonage cap is to change the competitive balance between in-state and out-of-state wineries in a way that benefits Massachusetts's wineries and significantly burdens out-of-state competitors. Massachusetts has used its 30,000 gallon grape wine cap to expand the distribution options available to "small" wineries, including all Massachusetts wineries, but not to similarly situated "large" wineries, all of which are outside Massachusetts. The advantages afforded to "small" wineries by these expanded distribution options bear little relation to the market challenges caused by the relative sizes of the wineries. Section 19F's statutory context, legislative history, and other factors also yield the unavoidable conclusion that this discrimination was purposeful. Nor does § 19F serve any legitimate local purpose that cannot be furthered by a nondiscriminatory alternative. We further hold that the Twenty-first Amendment cannot save § 19F from invalidation under the Commerce Clause. Section 2 of the Twenty-first Amendment does not exempt or otherwise immunize facially neutral but discriminatory state alcohol laws like § 19F from scrutiny under the Commerce Clause. We affirm the grant of injunctive relief. . . .

Most states, including Massachusetts, [impose] a three-tier system to control the sale of alcoholic beverages within their territories. The hallmark of the three-tier system is a rigid, tightly regulated separation between producers, wholesalers, and retailers of alcoholic beverages. Producers can ordinarily sell alcoholic beverages only to licensed in-state wholesalers. Wholesalers then must obtain licenses to sell to retailers. Retailers, which include stores, taverns, restaurants, and bars, must in turn obtain licenses to sell to consumers or to serve alcohol on their premises. . . .

The structure of the usual three-tier system is commonly described as an hourglass, with wholesalers at the constriction point. There are thousands of producers nationwide, a handful of licensed Massachusetts wholesalers, and approximately ten thousand licensed retailers in Massachusetts.

The three-tier system has had a particularly pronounced effect on wineries' access to the Massachusetts market. The economic incentives created by the three-tier system, in conjunction with the structure of the wine industry, severely limited certain wineries' ability to sell their wines in Massachusetts. In 2006, the year § 19F was enacted, . . . the five largest wineries in the U.S. produced approximately 70 percent of the country's wine. The . . . thirty largest wineries comprised approximately 92 percent of the market, and each produced between 680,000 and 150 million gallons per year. The rest of the commercial market — the 3,540 wineries which produce between one and 680,000 gallons per year — competed for 8 percent of the market share. . . .

[T]here are, broadly speaking, two categories of wine, high-volume, lower-cost wines and low-volume, higher-quality, higher-priced boutique wines. The largest wineries produce millions of gallons of wine per year because they have generally specialized in the former, but not to the exclusion of the latter. Wineries smaller than the largest producers have tended to specialize in low-volume boutique wines, which can be produced with a relatively small quantity of grapes and a much lower initial outlay of resources. At least until the current recession, consumer demand for boutique wines had grown exponentially, fueling a rise in the number of smaller U.S. wineries (which include many wineries producing more than 30,000 gallons annually).

Under Massachusetts's former three-tier system, all wineries could only distribute their wines through licensed Massachusetts wholesalers, and 75 percent of the wine sold in Massachusetts went through five wholesalers. This gave wholesalers, not wineries, the balance of the bargaining power. Wholesalers do not necessarily distribute a winery's entire range of wines; they often distribute the wines most likely to be profitable to them, which are lower-priced, high-volume wines. . . . The largest wineries, as the major producers of lower-priced, high-volume wines, have been best able to attract wholesalers. Only the country's fifty to one hundred largest wineries have consistently secured wholesaler representation. For most smaller wineries of whatever gallonage, which produce mostly boutique wines, obtaining wholesaler representation has been difficult, if not impossible. And even if a smaller winery obtained wholesaler representation, wholesalers were likely to distribute only one or two of its wines, limiting Massachusetts consumers' access to particular wines.

Wineries have heralded direct shipping as a supplemental avenue of distribution because of its economic advantages, especially for wineries that do not rank among the fifty to one hundred largest producers. Direct shipping lets consumers directly order wines from the winery, with access to their full range of wines, not just those a wholesaler is willing to distribute. Direct shipping also avoids added steps in the distribution chain, eliminating wholesaler and retailer price markups.

Before 2005, . . . Massachusetts . . . law . . . allowed only in-state wineries to obtain licenses to combine distribution methods through wholesalers, retailers, and direct shipping to consumers. Five months after *Granholm* invalidated similar facially discriminatory state laws, [this law] was held to be invalid under the Commerce Clause.

In 2006, the Massachusetts legislature enacted § 19F over then-Governor Romney's veto. During floor debates, § 19F's sponsor [noted that by § 19F] "we are really still giving an inherent advantage indirectly to the local wineries." [Another state senator successfully urged modification of § 19F to exclude a winery in his district producing over 30,000 gallons of fruit (non-grape) wine.]¹

[U]nder § 19F, "large" wineries can either choose to remain completely within the three-tier system and distribute their wines solely through wholesalers, or they can completely opt out of the three-tier system and sell their wines in Massachusetts exclusively through direct shipping. They cannot do both. . . . To put it differently, "large" wineries cannot distribute directly to consumers except at the cost of giving up distribution to retailers. By contrast, "small" wineries can simultaneously use the traditional wholesaler distribution method, direct distribution to retailers, and direct shipping to reach consumers. The practical effects of the distinctions Massachusetts has drawn are significant. In 2006, 637 U.S. wineries were "large" under § 19F's definition. They . . . accounted for 98 percent of all wine produced in the United States. . . . In 2007, there were thirty-one wineries in Massachusetts [and all were "small" wineries.]

Plaintiffs argue that [§ 19F] has both a discriminatory effect and purpose. The discriminatory effect is because § 19F's definition of "large" wineries encompasses the wineries which produce 98 percent of all wine in the United States, all of which are located out-of-state and all of which are deprived of the benefits of combining distribution methods. All wines produced in Massachusetts, on the other hand, are from "small" wineries that can use multiple distribution methods. Plaintiffs also say that Section 19F is discriminatory in purpose because the gallonage cap's [exclusion of fruit wines], along with legislators' statements and § 19F's process of enactment, show that § 19F's true purpose was to ensure that Massachusetts's wineries obtained advantages over their out-of-state counterparts. Plaintiffs also argue that Massachusetts cannot meet its burden of justifying § 19F because the law neither advances the three-tier system nor effectively assists small wineries in ways that available non-discriminatory alternatives could not. Finally, in the alternative, plaintiffs contend that § 19F impermissibly burdens interstate commerce under *Pike* even if it is not discriminatory.

Massachusetts counters that § 19F is not discriminatory in effect because most "small" wineries are located out-of-state. It says this proves that § 19F disproportionately benefits out-of-state, not in-state, wineries, especially since there are far more "small" § 19F wineries in the country than "large" . . . ones. Massachusetts argues that § 19F is not discriminatory in purpose because its aim is to level the economic playing field for all "small" wineries irrespective of

---

1. [4] Massachusetts tries to dismiss these statements as the isolated and unrepresentative comments of a few legislators. But such statements are precisely the kind of evidence the Supreme Court has looked to in previous Commerce Clause cases challenging a statute as discriminatory in purpose. Minnesota v. Clover Leaf Creamery Co., Hunt v. Wash. State Apple Adver. Comm'n. [While] the remarks of a single legislator are not controlling and do not compel any conclusion that the remarks reflect legislative intent . . . they are evidence.

where they are located, and the district court erroneously looked to comments by individual legislators, lobbyists, and intermediate steps in § 19F's process of enactment to find discriminatory purpose. Finally, Massachusetts says that § 19F poses no undue burden on interstate commerce under *Pike* and any . . . burden is surpassed by the local benefits of greater competition and consumer choice.

Because we hold that § 19F discriminates against interstate commerce, it is unnecessary for us to decide whether § 19F would also violate the Commerce Clause under *Pike*.

A. SECTION 19F IS DISCRIMINATORY IN EFFECT

A state law is discriminatory in effect when, in practice, it affects similarly situated entities in a market by imposing disproportionate burdens on out-of-state interests and conferring advantages upon in-state interests. [*Or. Waste Systems.*] One such form of discrimination is plainly when "the effect of a state regulation is to cause local goods to constitute a larger share, and goods with an out-of-state source to constitute a smaller share, of the total sales in the market." [Exxon v. Maryland.] State laws that alter conditions of competition to favor in-state interests over out-of-state competitors in a market have long been subject to invalidation. [*Hunt.*]

[The] totality of the evidence introduced by plaintiffs demonstrates that § 19F's . . . effect is to significantly alter the terms of competition between in-state and out-of-state wineries to the detriment of the out-of-state wineries that produce 98 percent of the country's wine. Section 19F confers a clear competitive advantage to "small" wineries, which include all Massachusetts's wineries, and creates a comparative disadvantage for "large" wineries, none of which are in Massachusetts. "Small" wineries . . . can use direct shipping to consumers, retailer distribution, and wholesaler distribution simultaneously, [which] allows "small" wineries to sell their full range of wines at maximum efficiency . . . . "Small" wineries that produce higher-volume wines can continue distributing those wines through wholesaler relationships. They can obtain new markets for all their wines by distributing their wines directly to retailers, including individual bars, restaurants, and stores. They can also use direct shipping to offer their full range of wines directly to Massachusetts consumers, resulting in greater overall sales. . . .

["Large"] out-of-state wineries . . . do not get these advantages and must instead choose between direct shipping and wholesaler distribution, [a choice which] carries a significant loss of potential profits, since using a single method results in a comparative loss of consumer sales. "Large" wineries also face comparatively greater distribution costs because they cannot always distribute a given wine through the most cost-effective method. . . .

Moreover, contrary to Massachusetts's assertions, § 19F does not level the playing field for all wineries unable to obtain consistent wholesaler distribution under the three-tier system. Section 19F . . . creates an especially acute competitive disadvantage for ["large"] wineries . . . which in practice face the same difficulties in distributing most of their wines as . . . "small" wineries. Massachusetts's own evidence shows that only the largest 50 to 100 wineries can distribute most of their wines through wholesalers under the three-tier system. The remaining 537 or so "large" wineries each produce . . . a mix of mass-market and boutique wines. . . . These smaller "large" wineries lose the most under [§ 19F.] Unlike the largest of the "large" wineries, which can distribute the vast majority of their wines through existing wholesale distribution, these smaller "large" wineries can only distribute a handful of their higher-volume wines through wholesalers. If they choose direct shipping, however, they are forced to terminate their existing wholesaler relationships, which also means that they lose all access to retailers in Massachusetts. Since this is a crucial way for a winery to build consumer awareness for the brand in Massachusetts, its unavailability means that these wineries are not able to compete on the same footing as § 19F "small" wineries. Importantly, these are also the wineries that would otherwise be most competitive in the market for boutique wines: their size affords them otherwise considerable advantages in terms of marketing, volume, transportation, and brand recognition. The ultimate effect of § 19F is to artificially limit the playing field in this market in a way that enables Massachusetts's wineries to gain market share against their out-of-state competitors. . . .

Massachusetts claims . . . that whatever the burden on out-of-state wineries . . . , § 19F does not create an in-state benefit, since Massachusetts's "small" wineries are made no better off than their out-of-state counterparts. Without evidence of in-state benefits, Massachusetts concludes, . . . *Exxon* dictates that we find no discriminatory effect. Massachusetts's argument ignores the effect of its statute. Section 19F's benefit to eligible "small" out-of-state wineries cannot be viewed separately from the much greater disadvantages that § 19F imposes on out-of-state wineries. Massachusetts's wineries uniquely receive a net competitive gain under § 19F, while the law impairs out-of-state wineries' competitive position. It deprives "large" wineries — and especially those "large" wineries that have trouble obtaining wholesale distribution — of the competitive advantages of specialization and higher-volume production. These disadvantages exceed the benefits that out-of-state "small" wineries receive.

Exxon does not support Massachusetts's argument. *Exxon* held that a law that restricts a market consisting entirely of out-of-state interests is not discriminatory because there is no local market to benefit. *Exxon* is not apposite where, as here, there is an in-state market and the law operates to its competitive benefit. . . .

B. SECTION 19F IS DISCRIMINATORY IN PURPOSE

We further hold that § 19F conferred a competitive advantage upon Massachusetts wineries by design. . . . That § 19F discriminates against out-of-state wineries in its effects strengthens the inference that the statute was discriminatory by design. . . . As to statutory context, § 19F is a new addition to a provision that covers an array of alcohol licensing rules. While § 19 generally includes licensing rules for producers that are typical of the three-tier system, § 19F is one of a number of recently appended subsections that sets out special exceptions to that system for particular entities. . . . Many of these subsections were enacted for the express purpose of assisting Massachusetts's domestic industries, including but not limited to § 19B, § 19F's facially discriminatory and unconstitutional predecessor. Though § 19F contains no stated statutory purpose, its placement in a licensing law that grants exceptions to the three-tier system for the predominant purpose of benefitting local industry is pertinent evidence of discriminatory intent. Based on statements made by various Massachusetts legislators, it is also clear that Massachusetts intended to benefit its local wine industry, and that it did so in particular ways whose effects on out-of-state wineries could easily be foreseen. . . . The gap between Massachusetts's professed neutrality and § 19F's practical effects also underscores the conclusion of discriminatory purpose. [*Hunt.*]

Massachusetts [claimed that the] 30,000 gallon cap and the fruit wine exception [from the gallonage cap] reflected the legislature's rational assessment of the kind of wineries that needed special assistance because they were suffering from the limitations of the three-tier system. [But the gallonage cap does not] correspond to the ability of the winery to obtain wholesaler representation. To the contrary, this choice prevents out-of-state, smaller "large" wineries from competing on equal terms with Massachusetts's "small" wineries even though these wineries faced similar difficulties in obtaining wholesaler distribution under the three-tier system. . . . Section 19F's unusual regulatory features do track one thing precisely: the unique attributes of Massachusetts's own wine industry. All of Massachusetts's thirty-one wineries are eligible for "small" winery licenses. All fall neatly within the 30,000 gallon cap, producing between 200 gallons and 24,000 gallons annually. And the record demonstrates — and Massachusetts does not contest — that legislators were well aware of these figures. . . . The fact that this gallonage cap excludes wines made from fruits other than grapes, no matter how many gallons a winery produces per year, is particularly probative. . . . Massachusetts's largest winery produced more than 30,000 gallons of wine annually because between half and three-quarters of its production came from apple wines. The main effect of the fruit wine exception was to guarantee that this winery, like all other Massachusetts wineries, could take advantage of § 19F's beneficial distribution rules for "small" wineries. Massachusetts has offered no other explanation for the fruit wine exception, and there is no obvious reason why it would serve § 19F's ostensible purposes. This exception, like similar, facially neutral statutory exemptions apparently motivated by a desire to shield in-state interests, "weaken[s] the presumption in favor of the validity of the [general provision], because [it] undermine[s] the assumption that the State's own political processes will act as a check on local regulations that unduly burden interstate commerce." Raymond Motor Transp., Inc. v. Rice, 434 U.S. 429, 447 (1978).

We conclude that § 19F altered the competitive balance to favor Massachusetts's wineries and disfavor out-of-state competition by design.

C. LACK OF LEGITIMATE LOCAL PURPOSE AND AVAILABILITY OF
   REASONABLE NON-DISCRIMINATORY ALTERNATIVES

Because plaintiffs have shown that § 19F discriminates against interstate commerce, Massachusetts bears the heavy burden of showing that the statute is nonetheless constitutional because it serves a legitimate local purpose that cannot be attained through reasonable non-discriminatory alternatives. The state can only carry this burden by presenting "concrete record evidence," and not "sweeping assertion[s]" or "mere speculation," to substantiate its claims that the discriminatory aspects of its challenged policy are necessary to achieve its asserted objectives. [*Granholm*.] Massachusetts has not even attempted to do so here. [Even so,] at least one viable non-discriminatory alternative existed when § 19F was under consideration: the Model Direct Shipment Bill . . . . As an alternative to § 19F, then-Governor Romney proposed a version of the Model Bill which would have allowed all wineries to ship directly to consumers, sell to retailers, and distribute through wholesalers. But the state legislature rejected this proposal and overrode his veto. . . .

III. [The Court of Appeals concluded that the Twenty-first Amendment does not immunize facially neutral alcohol statutes from scrutiny under the dormant commerce clause.] We also reject Massachusetts's alternate contention that the Twenty-first Amendment lessens the degree of Commerce Clause scrutiny for facially neutral but discriminatory state alcohol laws to mere rational basis review. The Supreme Court implicitly rejected this argument in *Granholm* when it applied the usual, searching degree of scrutiny to invalidate the facially discriminatory laws at issue. . . .

IV. We affirm the judgment of the district court.

C. Preemption and Consent: Congress Has the Final Word

1. Preemption

Page 328: Insert new Notes 3 and 4 at the end of the section:

3. Wyeth v. Levine and Justice Thomas's View of Preemption. Diana Levine, a professional musician who played bass, guitar, and piano, entered a Vermont emergency room to receive Demerol, a pain-killer, to treat a severe migraine headache. Because Demerol also induced nausea in Levine, she also received Phenergan, an anti-nausea drug manufactured by Wyeth. Normally Phenergan was administered by injection, but Levine received Phenergan intravenously (the "IV-push" method). The result of the IV-push method was that Levine developed gangrene, and her forearm was amputated. A Vermont jury awarded Levine substantial damages after concluding that Wyeth had caused the injury by its failure to provide an adequate warning about the significant risks of administering Phenergan by the IV-push method. Wyeth contended that Levine's failure-to-warn claim was preempted by federal law because Phenergan's labeling had been approved by the federal Food and Drug Administration (FDA). In Wyeth v. Levine, 555 U.S. 555 (2009), the Supreme Court held that Levine's claim was not preempted. It was possible for Wyeth to comply with both Vermont's duty to warn and the FDA's labeling requirements because under federal law Wyeth retained the power to make unilateral changes to its label to strengthen its warnings. There was inadequate evidence that Congress intended to confer upon the FDA the power to exercise exclusive control of drug labeling because the only indication of such an intent was in a preamble to the operative statute.

Justice Thomas concurred in the judgment:

> I write separately . . . because I cannot join the majority's implicit endorsement of far-reaching implied pre-emption doctrines. . . . Because implied pre-emption doctrines that wander far from the statutory text are inconsistent with the Constitution, I concur only in the judgment.
>
> In order "to ensure the protection of our fundamental liberties," the "Constitution establishes a system of dual sovereignty between the States and the Federal Government." . . . Under this federalist system, "the States possess sovereignty concurrent with that of the Federal Government, subject only to limitations imposed by the Supremacy Clause." [Thus, so] "long as it is acting within the powers granted it under the Constitution, Congress may impose its will on the States." . . . Nonetheless, the States retain substantial sovereign authority. U.S. Const., Amdt. 10. As a result, in order to protect the delicate balance of power mandated by the Constitution, the Supremacy Clause must operate only in accordance with its terms. [Because the Supremacy Clause makes "Laws of the United States . . . made in Pursuance" to the Constitution supreme, those laws consist only of those that are within the scope of the federal government's enumerated powers and which have complied with the Constitution's bicameralism and presentment requirements.] The Supremacy Clause thus requires that pre-emptive effect be given only those to federal standards and policies that are set forth in, or necessarily follow from, the statutory text that was produced through the constitutionally required bicameral and presentment procedures. . . . Under the Supremacy Clause, state law is pre-empted only by federal law "made in Pursuance" of the Constitution — not by extra-textual considerations of the purposes underlying congressional inaction. [T]his Court's "purposes and objectives" pre-emption jurisprudence . . . facilitates freewheeling, extra-textual, and broad evaluations of the "purposes and objectives" embodied within federal law [which] leads to decisions giving improperly broad pre-emptive effect to judicially manufactured policies, rather than to the statutory text enacted by Congress pursuant to the Constitution and the agency actions authorized thereby. Because such a sweeping approach to pre-emption leads to the illegitimate — and thus, unconstitutional — invalidation of state laws, I can no longer assent to a doctrine that pre-empts state laws merely because they "stan[d] as an obstacle to the accomplishment and execution of the full purposes and objectives" of federal law as perceived by this Court.

A similar issue arose in Pliva, Inc. v. Mensing, 2011 U.S. Lexis 4793. Long-term use of a generic drug, metoclopramide, has been linked to a severe neu-rological disorder. States began to require warning labels for the drug that were more stringent than those mandated by the Food and Drug Administration for Reglan, the brand-name version of metoclopramide. The FDA's rules limit the labeling of generic drugs to the same labels approved and required for the brand-name version. However, the FDA permits brand-name drug manufacturers to change the label for the brand-name drug in order to strengthen its warnings. It was this rule that caused the Court in *Wyeth* to conclude that the state laws at issue in that case were not pre-empted, because the manufacturer of a brand-name drug could comply with both federal and state law. However illogical it may be, the FDA does not permit manufacturers of generic drugs to deviate unilaterally from the approved brand-name label, thus creating a situation in which the manufacturer of Reglan could change its label to conform to state law but the manufacturers of metoclopramide, the generic version of Reglan, could not do so without FDA approval. Thus, the Court, in an opinion by Justice Thomas, ruled that the state laws were preempted because it was impossibile to comply with both federal and state law. The Court noted that Congress and the FDA could correct this anomaly, by which state law applies to brand-name drugs but not to their generic equivalents.

4. Pre-emption and Immigration. In Chamber of Commerce v. Whiting, 2011 U.S. Lexis 4018, the Supreme Court upheld an Arizona law that revoked the business licenses of businesses that knowingly hire a person unlawfully present in the United States. The same law also required Arizona employers to use the federal E-Verify system to determine if an applicant is lawfully present in the U.S. Federal law prohibits employers from knowingly hiring persons unlawfully present in the country. The federal government had created E-Verify and made it available throughout the country for voluntary use by employers. The relevant federal law that prohibits hiring illegal aliens knowingly also ex-pressly preempts "any State or local law imposing civil or criminal sanctions (other than through licensing and similar laws) upon those who employ . . . unauthorized aliens." The Court concluded that the Arizona law was within the exception and thus neither expressly or impliedly preempted. Although federal law forbids the federal government from mandating use of E-Verify it is silent on whether the states may do so. The Court found no implied preemption of Arizona's mandate that E-Verify be used because 1) federal law is silent on the point, 2) the federal government has authorized and promoted the use of E-Verify as a reliable means to determine an applicant's immigration status. There was no "impossibility" conflict with federal law and the Arizona law was in harmony with the federal government's objectives in creating E-Verify — to increase reliable determinations of immigration status.

Problem: California law permits persons who have attended a California high school for three years and who are unlawful residents of the United States to pay in-state tuition while denying those rates to lawful residents of the nation who are not California residents. Federal law prohibits a state from offering in-state tuition to unlawfully present aliens on the basis of their residence within the state unless the state permits non-residents of the state who are lawfully present in the United States the same benefit. In Martinez v. Regents of the University of California, 50 Cal. 4th 1277 (2010), the California Supreme Court upheld this law, reasoning that California did not offer the tuition benefit on the basis of *residence* within California. Is the California law pre-empted? The Supreme Court denied certiorari, 2011 U.S. Lexis 4299.

Chapter 5
Separation of Powers

B. Executive Action

1. In Domestic Affairs

a. The Appointment Power

Page 349: Insert as new note 1a:

1a. More on Inferior Officers. In Edmond v. United States, 520 U.S. 651 (1997), the Court held that judges of the Coast Guard Court of Criminal Appeals were inferior officers and thus could constitutionally be appointed by the Secretary of Transportation, a head of a department. In so doing, Justice Scalia, writing for the Court, stated:

> Generally speaking, the term "inferior officer" connotes a relationship with some higher ranking officer or officers below the President: whether one is an "inferior" officer depends on whether he has a superior. It is not enough that other officers may be identified who formally maintain a higher rank, or possess responsibilities of a greater magnitude. If that were the intention, the Constitution might have used the phrase "lesser officer." Rather, in the context of a clause designed to preserve political accountability relative to important government assignments, we think it evident that "inferior officers" are officers whose work is directed and supervised at some level by others who were appointed by presidential nomination with the advice and consent of the Senate.

Page 350: Insert at the end of note 2:

Following a series of spectacular accounting frauds involving public companies, Congress created the Public Company Accounting Oversight Board, an arm of government clothed with the power to investigate and discipline accounting firms that audit publicly held companies. The Board was composed of five members appointed by the commissioners of the Securities and Exchange Commission and subject to removal for good cause by the SEC commissioners. In Free Enterprise Fund v. Public Company Accounting Oversight Board, 130 S. Ct. 3138 (2010), the Court upheld the validity of the appointment of the Board by the SEC commissioners. First, the Court invoked *Edmond* to conclude that the Board members were inferior officers because they have a superior and their work is subject to supervision or direction by the SEC commissioners. Next, the Court ruled that the SEC is a "department" for purposes of the appointments power because it is "a freestanding component of the Executive Branch, not subordinate to or contained within any other such component," a conclusion consistent with practice in the immediate aftermath of the Constitution's adoption. The SEC commissioners, as a body, were deemed to be the "head" of the department, rather than the Chairman of the SEC, because the SEC acts a body and the Chairman exercises no supervisory control over the actions of the SEC as a whole.

b. The Removal Power

Page 354: Insert new note 1a:

1a. The Outer Boundaries of *Morrison*. When Congress created the Public Company Accounting Oversight Board it vested the power to remove Board members in the commissioners of the Securities and Exchange Commission, but only for "good cause shown." The SEC commissioners, in turn, are removable by the President only for "inefficiency, neglect of duty, or malfeasance in office." In Free Enterprise Fund v. Public Company Accounting Oversight Board, 130 S. Ct. 3138 (2010), the Court invalidated this double-layered limitation on the President's removal power. Chief Justice Roberts wrote for 5-4 majority:

> May the President be restricted in his ability to remove a principal officer, who is in turn restricted in his ability to remove an inferior officer, even though that inferior officer determines the policy and enforces the laws of the United States? We hold that such multilevel protection from removal is contrary to Article II's vesting of the executive power in the President. The President cannot "take Care that the Laws be faithfully executed" if he cannot oversee the faithfulness of the officers who execute them. Here the President cannot remove an officer who enjoys more than one level of good-cause protection, even if the President determines that the officer is neglecting his duties or discharging them improperly. That judgment is instead committed to another officer, who may or may not agree with the President's determination, and whom the President cannot remove simply because that officer disagrees with him. This contravenes the President's "constitutional obligation to ensure the faithful execution of the laws."
>
> [While] we have previously upheld limited restrictions on the President's removal power[, in] those cases . . . only one level of protected tenure separated the President from an officer exercising executive power. It was the President — or a subordinate he could remove at will — who decided whether the officer's conduct merited removal under the good-cause standard. The Act before us does something quite different. It not only protects Board members from removal except for good cause, but withdraws from the President any decision on whether that good cause exists. That decision is vested instead in other tenured officers — the Commissioners —

none of whom is subject to the President's direct control. The result is a Board that is not accountable to the President, and a President who is not responsible for the Board. The added layer of tenure protection makes a difference. Without a layer of insulation between the Commission and the Board, the Commission could remove a Board member at any time, and therefore would be fully responsible for what the Board does. The President could then hold the Commission to account for its supervision of the Board, to the same extent that he may hold the Commission to account for everything else it does.

A second level of tenure protection changes the nature of the President's review. [Because] the Commission cannot remove a Board member at will [the] President . . . cannot hold the Commission fully accountable for the Board's conduct, to the same extent that he may hold the Commission accountable for everything else that it does. The Commissioners are not responsible for the Board's actions [but only] for their own determination of whether the Act's rigorous good-cause standard is met. And even if the President disagrees with their determination, he is powerless to intervene — unless that determination is so unreasonable as to constitute "inefficiency, neglect of duty, or malfeasance in office."

This novel structure does not merely add to the Board's independence, but transforms it. Neither the President, nor anyone directly responsible to him, nor even an officer whose conduct he may review only for good cause, has full control over the Board. The President is stripped of the power our precedents have preserved, and his ability to execute the laws — by holding his subordinates accountable for their conduct — is impaired. That arrangement is contrary to Article II's vesting of the executive power in the President. Without the ability to oversee the Board, or to attribute the Board's failings to those whom he *can* oversee, the President is no longer the judge of the Board's conduct. . . . He can neither ensure that the laws are faithfully executed, nor be held responsible for a Board member's breach of faith. This violates the basic principle that the President "cannot delegate ultimate responsibility or the active obligation to supervise that goes with it," because Article II "makes a single President responsible for the actions of the Executive Branch."

Indeed, if allowed to stand, this dispersion of responsibility could be multiplied. If Congress can shelter the bureaucracy behind two layers of good-cause tenure, why not a third? At oral argument, the Government was unwilling to concede that even *five* layers between the President and the Board would be too many. The officers of such an agency — safely encased within a Matryoshka doll of tenure protections — would be immune from Presidential oversight, even as they exercised power in the people's name. The diffusion of power carries with it a diffusion of accountability. . . . Without a clear and effective chain of command, the public cannot "determine on whom the blame or the punishment of a pernicious measure, or series of pernicious measures ought really to fall." . . . By granting the Board executive power without the Executive's oversight, this Act subverts the President's ability to ensure that the laws are faithfully executed — as well as the public's ability to pass judgment on his efforts. . . .

No one doubts Congress's power to create a vast and varied federal bureaucracy. But where, in all this, is the role for oversight by an elected President? The Constitution requires that a President chosen by the entire Nation oversee the execution of the laws. And the "'fact that a given law or procedure is efficient, convenient, and useful in facilitating functions of government, standing alone, will not save it if it is contrary to the Constitution,'" for "'[c]onvenience and efficiency are not the primary objectives — or the hallmarks — of democratic government.'" One can have a government that functions without being ruled by functionaries, and a government that benefits from expertise without being ruled by experts. Our Constitution was adopted to enable the people to govern themselves, through their elected leaders. The growth of the Executive Branch, which now wields vast power and touches almost every aspect of daily life, heightens the concern that it may slip from the Executive's control, and thus from that of the people. . . .

2.   In Foreign Affairs

b.   War

Page 368: Insert Problem 2a after existing note 2:

2a. Problem. In February 2011, the Libyan people began to protest the regime of Moammar Gaddafi, an uprising that quickly escalated into armed combat between protesters, mostly centered in eastern Libya, and the Libyan military loyal to Gaddafi. On March 19, 2011, after the United Nations had condemned the Gaddafi regime for its brutal treatment of civilians and authorized actions to protect civilians, including imposition of a "no-fly" zone over Libya, President Obama directed American armed forces to attack military targets in Libya to implement the United Nations resolutions. On March 31, 2011 the United States turned over full command and control of the military operations to a NATO coalition. By late May, the 60 day period prescribed in section 5 of the War Powers Resolution had expired. Even so, American armed forces provided about 70% of the military intelligence in the Libya campaign and a majority of the assets used in refueling of warplanes (including mid-air refueling), flew approximately 2,500 sorties in Libya (about 25% of all sorties) and a lesser proportion of air strikes against Libyan air defense targets, and sent numerous armed but unmanned "drone" aircraft to strike Libyan targets. The cost of American military involvement in the Libyan campaign from March through September 2011 is estimated to be about $1.1 billion.

On June 15, 2011, the President transmitted to Speaker John Boehner a report, "United States Activities in Libya," that summarized these matters and explained why the President believed that the War Powers Resolution was in-applicable:

> The President is of the view that the current U.S. military operations in Libya are consistent with the War Powers Resolution and do not under that law require further congressional authorization, because U.S military operations are distinct from the kind of "hostilities" contemplated by the Resolution's 60-day termination provi-sion. ... U.S. operations do not involve sustained fighting or active exchanges of fire with hostile forces, nor do they involve the presence of U.S. ground troops, U.S.

casualties or a serious threat thereof, or any significant chance of escalation into a conflict characterized by those factors.

Within days of this report, ten members of Congress filed suit in the U.S. District Court for the District of Columbia, seeking a declaration that the Libyan conflict is a war and President Obama's commitment of U.S. military assets to the Libyan conflict is unconstitutional. The suit, Kucinich v. Obama, also seeks an injunction to suspend further U.S. military operations in Libya absent a congressional declaration of war.

Has President Obama violated the War Powers Resolution? Analyze the issues presented in Kucinich v. Obama and assess the prospects for success of the claims presented in that suit.

D. *Immunities and Privileges*

2. Executive Immunities

Page 416: Insert at the end of the first paragraph, immediately before Clinton v. Jones:

Saucier required that a court first determine whether the alleged conduct violates a constitutional right and, if so, whether that right was "clearly established" at the time of the alleged violation. In Pearson v. Callahan, 555 U.S. 223 (2009), the Court ruled that *Saucier*'s two-step inquiry was not mandatory. Determination of whether a constitutional violation occurred is not easy at the pleading stage, and requiring such a determination departs from the general rule of avoiding deciding constitutional questions when it is not necessary to do so. Moreover, because qualified immunity is "an immunity from suit rather than a mere defense to liability [and] is effectively lost if a case is erroneously permitted to go to trial," judges should have discretion to determine whether the claimed constitutional right, whether or not violated, was "clearly established" at the time of the official conduct. After *Pearson*, qualified immunity continues to depend on the "objective legal reasonableness of the action, assessed in light of the legal rules that were clearly established at the time it was taken."

Chapter 6
Due Process

B. Substantive Due Process

1. The Incorporation Doctrine

Page 458: Insert new note 4 at the end of the subsection:

4. The Continuing Evolution of Incorporation. In McDonald v. City of Chicago, 130 S. Ct. 3020 (2010), the Supreme Court, by a margin of 5 to 4, ruled that the Second Amendment right to possession of a firearm for purposes of self-defense was "fundamental to *our* scheme of ordered liberty" and thus applicable to the states by the Fourteenth Amendment. But the justices could not agree on the rationale. Justice Alito, joined by Chief Justice Roberts and Justices Scalia and Kennedy, concluded that the Second Amendment right is one of the fundamental rights that are made applicable to the states via the due process guarantee. "Self-defense is a basic right [and] individual self-defense is the *'central component'* of the Second Amendment right." The fundamental nature of armed self-defense was buttressed by the repeated assertion of the right in historical practice, state constitutional provisions, and the action of the 39th Congress, which in 1866 enacted a provision guaranteeing all citizens, regardless of "race, . . . color, or previous condition of slavery" the "constitutional right to bear arms." Thus, the Second Amendment right was not only fundamental but deeply rooted in the nation's history and tradition. An excerpt of this opinion is at the end of note 3, following *Heller*, in Chapter 12 of this supplement.

Justice Thomas concurred in the judgment, but thought that the Second Amendment right was a privilege of national citizenship encompassed in the Fourteenth Amendment's command that no state may "abridge the privileges or immunities of citizens of the United States." Reliance upon the due process clause to protect certain substantive liberties is "a legal fiction," said Justice Thomas. "The notion that a constitutional provision that guarantees only 'process' before a person is deprived of life, liberty, or property could define the substance of those rights strains credulity for even the most casual user of words. Moreover, this fiction is a particularly dangerous one. The one theme that links the Court's substantive due process precedents together is their lack of a guiding principle to distinguish 'fundamental' rights that warrant protection from nonfundamental rights that do not." Justice Thomas relied on historical evidence to support his claim that the privileges of federal citizenship included what colonists regarded as their inalienable rights and that the term, as used in the Fourteenth Amendment, was intended to make the Bill of Rights applicable to the states. An excerpt of his opinion is in note 4, following *Heller*, in Chapter 12 of this supplement.

Page 549: Insert this subsection at the end of the chapter:

3. The Modern Revival: "Privacy" Rights

g. *The Methodology of Substantive Due Process: A Debate*

Substantive due process is controversial in part because there is marked disagreement concerning the appropriate methodology to be employed in determining which rights may be constitutionally fundamental. Much of that controversy has been revealed in the cases you have studied in this chapter, but an explicit debate on the issue erupted between Justices Stevens and Scalia in the following case.

McDONALD v. CITY OF CHICAGO

130 S. Ct. 3020 (2010)

[The Court held that the Second Amendment right to possess a firearm for purposes of self-defense was constitutionally fundamental and made applicable to the states through the Fourteenth Amendment. Four justices thought the right was incorporated into the due process guarantee; Justice Thomas, concurring in the judgment, thought the right was one of the privileges or immunities protected by the Fourteenth Amendment.]

JUSTICE STEVENS, dissenting:
This is a substantive due process case. . . . [The] vast corpus of substantive due process opinions . . . confirm several important principles that ought to guide our resolution of this case. . . . The first, and most basic, principle established by our cases is that the rights protected by the Due Process Clause are not merely procedural in nature. . . . [S]ubstance and procedure are often deeply entwined. [The clause] can be read to "impos[e] nothing less than an obligation to give substantive content to the words 'liberty' and 'due process of law,'" lest superficially fair procedures be permitted to "destroy the enjoyment" of life, liberty, and property . . . . Procedural guarantees are hollow unless linked to substantive interests; and no amount of process can legitimize some deprivations. . . . [H]istorical evidence suggests that, at least by the time of the Civil War if not much earlier, the phrase "due process of law" had acquired

substantive content as a term of art within the legal community. . . . The second principle woven through our cases is that substantive due process is fundamentally a matter of personal liberty. . . . It follows that the term "incorporation," like the term "unenumerated rights," is something of a misnomer. Whether an asserted substantive due process interest is explicitly named in one of the first eight Amendments to the Constitution or is not mentioned, the underlying inquiry is the same: We must ask whether the interest is "comprised within the term liberty." . . .

How should a court go about the analysis, then? Our precedents have established, not an exact methodology, but rather a framework for decisionmaking. . . . The basic inquiry was described by Justice Cardozo more than 70 years ago. When confronted with a substantive due process claim, we must ask whether the allegedly unlawful practice violates values "implicit in the concept of ordered liberty." *Palko*. . . . Justice Cardozo's test undeniably requires judges to apply their own reasoned judgment, but that does not mean it involves an exercise in abstract philosophy. In addition to other constraints . . . [t]extual commitments laid down elsewhere in the Constitution, judicial precedents, English common law, legislative and social facts, scientific and professional developments, practices of other civilized societies, and, above all else, the "'traditions and conscience of our people'" are critical variables. They can provide evidence about which rights really are vital to ordered liberty, as well as a spur to judicial action. A rigid historical test is inappropriate in this case, most basically, because our substantive due process doctrine has never evaluated substantive rights in purely, or even predominantly, historical terms.

More fundamentally, a rigid historical methodology is unfaithful to the Constitution's command. For if it were really the case that the Fourteenth Amendment's guarantee of liberty embraces only those rights "so rooted in our history, tradition, and practice as to require special protection," then the guarantee would serve little function, save to ratify those rights that state actors have *already* been according the most extensive protection. That approach is unfaithful to the expansive principle Americans laid down when they ratified the Fourteenth Amendment and to the level of generality they chose when they crafted its language; it promises an objectivity it cannot deliver and masks the value judgments that pervade any analysis of what customs, defined in what manner, are sufficiently "'rooted'"; it countenances the most revolting injustices in the name of continuity . . . ; and it effaces this Court's distinctive role in saying what the law is, leaving the development and safekeeping of liberty to majoritarian political processes. It is judicial abdication in the guise of judicial modesty. . . .

[The] liberty safeguarded by the Fourteenth Amendment is not merely preservative in nature but rather is a "dynamic concept." . . . The judge who would outsource the interpretation of "liberty" to historical sentiment has turned his back on a task the Constitution assigned to him and drained the document of its intended vitality. . . . [H]ow are we to do justice to its urgent call and its open texture — and to the grant of interpretive discretion the latter embodies —

without injecting excessive subjectivity or unduly restricting the States "broad latitude in experimenting with possible solutions to problems of vital local concern"? . . .

[We] have eschewed attempts to provide any all-purpose, top-down, totalizing theory of "liberty." . . . [The] meaning of liberty cannot be "reduced to any formula; its content cannot be determined by reference to any code." . . . We have insisted that only certain types of especially significant personal interests may qualify for especially heightened protection. . . . Government action that shocks the conscience, pointlessly infringes settled expectations, trespasses into sensitive private realms or life choices without adequate justification, perpetrates gross injustice, or simply lacks a rational basis will always be vulnerable to judicial invalidation. Nor does the fact that an asserted right falls within one of these categories end the inquiry. More fundamental rights may receive more robust judicial protection, but the strength of the individual's liberty interests and the State's regulatory interests must always be assessed and compared. No right is absolute. . . .

The clause safeguards, most basically, "the ability independently to define one's identity," "the individual's right to make certain unusually important decisions that will affect his own, or his family's, destiny," and the right to be respected as a human being. Self-determination, bodily integrity, freedom of conscience, intimate relationships, political equality, dignity and respect — these are the central values we have found implicit in the concept of ordered liberty. . . .

Another key constraint on substantive due process analysis is respect for the democratic process. If a particular liberty interest is already being given careful consideration in, and subjected to ongoing calibration by, the States, judicial enforcement may not be appropriate. . . .

[S]ensitivity to the interaction between the intrinsic aspects of liberty and the practical realities of contemporary society provides an important tool for guiding judicial discretion. This sensitivity is an aspect of a deeper principle: the need to approach our work with humility and caution. Because the relevant constitutional language is so "spacious," I have emphasized that "[t]he doctrine of judicial self-restraint requires us to exercise the utmost care whenever we are asked to break new ground in this field." . . .

First, firearms have a fundamentally ambivalent relationship to liberty. Just as they can help homeowners defend their families and property from intruders, they can help thugs and insurrectionists murder innocent victims. . . . *Your* interest in keeping and bearing a certain firearm may diminish *my* interest in being and feeling safe from armed violence. And while granting you the right to own a handgun might make you safer on any given day — assuming the handgun's marginal contribution to self-defense outweighs its marginal contribution to the risk of accident, suicide, and criminal mischief — it may make you and the community you live in less safe overall, owing to the increased number of handguns in circulation. It is at least reasonable for a democratically elected legislature to take such concerns into account in considering what sorts of regulations would best serve the public welfare. . . .

Second, the right to possess a firearm of one's choosing is different in kind from the liberty interests we have recognized under the Due Process Clause. . . . [It] does not appear to be the case that the ability to own a handgun, or any particular type of firearm, is critical to leading a life of autonomy, dignity, or political equality . . . . The liberty interest asserted [here] is also dissimilar from those we have recognized in its capacity to undermine the security of others. . . .

Third, the experience of other advanced democracies, including those that share our British heritage, undercuts the notion that an expansive right to keep and bear arms is intrinsic to ordered liberty. . . .

Fourth, the Second Amendment differs in kind from the Amendments that surround it, with the consequence that its inclusion in the Bill of Rights is not merely unhelpful but positively harmful to petitioners' claim. . . . The Second Amendment, in other words, "is a federalism provision" . . . .

Nor will the Court's intervention bring any clarity to this enormously complex area of law. Quite to the contrary, today's decision invites an avalanche of litigation that could mire the federal courts in fine-grained determinations about which state and local regulations comport with the *Heller* right — the precise contours of which are far from pellucid — under a standard of review we have not even established. . . .

[The] Court's imposition of a national standard is still more unwise because the elected branches have shown themselves to be perfectly capable of safeguarding the interest in keeping and bearing arms. . . .

Under the "historically focused" approach [Justice Scalia] advocates, numerous threshold questions arise before one ever gets to the history. At what level of generality should one frame the liberty interest in question? What does it mean for a right to be "deeply rooted in this Nation's history and tradition"? By what standard will that proposition be tested? Which types of sources will count, and how will those sources be weighed and aggregated? There is no objective, neutral answer to these questions. . . . It is hardly a novel insight that history is not an objective science, and that its use can therefore "point in any direction the judges favor . . . ." The historian must choose which pieces to credit and which to discount, and then must try to assemble them into a coherent whole. . . .

Justice Scalia's . . . method . . . is unsatisfying on its own terms. For a limitless number of subjective judgments may be smuggled into his historical analysis. Worse, they may be *buried* in the analysis. At least with my approach, the judge's cards are laid on the table for all to see, and to critique. The judge must exercise judgment, to be sure. When answering a constitutional question to which the text provides no clear answer, there is always some amount of discretion; our constitutional system has always depended on judges' filling in the document's vast open spaces. But there is also transparency. . . .

Justice Scalia's method invites not only bad history, but also bad constitutional law. [It] makes little sense to give history dispositive weight in every case. And it makes *especially* little sense to answer questions like whether the right to bear arms is "fundamental" by focusing only on the past, given that both the practical significance and the public understandings of such a right often change as society changes. What if the evidence had shown that, whereas at one time firearm possession contributed substantially to personal liberty and safety, nowadays it contributes nothing, or even tends to undermine them? Would it still have been reasonable to constitutionalize the right? The concern runs still deeper. Not only can historical views be less than completely clear or informative, but they can also be wrong. Some notions that many Americans deeply believed to be true, at one time, turned out not to be true. Some practices that many Americans believed to be consistent with the Constitution's guarantees of liberty and equality, at one time, turned out to be inconsistent with them. . . .

JUSTICE SCALIA, concurring:
 . . . [M]uch of what Justice Stevens writes is a broad condemnation of the theory of interpretation which underlies the Court's opinion, a theory that makes the traditions of our people paramount. He proposes a different theory, which he claims is more "cautiou[s]" and respectful of proper limits on the judicial role. It is that claim I wish to address. . . .

Justice Stevens [urges] readoption of the theory of incorporation articulated in *Palko*. But in fact he does not favor application of that theory at all. . . . That Justice Stevens is not applying any version of *Palko* is clear from comparing, on the one hand, the rights he believes *are* covered, with, on the other hand, his conclusion that the right to keep and bear arms is *not* covered. Rights that pass his test include not just those "relating to marriage, procreation, contraception, family relationships, and child rearing and education," but also rights against "[g]overnment action that shocks the conscience, pointlessly infringes settled expectations, trespasses into sensitive private realms or life choices without adequate justification, [or] perpetrates gross injustice." Not *all* such rights are in, however, since only "*some* fundamental aspects of personhood, dignity, and the like" are protected. Exactly what is covered is not clear. But whatever else is in, he *knows* that the right to keep and bear arms is out, despite its being as "deeply rooted in this Nation's history and tradition" as a right can be. I can find no other explanation for such certitude except that Justice Stevens, despite his forswearing of "personal and private notions," deeply believes it should be out. . . .

The subjective nature of Justice Stevens' standard is also apparent from his claim that it is the courts' prerogative — indeed their *duty* — to update the Due Process Clause so that it encompasses new freedoms the Framers were too narrow-minded to imagine. Courts, he proclaims, must "do justice to [the Clause's] urgent call and its open texture" by exercising the "interpretive discretion the latter embodies." (Why the *people* are not up to the task of deciding what new rights to protect, even though it is *they* who are authorized to make changes [by constitutional amendment] is never explained.) And it would be "judicial abdication" for a judge to "tur[n] his back" on *his* task of determining what the Fourteenth Amendment covers by "outsourc[ing]" the job to "historical sentiment" — that is, by being guided by what the American people throughout our history have thought. It is only we judges, exercising our "own reasoned judgment," who can be entrusted with deciding the Due Process Clause's scope — which rights serve the Amendment's "central values" — which basically means picking the rights we want to protect and discarding those we do not.

Justice Stevens resists this description, insisting that his approach provides plenty of "guideposts" and "constraints" to keep courts from "injecting excessive subjectivity" into the process. Plenty indeed — and that alone is a problem. The ability of omnidirectional guideposts to constrain is inversely proportional to their number. But even individually, each lodestar or limitation he lists either is incapable of restraining judicial whimsy or cannot be squared with the precedents he seeks to preserve. . . .

Justice Stevens moves on to the "most basic" constraint on subjectivity his theory offers: that he would "esche[w] attempts to provide any all-purpose, top-down, totalizing theory of 'liberty.'" The notion that the absence of a coherent theory of the Due Process Clause will somehow *curtail* judicial caprice is at war with reason. Indeterminacy means opportunity for courts to impose whatever rule they like; it is the problem, not the solution. The idea that interpretive pluralism would *reduce* courts' ability to impose their will on the ignorant masses is not merely naive, but absurd. If there are no right answers, there are no wrong answers either.

Justice Stevens also argues that requiring courts to show "respect for the democratic process" should serve as a constraint. That is true, but Justice Stevens would have them show respect in an extraordinary manner. In his view, if a right "is already being given careful consideration in, and subjected to ongoing calibration by, the States, judicial enforcement may not be appropriate." In other words, a right, such as the right to keep and bear arms, that has long been recognized but on which the States are considering restrictions, apparently deserves *less* protection, while a privilege the political branches (instruments of the democratic process) have withheld entirely and continue to withhold, deserves *more*. That topsy-turvy approach conveniently accomplishes the objective of ensuring that the rights this Court held protected in *Casey*, *Lawrence*, and other such cases fit the theory — but at the cost of insulting rather than respecting the democratic process.

The next constraint Justice Stevens suggests is harder to evaluate. He describes as "an important tool for guiding judicial discretion" "sensitivity to the interaction between the intrinsic aspects of liberty and the practical realities of contemporary society." I cannot say whether that sensitivity will really guide judges because I have no idea what it is. Is it some sixth sense instilled in judges when they ascend to the bench? Or does it mean judges are more constrained when they agonize about the cosmic conflict between liberty and its potentially harmful consequences? Attempting to give the concept more precision, Justice Stevens explains that "sensitivity is an aspect of a deeper principle: the need to approach our work with humility and caution." Both traits are undeniably admirable, though what relation they bear to sensitivity is a mystery. But it makes no difference, for the first case Justice Stevens cites in support, *Casey*, dispels any illusion that he has a meaningful form of judicial modesty in mind. . . .

If Justice Stevens' account of the constraints of his approach did not demonstrate that they do not exist, his application of that approach to the case before us leaves no doubt. He offers several reasons for concluding that the Second Amendment right to keep and bear arms is not fundamental enough to be applied against the States. None is persuasive [and] each is either intrinsically indeterminate, would preclude incorporation of rights we have already held incorporated, or both. His approach therefore does nothing to stop a judge from arriving at any conclusion he sets out to reach. . . .

Justice Stevens begins with the odd assertion that "firearms have a fundamentally ambivalent relationship to liberty," since sometimes they are used to cause (or sometimes accidentally produce) injury to others. The source of the rule that only nonambivalent liberties deserve Due Process protection is never explained — proof that judges applying Justice Stevens' approach can add new elements to the test as they see fit. The criterion, moreover, is inherently manipulable. Surely Justice Stevens does not mean that the Clause covers only rights that have *zero* harmful effect on *anyone*. Otherwise even the First Amendment is out. Maybe what he means is that the right to keep and bear arms imposes *too great* a risk to others' physical well-being. But as the plurality explains, other rights we have already held incorporated pose similarly substantial risks to public safety. In all events, Justice Stevens supplies neither a standard for how severe the impairment on others' liberty must be for a right to be disqualified, nor (of course) any method of measuring the severity.

Justice Stevens next suggests that the Second Amendment right is not fundamental because it is "different in kind" from other rights we have recognized. In one respect, of course, the right to keep and bear arms *is* different from some other rights we have held the Clause protects and he would recognize: It is deeply grounded in our nation's history and tradition. But Justice Stevens has a different distinction in mind: Even though he does "not doubt for a moment that many Americans . . . see [firearms] as critical to their way of life as well as to their security," he pronounces that owning a handgun is not "critical to leading a life of autonomy, dignity, or political equality." Who says? Deciding what is essential to an enlightened, liberty-filled life is an inherently political, moral judgment — the antithesis of an objective approach that reaches conclusions by applying neutral rules to verifiable evidence. . . .

No determination of what rights the Constitution of the United States covers would be complete, of course, without a survey of what *other* countries do. When it comes to guns, Justice Stevens explains, our Nation is *already* an outlier among "advanced democracies"; not even our "oldest allies" protect as robust a right as we do, and we should not widen the gap. Never mind that he explains neither which countries qualify as "advanced democracies" nor why others are irrelevant. For there is an even clearer indication that this criterion lets judges pick which rights States must respect and those they can ignore: As the plurality shows, this follow-the-foreign-crowd requirement would foreclose rights that we have held (and Justice Stevens accepts) are incorporated, but that other "advanced" nations do not recognize — from the exclusionary rule to the Establishment Clause. A judge applying Justice Stevens' approach must either throw all of those rights overboard or, as cases Justice Stevens approves have done in considering unenumerated rights, simply ignore foreign law when it undermines the desired conclusion. [S]ee, *e.g., Casey* (making no mention of foreign law).

Justice Stevens also argues that since the right to keep and bear arms was *codified* for the purpose of "prevent[ing] elimination of the militia," it should be viewed as "a federalism provision" logically incapable of incorporation. This criterion, too, evidently applies only when judges want it to. The opinion Justice Stevens quotes for the "federalism provision" principle . . . argued that incorporation of the Establishment Clause "makes little sense" because that Clause was originally understood as a limit on congressional interference with state establishments of religion. Justice Stevens, of course, has no problem with applying the Establishment Clause to the States. While he insists *that* Clause is not a "federalism provision," he does not explain why *it* is not, but the right to keep and bear arms *is* (even though only the latter refers to a "right of the people"). The "federalism" argument prevents the incorporation of only *certain* rights.

Justice Stevens' final reason for rejecting incorporation of the Second Amendment reveals, more clearly than any of the others, the game that is afoot. Assuming that there is a "plausible constitutional basis" for holding that the right to keep and bear arms is incorporated, he asserts that we ought not to do so *for prudential reasons*. Even if we had the authority to withhold rights that are within the Constitution's command (and we assuredly do not), two of the reasons Justice Stevens gives for abstention show just how much power he would hand to judges. The States' "right to experiment" with solutions to the problem of gun violence, he says, is at its apex here because "the best solution is far from clear." That is true of most serious social problems — whether, for example, "the best solution" for rampant crime is to admit confessions unless they are affirmatively shown to have been coerced . . . . The implication of Justice Stevens' call for abstention is that if We The Court conclude that They The People's answers to a problem are silly, we are free to "interven[e]," but if we too are uncertain of the right answer, or merely think the States may be on to something, we can loosen the leash.

A second reason Justice Stevens says we should abstain is that the States have shown they are "capable" of protecting the right at issue, and if anything have protected it too much. That reflects an assumption that judges can distinguish between a *proper* democratic decision to leave things alone (which we should honor), and a case of democratic market failure (which we should step in to correct). I would not — and no judge should — presume to have that sort of omniscience, which seems to me far more "arrogant" than confining courts' focus to our own national heritage.

Justice Stevens . . . makes the usual rejoinder of "living Constitution" advocates to the criticism that it empowers judges to eliminate or expand what the people have prescribed: The traditional, historically focused method, he says, reposes discretion in judges as well. Historical analysis can be difficult; it sometimes requires resolving threshold questions, and making nuanced judgments about which evidence to consult and how to interpret it. I will stipulate to that. But the question to be decided is not whether the historically focused method is a *perfect means* of restraining aristocratic judicial Constitution-writing; but whether it is the *best means available* in an imperfect world. Or indeed, even more narrowly than that: whether it is demonstrably much better than what Justice Stevens proposes. I think it beyond all serious dispute that it is much less subjective, and intrudes much less upon the democratic process. It is less subjective because it depends upon a body of evidence susceptible of reasoned analysis rather than a variety of vague ethico-political First Principles whose combined conclusion can be found to point in any direction the judges favor. In the most controversial matters brought before this Court — for example, the constitutionality of prohibiting abortion, assisted suicide, or homosexual sodomy, or the constitutionality of the death penalty — *any* historical methodology, under *any* plausible standard of proof, would lead to the same conclusion. Moreover, the methodological differences that divide historians, and the varying interpretive assumptions they bring to their work, are nothing compared to the differences among the American people (though perhaps not among graduates of prestigious law schools) with regard to the moral judgments Justice Stevens would have courts pronounce. And whether or not special expertise is needed to answer historical questions, judges most certainly have no "comparative . . . advantage" in resolving moral disputes. What is more, his approach would not eliminate, but multiply, the hard questions courts must confront, since he would not *replace* history with moral philosophy, but would have courts consider *both*.

[The] Court's approach intrudes less upon the democratic process because the rights it acknowledges are those established by a constitutional history formed by democratic decisions; and the rights it fails to acknowledge are left to be democratically adopted or rejected by the people, with the assurance that their decision is not subject to judicial revision. Justice Stevens' approach, on the other hand, deprives the people of that power, since whatever the Constitution and laws may say, the list of protected rights will be whatever courts wish it to be. After all, he notes, the people have been wrong before, and courts may conclude they are wrong in the future. Justice Stevens abhors a system in which "majorities or powerful interest groups always get their way," but replaces it with a system in which unelected and life-tenured judges always get their way. That such usurpation is effected unabashedly — with "the judge's cards . . . laid on the table" — makes it even worse. In a vibrant democracy, usurpation should have to be accomplished in the dark. It is Justice Stevens' approach, not the Court's, that puts democracy in peril.

Page 459: Insert the following section at the end of the chapter:

4. The Modern Revival: Excessive Punitive Damages

The question of whether the Constitution imposes any limits on the amount of punitive damages has produced a growing body of law that unites procedural and substantive due process in a somewhat awkward fashion. When the issue was initially presented to the Supreme Court in the late 1980s, it was contended that the excessive fines clause of the Eighth Amendment operated to limit the amount of punitive damages. A small corpus of commentary had so argued[1] but the Court, in Browning-Ferris Industries of Vermont, Inc. v. Kelco Disposal, Inc., 492 U.S. 257 (1989), concluded that the excessive fines clause placed no limits on punitive damage awards. That decision merely shifted the argument to the due process clause.

In Honda Motor Company v. Oberg, 512 U.S. 415 (1994), the Court held that due process requires judicial review of the size of punitive awards and forbids those that are "grossly excessive." Cooper Industries, Inc. v. Leatherman Tool Group, Inc., 532 U.S. 424 (2001), concluded that such review must be *de novo*. The Court fleshed out this nascent doctrine in the following case.

BMW OF NORTH AMERICA, INC. v. GORE
517 U.S. 559 (1996)

STEVENS, J., delivered the opinion of the Court.

The Due Process Clause of the Fourteenth Amendment prohibits a State from imposing a "grossly excessive" punishment on a tortfeasor. The wrongdoing involved in this case was the decision by a national distributor of automobiles not to advise its dealers, and hence their customers, of predelivery damage to new cars when the cost of repair amounted to less than 3 percent of the car's suggested retail price. The question presented is whether a $2 million punitive damages award to the purchaser of one of these cars exceeds the constitutional limit.

I. [After purchasing a new BMW for about $41,000, respondent Ira Gore learned that auto's paint finish had been damaged in transit from Germany and that it has been repainted at a cost of $601.37. Gore sued BMW in the Alabama courts for fraud. At trial, he introduced expert testimony that, due to the repainting, his car was worth $4,000 less than he paid for it. Gore also introduced evidence that "since 1983 BMW had sold 983 refinished cars as new, including

---

1. See Boston, Punitive Damages and the Eighth Amendment: Application of the Excessive Fines Clause, 5 Cooley L. Rev. 667 (1988); Massey, The Excessive Fines Clause and Punitive Damages: Some Lessons from History, 40 Vand. L. Rev. 1233 (1987); Jeffries, A Comment on the Constitutionality of Punitive Damages, 72 Va. L. Rev. 139 (1986); Note, The Constitutionality of Punitive Damages Under the Excessive Fines Clause of the Eighth Amendment, 85 Mich. L. Rev. 1699 (1987).

14 in Alabama, without disclosing that the cars had been repainted before sale."
Gore argued that BMW should be assessed punitive damages of $4 million,
being the product of $4,000 times 1000 cars. The jury delivered a verdict for
Gore, awarding him $4,000 in compensatory damages and $4 million in punitive
damages.]

[In] a post-trial motion to set aside the punitive damages award[, BMW]
introduced evidence to establish that its nondisclosure policy was consistent with
the laws of roughly 25 States defining the disclosure obligations of automobile
manufacturers, distributors, and dealers. . . . Relying on these statutes, BMW
contended that its conduct was lawful in these States and therefore could not
provide the basis for an award of punitive damages. . . . When the $4 million
verdict was returned in this case, BMW promptly instituted a nationwide policy
of full disclosure of all repairs, no matter how minor. . . . Gore asserted that the
policy change demonstrated the efficacy of the punitive damages award [and]
noted that . . . BMW had received a number of customer complaints relating to
undisclosed repairs and had settled some lawsuits. . . .

The trial judge denied BMW's post-trial motion. [The] Alabama Supreme
Court also rejected BMW's claim that the award exceeded the constitutionally
permissible amount, [but] found that the jury improperly computed the amount
of punitive damages by multiplying Dr. Gore's compensatory damages by the
number of similar sales in other jurisdictions. [Without relying on BMW's
conduct outside Alabama,] the court held that "a constitutionally reasonable
punitive damages award in this case is $2,000,000," and therefore ordered a
remittitur in that amount. . . .

II. Punitive damages may properly be imposed to further a State's legitimate
interests in punishing unlawful conduct and deterring its repetition. . . . States
necessarily have considerable flexibility in determining the level of punitive
damages. . . . Only when an award can fairly be categorized as "grossly excessive" in relation to these interests does it enter the zone of arbitrariness that
violates the Due Process Clause of the Fourteenth Amendment. For that reason,
the federal excessiveness inquiry appropriately begins with an identification of
the state interests that a punitive award is designed to serve. . . .

No one doubts that a State may protect its citizens by prohibiting deceptive
trade practices and by requiring automobile distributors to disclose presale repairs
that affect the value of a new car. But the States need not, and in fact do not,
provide such protection in a uniform manner. Some States rely on the judicial
process to formulate and enforce an appropriate disclosure requirement by applying principles of contract and tort law. Other States have enacted various
forms of legislation that define the disclosure obligations of automobile manufacturers, distributors, and dealers. The result is a patchwork of rules representing
the diverse policy judgments of lawmakers in 50 States. [It] is clear that no single
State could . . . impose its own policy choice on neighboring States. . . .

We think it follows from these principles of state sovereignty and comity that
a State may not impose economic sanctions on violators of its laws with the
intent of changing the tortfeasors' lawful conduct in other States. . . . Gore

argued that the large punitive damages award was necessary to induce BMW to change the nationwide policy that it adopted in 1983. But by attempting to alter BMW's nationwide policy, Alabama would be infringing on the policy choices of other States. To avoid such encroachment, the economic penalties that a State such as Alabama inflicts on those who transgress its laws, whether the penalties take the form of legislatively authorized fines or judicially imposed punitive damages, must be supported by the State's interest in protecting its own consumers and its own economy. Alabama may insist that BMW adhere to a particular disclosure policy in that State. Alabama does not have the power, however, to punish BMW for conduct that was lawful where it occurred and that had no impact on Alabama or its residents. Nor may Alabama impose sanctions on BMW in order to deter conduct that is lawful in other jurisdictions. . . .

The Alabama Supreme Court . . . properly eschewed reliance on BMW's out-of-state conduct, and based its remitted award solely on conduct that occurred within Alabama. The award must be analyzed in . . . light of . . . the interests of Alabama consumers, rather than those of the entire Nation. When [so] limited, it is apparent . . . that this award is grossly excessive.

III. Elementary notions of fairness enshrined in our constitutional jurisprudence dictate that a person receive fair notice . . . of the severity of the penalty that a State may impose. Three guideposts, each of which indicates that BMW did not receive adequate notice of the magnitude of the sanction that Alabama might impose for adhering to the nondisclosure policy adopted in 1983, lead us to the conclusion that the $2 million award against BMW is grossly excessive: the degree of reprehensibility of the nondisclosure; the disparity between the harm or potential harm suffered by Dr. Gore and his punitive damages award; and the difference between this remedy and the civil penalties authorized or imposed in comparable cases. We discuss these considerations in turn.

Degree of Reprehensibility

Perhaps the most important indicium of the reasonableness of a punitive damages award is the degree of reprehensibility of the defendant's conduct. . . . This principle reflects the accepted view that some wrongs are more blameworthy than others. Thus, we have said that . . . "trickery and deceit" are more reprehensible than negligence. [In TXO Production Corp. v. Alliance Resources Corp., 509 U.S. 443 (1993),] the Justices of this Court placed special emphasis on the principle that punitive damages may not be "grossly out of proportion to the severity of the offense." [For] Justice Kennedy, the defendant's intentional malice was the decisive element in a "close and difficult" case.

In this case, none of the aggravating factors associated with particularly reprehensible conduct is present. The harm BMW inflicted on Dr. Gore was purely economic in nature. The presale refinishing of the car had no effect on its performance or safety features, or even its appearance for at least nine months after his purchase. BMW's conduct evinced no indifference to or reckless disregard for the health and safety of others. To be sure, infliction of economic injury, especially when done intentionally through affirmative acts of misconduct, or when the target is financially vulnerable, can warrant a substantial penalty. But this observation does not convert all acts that cause economic harm into torts that are sufficiently reprehensible to justify a significant sanction in addition to compensatory damages. . . . Finally, the record in this case discloses no deliberate false statements, acts of affirmative misconduct, or concealment of evidence of improper motive, such as were present in [Pacific Mut. Life Ins. Co. v. Haslip, 499 U.S. 1 (1991)] and *TXO*. . . . That conduct is sufficiently reprehensible to give rise to tort liability, and even a modest award of exemplary damages does not establish the high degree of culpability that warrants a substantial punitive damages award.

RATIO

The second . . . indicium of an unreasonable or excessive punitive damages award is its ratio to the actual harm inflicted on the plaintiff. The principle that exemplary damages must bear a "reasonable relationship" to compensatory damages has a long pedigree. . . . Some 65 different [English] enactments during the period between 1275 and 1753 provided for double, treble, or quadruple damages. Our decisions in both *Haslip* and *TXO* endorsed the proposition that a comparison between the compensatory award and the punitive award is significant. [The] proper inquiry is "'Whether there is a reasonable relationship between the punitive damages award and *the harm likely to result* from the defendant's conduct as well as the harm that actually has occurred.'" *TXO*, 509 U.S. at 460 (emphasis in original), quoting *Haslip*, 499 U.S. at 21. Thus, in upholding the $10 million award in *TXO*, we relied on the difference between that figure and the harm to the victim that would have ensued if the tortious plan had succeeded. That difference suggested that the relevant ratio was not more than 10 to 1.

The $2 million in punitive damages awarded to Dr. Gore . . . is 500 times the amount of his actual harm as determined by the jury [and] there is no suggestion that Dr. Gore or any other BMW purchaser was threatened with any additional potential harm by BMW's nondisclosure policy. The disparity in this case is thus dramatically greater than those considered in *Haslip* and *TXO*.

Of course, we have consistently rejected the notion that the constitutional line is marked by a simple mathematical formula. . . . [Low] awards of compensatory damages may properly support a higher ratio than high compensatory awards if . . . a particularly egregious act has resulted in only a small amount of economic damages[, or when] the injury is hard to detect or the monetary value of noneconomic harm might have been difficult to determine. . . .

SANCTIONS FOR COMPARABLE MISCONDUCT

Comparing the punitive damages award and the civil or criminal penalties that could be imposed for comparable misconduct provides a third indicium of excessiveness. [A] reviewing court engaged in determining whether an award of punitive damages is excessive should "accord 'substantial deference' to legislative judgments concerning appropriate sanctions for the conduct at issue." . . . In this case the $2 million economic sanction imposed on BMW is substantially greater than the statutory fines available in Alabama and elsewhere for similar malfeasance. The maximum civil penalty authorized by the Alabama Legislature for a violation of its Deceptive Trade Practices Act is $2,000; other States authorize more severe sanctions, with the maxima ranging from $5,000 to $10,000.

IV. . . . As in *Haslip*, we are not prepared to draw a bright line marking the limits of a constitutionally acceptable punitive damages award. Unlike that case, however, we are fully convinced that the grossly excessive award imposed in this case transcends the constitutional limit. . . . The judgment is reversed, and the case is remanded for further proceedings not inconsistent with this opinion.

JUSTICE BREYER, joined by JUSTICES O'CONNOR and SOUTER, concurring.

[This] award . . . was "grossly excessive" in relation to legitimate punitive damages objectives, and hence an arbitrary deprivation of life, liberty, or property in violation of the Due Process Clause. . . . Members of this Court have generally thought, however, that if "fair procedures were followed, a judgment that is a product of that process is entitled to a strong presumption of validity." And the Court also has found that punitive damages procedures very similar to those followed here were not, by themselves, fundamentally unfair. Thus, I believe it important to explain why this presumption of validity is overcome in this instance.

The reason flows from the . . . constitutional importance of legal standards that provide "reasonable constraints" within which "discretion is exercised," that assure "meaningful and adequate review by the trial court whenever a jury has fixed the punitive damages," and permit "appellate review [that] makes certain that the punitive damages are reasonable in their amount and rational in light of their purpose to punish what has occurred and to deter its repetition." . . . This constitutional concern, itself harkening back to the Magna Carta, arises out of the basic unfairness of depriving citizens of life, liberty, or property, through the application, not of law and legal processes, but of arbitrary coercion. . . .

Legal standards need not be precise in order to satisfy this constitutional concern[, but] they must offer some kind of constraint upon a jury or court's discretion, and thus protection against purely arbitrary behavior. The standards the Alabama courts applied here are vague and open ended to the point where they risk arbitrary results. In my view, although the vagueness of those standards does not, by itself, violate due process, it does invite the kind of scrutiny the Court has given the particular verdict before us. [Justice Breyer canvassed Alabama statutory and case law to conclude that neither source adequately cabined discretion in the award of punitive damages. The result is that] the award in this case was both (a) the product of a system of standards that did not significantly constrain . . . discretion in making that award; and (b) grossly excessive in light of the State's legitimate punitive damages objectives. . . .

To the extent that neither clear legal principles nor fairly obvious historical or community-based standards (defining, say, especially egregious behavior) significantly constrain punitive damages awards, is there not a substantial risk of outcomes so arbitrary that they become difficult to square with the Constitution's assurance, to every citizen, of the law's protection? The standards here . . . make this threat real and not theoretical [and this fact] warrants this Court's detailed examination of the award. The second reason — the severe disproportionality between the award and the legitimate punitive damages objectives — reflects a judgment about a matter of degree. [Whatever] the difficulties of drawing a precise line, . . . it is not difficult to say that this award lies on the line's far side. . . .

JUSTICE SCALIA, with whom JUSTICE THOMAS joins, dissenting.

Today we see the latest manifestation of this Court's recent and increasingly insistent "concern about punitive damages that 'run wild.' " Since the Constitution does not make that concern any of our business, the Court's activities in this area are an unjustified incursion into the province of state governments. . . . I do not regard the Fourteenth Amendment's Due Process Clause as a secret repository of substantive guarantees against "unfairness" — neither the unfairness of an excessive civil compensatory award, nor the unfairness of an "unreasonable" punitive award. What the Fourteenth Amendment's procedural guarantee assures is an opportunity to contest the reasonableness of a damages judgment in state court; but there is no federal guarantee a damages award actually *be* reasonable.

This view . . . has not prevailed in our punitive damages cases. When, however, a constitutional doctrine adopted by the Court is not only mistaken but also insusceptible of principled application, I do not feel bound to give it *stare decisis* effect — indeed, I do not feel justified in doing so. Our punitive damages jurisprudence compels such a response. The Constitution provides no warrant for federalizing yet another aspect of our Nation's legal culture (no matter how much in need of correction it may be), and the application of the Court's new rule of constitutional law is constrained by no principle other than the Justices' subjective assessment of the "reasonableness" of the award in relation to the conduct for which it was assessed.

[T]oday's decision [identifies] a "substantive due process" right against a "grossly excessive" award, and [assumes] ultimate authority to decide anew a matter of "reasonableness" resolved in lower court proceedings. . . . Today's decision, though dressed up as a legal opinion, is really no more than a disagreement with the community's sense of indignation or outrage expressed in the punitive award of the Alabama jury, as reduced by the State Supreme Court. It reflects not merely, as the concurrence candidly acknowledges, "a judgment about a matter of degree," but a judgment about the appropriate degree of indignation or outrage, which is hardly an analytical determination.

There is no precedential warrant for giving our judgment priority over the judgment of state courts and juries on this matter. The only support for the Court's position is to be found in a handful of errant federal cases, bunched within a few years of one other, which invented the notion that an unfairly severe civil sanction amounts to a violation of constitutional liberties. [These cases] simply fabricated the "substantive due process" right at issue. . . . These cases fall far short of what is needed to supplant this country's longstanding practice regarding exemplary awards. . . .

One might understand the Court's eagerness to enter this field . . . if it had something useful to say. In fact, however, its opinion provides virtually no guidance . . . as to what a "constitutionally proper" level of punitive damages might be. . . .

"Alabama does not have the power," the Court says, "to punish BMW for conduct that was lawful where it occurred and that had no impact on Alabama or its residents." That may be true, though only in the narrow sense that a person cannot be *held liable to be punished* on the basis of a lawful act. But if a person has been held subject to punishment because he committed an *un*lawful act, the *degree* of his punishment assuredly *can* be increased on the basis of any other conduct of his that displays his wickedness, unlawful or not. . . . Why could the Supreme Court of Alabama not consider lawful (but disreputable) conduct, both inside and outside Alabama, for the purpose of assessing just how bad an actor BMW was?

[Because the reduced award of punitive damages was not based on any conduct outside Alabama,] the only question presented . . . is whether that award, limited to petitioner's Alabama conduct and viewed in light of the factors identified as properly informing the inquiry, is excessive. The Court's sweeping (and largely unsupported) statements regarding the relationship of punitive awards to lawful or unlawful out-of-state conduct are the purest dicta.

[The Court's three guideposts — reprehensibility, ratio, and comparable sanctions — necessarily] establish federal standards governing the hitherto exclusively state law of damages. . . . Of course it will not be easy for the States to comply with this new federal law of damages, no matter how willing they are to do so. In truth, the "guideposts" mark a road to nowhere; they provide no real guidance at all. [The Court's] criss-crossing platitudes yield no real answers in no real cases. And it must be noted that the Court nowhere says that these three "guideposts" are the *only* guideposts; indeed, it makes very clear that they are not. . . . [Even] these utter platitudes, if they should ever happen to produce an answer, may be overridden by other unnamed considerations. The Court has constructed a framework that does not genuinely constrain, that does not inform state legislatures and lower courts — that does nothing at all except confer an artificial air of doctrinal analysis upon its essentially ad hoc determination that this particular award of punitive damages was not "fair."

[As] a matter of logic there is no more justification for ignoring the jury's determination as to *how* reprehensible petitioner's conduct was (*i.e.*, how much it deserves to be punished), than there is for ignoring its determination that it was reprehensible *at all* (*i.e.*, that the wrong was willful and punitive damages are therefore recoverable). [The] logical and necessary consequence of the Court's approach is the recognition of a constitutional right against unreasonably *imposed* awards as well. The elevation of "fairness" in punishment to a principle of "substantive due process" means that every punitive award unreasonably imposed is unconstitutional; such an award is by definition excessive, since it attaches a penalty to conduct undeserving of punishment. Indeed, if the Court is correct, it must be that every claim that a state jury's award of *compensatory* damages is "unreasonable" (because not supported by the evidence) amounts to an assertion of constitutional injury. And the same would be true for determinations of liability. By today's logic, *every* dispute as to evidentiary sufficiency in a state civil suit poses a question of constitutional moment, subject to review in this Court. That is a stupefying proposition.

For the foregoing reasons, I respectfully dissent. [A dissent by Justice Ginsburg, in which Chief Justice Rehnquist joined, is omitted.]

* * *

In State Farm Mutual Automobile Insurance Company v. Campbell, 538 U.S. 408 (2003), the Court suggested that awards of ten times or more compensatory damages might be presumed to be void. Although that issue was present in the following case, the Court declined to rule on it, preferring to rest its decision on another ground.

PHILIP MORRIS, USA v. WILLIAMS
549 U.S. 346 (2007)

JUSTICE BREYER delivered the opinion of the Court.

[Jesse Williams smoked Marlboro^{TM} cigarettes. They killed him. In Oregon state court his widow, Mayola, sued Philip Morris, the Marlboro^{TM} manufacturer, for negligence and deceit. Mayola Williams contended that Philip Morris had knowingly and falsely led Jesse to believe that smoking posed no danger to health. Williams urged the jury to consider how many other people in Oregon had died and would die from smoking. She argued that 10% of smokers would die from their habit and that, due to Philip Morris's share of the cigarette market, it was responsible for one-third of those deaths. Philip Morris unsuccessfully asked the judge to instruct the jury that "you may consider the extent of harm suffered by others in determining what [the] reasonable relationship is" between punitive damages and "the harm caused to Jesse Williams" by Philip Morris, but "you are not to punish the defendant for the impact of its alleged misconduct on other persons, who may bring lawsuits of their own in which other juries can resolve their claims. . . . " Instead, the trial judge told the jury that "punitive damages are awarded against a defendant to punish misconduct and to deter misconduct, [and] are not intended to compensate the plaintiff or anyone else for damages caused by the defendant's conduct." The jury returned a verdict for

Williams and awarded her $821,000 in compensatory damages and $79.5 million in punitive damages. The trial judge reduced the award to $32 million, the Oregon intermediate appeals court reinstated the jury's award, and the Oregon Supreme Court ultimately affirmed the appeals court.]

. . . We are asked whether the Constitution's Due Process Clause permits a jury to base that award in part upon its desire to *punish* the defendant for harming persons who are not before the court (*e.g.*, victims whom the parties do not represent). We hold that such an award would amount to a taking of "property" from the defendant without due process. . . . In our view, the Constitution's Due Process Clause forbids a State to use a punitive damages award to punish a defendant for injury that it inflicts upon nonparties or those whom they directly represent, *i.e.*, injury that it inflicts upon those who are, essentially, strangers to the litigation. For one thing, . . . a defendant threatened with punishment for injuring a nonparty victim has no opportunity to defend against the charge, by showing, for example in a case such as this, that the other victim was not entitled to damages because he or she knew that smoking was dangerous or did not rely upon the defendant's statements to the contrary. For another, to permit punishment for injuring a nonparty victim would add a near standardless dimension to the punitive damages equation. How many such victims are there? How seriously were they injured? Under what circumstances did injury occur? The trial will not likely answer such questions as to nonparty victims. The jury will be left to speculate. And the fundamental due process concerns to which our punitive damages cases refer — risks of arbitrariness, uncertainty and lack of notice — will be magnified. Finally, we can find no authority supporting the use of punitive damages awards for the purpose of punishing a defendant for harming others. . . .

[Williams] argues that she is free to show harm to other victims because it is relevant to a different part of the punitive damages constitutional equation, namely, reprehensibility. That is to say, harm to others shows more reprehensible conduct. Philip Morris . . . does not deny that a plaintiff may show harm to others in order to demonstrate reprehensibility. Nor do we. Evidence of actual harm to nonparties can help to show that the conduct that harmed the plaintiff also posed a substantial risk of harm to the general public, and so was particularly reprehensible. . . . Yet for the reasons given above, a jury may not go further than this and use a punitive damages verdict to punish a defendant directly on account of harms it is alleged to have visited on nonparties.

[It] is constitutionally important for a court to provide assurance that the jury will ask the right question, not the wrong one. . . . We therefore conclude that the Due Process Clause requires States to provide assurance that juries are not asking the wrong question, *i.e.*, seeking, not simply to determine reprehensibility, but also to punish for harm caused strangers. [There is, however,] a practical problem. How can we know whether a jury, in taking account of harm caused others under the rubric of reprehensibility, also seeks to *punish* the defendant for having caused injury to others? Our answer is that state courts cannot authorize procedures that create an unreasonable and unnecessary risk of any such confusion occurring. In particular, we believe that where the risk of that misunderstanding is a significant one — because, for instance, of the sort of evidence that was introduced at trial or the kinds of argument the plaintiff made to the jury — a court, upon request, must protect against that risk. Although the States have some flexibility to determine what *kind* of procedures they will implement, federal constitutional law obligates them to provide *some* form of protection in appropriate cases.

[Because] the Oregon Supreme Court applied the wrong constitutional standard when considering Philip Morris'[s] appeal [we] remand this case so that the Oregon Supreme Court can apply the standard we have set forth. [We do] not consider whether the award is constitutionally "grossly excessive."

JUSTICE STEVENS, dissenting.

. . . Unlike the Court, I see no reason why an interest in punishing a wrong-doer "for harming persons who are not before the court" should not be taken into consideration when assessing the appropriate sanction for reprehensible conduct. [P]unitive damages are a sanction for the public harm the defendant's conduct has caused or threatened. There is little difference between the justification for a criminal sanction, such as a fine or a term of imprisonment, and an award of punitive damages. . . . To award compensatory damages to remedy . . . third-party harm might well constitute a taking of property from the defendant without due process, [but] a punitive damages award, instead of serving a compensatory purpose, serves the entirely different purposes of retribution and deterrence that underlie every criminal sanction. This justification for punitive damages has even greater salience when, as in this case, the award is payable in whole or in part to the State rather than to the private litigant. [The] majority relies on a distinction between taking third-party harm into account in order to assess the reprehensibility of the defendant's conduct — which is permitted — and from doing so in order to punish the defendant "directly" — which is forbidden. This nuance eludes me. When a jury increases a punitive damages award because injuries to third parties enhanced the reprehensibility of the defendant's conduct, the jury is by definition punishing the defendant — directly — for third-party harm. A murderer who kills his victim by throwing a bomb that injures dozens of bystanders should be punished more severely than one who harms no one other than his intended victim. Similarly, there is no reason why the measure of the appropriate punishment for engaging in a campaign of deceit in distributing a poisonous and addictive substance to thousands of cigarette smokers statewide should not include consideration of the harm to those "bystanders" as well as the harm to the individual plaintiff. The Court endorses a contrary conclusion without providing us with any reasoned justification. . . .

It is far too late in the day to argue that the Due Process Clause merely guarantees fair procedure and imposes no substantive limits on a State's law-making power. It remains true, however, that the Court should be "reluctant to expand the concept of substantive due process because guideposts for responsible decisionmaking in this unchartered area are scarce and open-ended." Judicial restraint counsels us to "exercise the utmost care whenever we are asked to break new ground in this field." Today the majority ignores that sound advice when it announces its new rule of substantive law.

JUSTICE THOMAS, dissenting.

. . . I write separately to reiterate my view that "'The Constitution does not constrain the size of punitive damages awards.'" It matters not that the Court styles today's holding as "procedural" because the "procedural" rule is simply a confusing implementation of the substantive due process regime this Court has created for punitive damages. . . . Today's opinion proves once again that this Court's punitive damages jurisprudence is "insusceptible of principled application"

[A dissent by Justice Ginsburg, which was joined by Justices Scalia and Thomas, is omitted.]

NOTES

1. Substantive or Procedural Due Process?   The Court says that the due process clause imposes constitutional limits on the size of punitive damages. Are these limits rooted in procedural or substantive due process? Recall that the Court's view is that a property interest is to be determined by state law sources, such as statutory or common law, contracts, or anything else that might reasonably cause a person to have more than a unilateral expectation of some right or benefit. Yet, in these cases, state statutory and common law provide for imposition of punitive damages. Perhaps the procedural issue is that the size of punitive damage awards is arbitrary because the states inadequately confine jury discretion. But if that is so, does the Court's doctrine effectively eliminate arbitrariness? The majority in *Philip Morris* says that its ruling is procedural, but is it? According to the Court, Oregon may not punish civil defendants for harm they have inflicted on third parties. What sort of *procedure* could Oregon devise that would permit it to do so? If there are none, does that mean that the holding in *Philip Morris* is in fact substantive?

2. *Sui Generis* Substantive Due Process?   Suppose that the limits on punitive damages are an aspect of substantive due process. Are these limits "deeply rooted in [our] Nation's history and tradition"? Is freedom from excessive punitive damages a constitutionally fundamental liberty interest that can only be infringed upon proof that the infringement is necessary to accomplish a compelling governmental interest? If not, what is the standard of review that the Court uses in this area? The Court says three factors are important to resolve whether an award of punitive damages is constitutionally valid, but admits that they do not exhaust the relevant factors that control resolution of the question. The Court says that the analytical process in substantive due process cases is to first frame the alleged right with careful specificity, then to determine whether it is within our history and tradition to recognize it as a constitutionally fundamental liberty interest and, if so, to presume that infringements of the right are void unless the government can justify them under strict scrutiny. Yet, the Court departs from this framework with some regularity. The undue burden test in abortion cases relies on neither fundamental rights nor strict scrutiny; *Lawrence* observed the form of this analysis but used a moral judgment of its own to declare that Texas's moral justification was inadequate; *Moore* evaded the question of the level of scrutiny applicable to the right to live with one's relatives, even though that right was found to be "deeply rooted"; and the "right to die" cases assume the existence of such a right but never find that it is present in the cases that consider the problem. Are the punitive damages cases simply another analytical exception to the stated doctrine? If so, what significance, if any, does that conclusion have with respect to the entire project of substantive due process?

3. Federal Common Law Limits.   In Exxon Shipping Company v. Baker, 554 U.S. 471 (2008), the Supreme Court reviewed, under federal maritime common law, punitive damages of $5 billion (reduced by the Ninth Circuit to $2.5 billion) assessed against Exxon for the 1989 *Exxon Valdez* oil spill in Prince William Sound, Alaska. The original award was ten times the compensatory damages. Ruling only under federal maritime common law, rather than the Constitution's due process clause, the Court declared:

> The real problem . . . is the stark unpredictability of punitive awards. [T]he spread [of awards] is great, and the outlier cases subject defendants to punitive damages that dwarf the corresponding compensatories. . . . [E]vidence of an accepted limit of [a] reasonable civil penalty [is] in several studies . . . showing the median ratio of punitive to compensatory verdicts, reflecting what juries and judges have considered reasonable across many hundreds of punitive awards. . . . The data put the median ratio for the entire gamut of circumstances at less than 1:1, meaning that the compensatory award exceeds the punitive award in most cases. . . . [W]e we would expect that awards at the median or lower would roughly express jurors' sense of reasonable penalties in cases with no earmarks of exceptional blameworthiness . . . (cases like this one, without intentional or malicious conduct, and without behavior driven primarily by desire for gain . . .) and cases (again like this one) without the modest economic harm or odds of detection that have opened the door to higher awards. [Thus,] we consider that a 1:1 ratio . . . is a fair upper limit in such maritime cases.

Though not a constitutional case, is *Exxon Shipping* an augury of future due process limits on punitive damages?

Chapter 7
Economic Rights: The Takings and Contracts Clauses

A. The Takings Clause

Page 552: Insert the following after the first paragraph:

In Stop the Beach Renourishment, Inc. v. Florida Department of Environmental Conservation, 130 S. Ct. 2592 (2010), the Supreme Court affirmed the Florida Supreme Court's ruling that a Florida statutory scheme that allegedly curtailed the common law rights of beachfront landowners in order to restore hurricane-eroded beaches was not a taking. In reaching that decision, four justices (Chief Justice Roberts and Justices Scalia, Thomas, and Alito) opined that

> "States effect a taking if they recharacterize as public property what was previously private property," whether the actor accomplishing the recharacterization is the legislature, executive, or judiciary. "The Takings Clause . . . is concerned simply with the act, and not with the governmental actor. . . . There is no textual justification for saying that the existence or the scope of a State's power to expropriate private property without just compensation varies according to the branch of government effecting the expropriation. Nor does common sense recommend such a principle. It would be absurd to allow a State to do by judicial decree what the Takings Clause forbids it to do by legislative fiat. Our precedents provide no support for the proposition that takings effected by the judicial branch are entitled to special treatment, and in fact suggest the contrary. [PruneYard Shopping Center v. Robins, 447 U.S. 74 (1980); Webb's Fabulous Pharmacies, Inc. v. Beckwith, 449 U.S. 155 (1980).] . . . If a legislature *or a court* declares that what was once an established right of private property no longer exists, it has taken that property, no less than if the State had physically appropriated it or destroyed its value by regulation." [emphasis in original]

Even so, the Court ruled that the Florida Supreme Court's ruling that there was no taking was correct because the Florida law, as interpreted by the Florida court, did not eliminate any right of private property that was previously established in Florida law. Justice Kennedy, joined by Justice Sotomayor, concurred in the judgment in order to suggest that the due process clauses, rather than the takings clause, might be the vehicle to address alleged judicial takings. Justice Breyer, concurring in the judgment, claimed that it was unnecessary to decide the question of whether judicial decisions are subject to the takings clause, but then opined that, in any case, the Florida Supreme Court's ruling was not a judicial taking, a view that led Justice Scalia to retort that Justice Breyer's position required him to "either (a) grapple with the artificial question of what would constitute a judicial taking if there were such a thing as a judicial taking (reminiscent of the perplexing question how much wood would a woodchuck chuck if a woodchuck could chuck wood?), or (b) answer in the negative what he considers to be the 'unnecessary' constitutional question whether there is such a thing as a judicial taking."

1.   The Public Use Requirement

Page 562: Insert the following at the end of note 3:

In light of *Midkiff* and *Kelo*, consider whether the following case satisfies the public use requirement.

DIDDEN v. VILLAGE OF PORT CHESTER
173 Fed. Appx. 931 (2d Cir. 2006); 2006 U.S. LEXIS 8653

Plaintiffs-Appellants appeal from a . . . decision and order of the United States District Court for the Southern District of New York dismissing their complaint alleging various constitutional violations under 42 U.S.C. § 1983 against the Village of Port Chester and others. . . . In April 1998, Defendant-Appellee G&S Port Chester, LLC, ("G&S"), entered into a development agreement with Defendant-Appellee Village of Port Chester that named G&S as the designated developer of a marina redevelopment project. On July 14, 1999, after a public hearing, the Defendant-Appellee Village Board of Trustees adopted a resolution in which it made a finding of public purpose for con-demnation of the properties located in the redevelopment district. In March 2003, Appellants discussed with representatives of [CVS,] a pharmacy chain[,] the possibility of constructing a pharmacy on their property. A portion of Appellants' property adjoined the redevelopment district and another portion lay within the redevelopment district. According to Appellants, at a November 2003 negotiation session with Defendants-Appellees G&S and Wasser [G&S's prin-cipal representative], Wasser demanded $800,000 from them in order to avert a condemnation proceeding of their property within the redevelopment district, and offered to allow them to proceed if [G&S and Wasser] were given a [50%] partnership interest in the project. Appellants refused both demands and, two days later, they received a petition seeking to condemn their property. On appeal, Appellants advance constitutional claims based on the Fifth and Fourteenth Amendments asserting . . . that they have a right "not to have their property taken by the State through the power of eminent domain for a private use, regardless of whether just compensation is given." . . .

[To] the extent that Appellants assert that the Takings Clause prevents the State from condemning their property for a private use within a redevelopment district, regardless of whether they have been provided with just compensation, the recent Supreme Court decision in Kelo v. City of New London obliges us to conclude that they have articulated no basis upon which relief can be granted. ("Just as we decline to second-guess the City's considered judgments about the efficacy of its development plan, we also decline to second-guess the City's determinations as to what lands it needs to acquire in order to effectuate the project.") Finally, we agree with the district court that Appellees' voluntary attempts to resolve Appellants' demands was neither an unconstitutional exaction in the form of extortion nor an equal protection violation. . . .

NOTE

Developer Wasser's plans for the condemned property are reported to have been to construct a Walgreen's pharmacy. Does this establish that the putative public use was pretextual? Would it make any difference if Wasser had intended to develop the condemned site as low-income housing, or luxury housing?

B. The Contracts Clause

1. Public Contracts After *Blaisdell*

Page 601: Insert new Note after existing Note following U.S. Trust:

Burden of Proof. Who has the burden of proving that a state's impairment of a contract to which it is a party is or is not reasonable and necessary? Does *U.S. Trust* provide an answer? The Court said that in applying the reasonable and necessary standard "complete deference . . . is not appropriate because the State's self-interest is at stake." Does (or should) that statement indicate that the state has the burden of proof of reasonableness and necessity?

The circuit courts are divided on the issue. Southern Cal. Gas Co. v. City of Santa Ana, 336 F.3d 885, 894 (9th Cir. 2003), and Toledo Area AFL-CIO Council v. Pizza, 154 F.3d 307, 323 (6th Cir. 1998) allocate the burden to the defendant state. Conversely, United Auto., Aero., Agric. Implement Workers of America Int'l Union v. Fortuo, 633 F.3d 37, 42, 45 (2011), assigned that burden to the plaintiff private party. Cf. Buffalo Teachers Federation v. Tobe, 464 F.3d 362, 365 (2d Cir. 2006) (plaintiffs must "produce evidence that the state's self-interest rather than the general welfare of the public motivated the state's conduct).

Chapter 8
Equal Protection

C. Strict Scrutiny and Suspect Classifications: Race and Ethnicity

4. Affirmative Action

b. General Principles

Page 679: Insert the following after note 3 (Problems), immediately before Section C.4.c:

4. *Wygant* and Title VII of the Civil Rights Act. The City of New Haven, Connecticut used a written and oral examination system to determine which city firefighters would be eligible for promotion to Lieutenant and Captain. Substantially more white and Hispanic firefighters qualified for promotion than black firefighters. The test results were then challenged as producing a racially disparate result that, it was contended, would violate 42 U.S.C. § 2000e-2(k)(1)(A), which forbids the use of any "employment practice that causes a disparate impact on the basis of race," unless the employer can prove that the practice is "job related . . . and consistent with business necessity," unless the plaintiff can show that the employer refuses to use an alternative practice that will serve the employer's needs with less disparate impact. The City agreed and decided to ignore the test results. The white and Hispanic firefighters denied promotions then sued, contending that New Haven's actions constituted a violation of the disparate treatment section of Title VII of the Civil Rights Act, 42 U.S.C. § 2000e-2(a)(1), which prohibits any form of intentional employment discrimination on the basis of race, and the Equal Protection guarantee. In Ricci v. DeStefano, 129 S. Ct. 2658 (2009), the Court ruled for the plaintiff firefighters on the statutory issue and did not reach the constitutional question.

The Court declared that the City's refusal to honor the test results was, on its face, a violation of the disparate treatment section of Title VII, because it was motivated entirely by race, but then considered whether the City's "purpose to avoid disparate-impact liability excuses what otherwise would be prohibited disparate-treatment discrimination." The standard the Court used to conclude that the City had failed to establish such an excuse was derived from Justice Powell's plurality opinion in Wygant v. Jackson Board of Education (Casebook,

p. 665). The Court in *Ricci* noted "that certain government actions to remedy past racial discrimination — actions that are themselves based on race — are constitutional only where there is a 'strong basis in evidence' that the remedial actions were necessary." Although the Court said it need not decide whether "the statutory constraints under Title VII must be parallel in all respects to those under the Constitution," it ruled that an employer must have a "strong basis in evidence" of disparate impact liability in order to justify the employer's use of a race-based remedy to avoid disparate impact liability. The Court expressly noted, however, that it was *not* holding "that meeting the strong-basis-in-evidence standard would satisfy the Equal Protection Clause in a future case. . . . [W]e need not decide whether a legitimate fear of disparate impact is ever sufficient to justify discriminatory treatment under the Constitution."

The City failed to show the strong basis in evidence of disparate impact liability. A "prima facie case of disparate-impact liability — essentially, a threshold showing of a significant statistical disparity and nothing more — is far from a strong basis in evidence that the City would have been liable under Title VII had it certified the results." New Haven failed to prove either that "the examinations were not job related and consistent with business necessity, or [that] there existed an equally valid, less-discriminatory alternative that served the City's needs but that the City refused to adopt."

Justice Scalia, concurring in full, noted that the Court must eventually decide the constitutional question of whether equal protection principles forbid the federal government from requiring employers to discriminate on the basis of race in order to avoid statutory liability for employment practices that have a racially disparate impact. Justice Ginsburg, joined by Justices Stevens, Souter, and Breyer, dissented. They argued that New Haven had "ample cause" or "good cause" to use race to avoid statutory disparate impact liability. The dissent did not reveal exactly what constitutes ample or good cause.

Chapter 9

Free Expression of Ideas

B. Content-Based Regulation of Speech

1. Incitement of Immediate Crime

c. The Contemporary Standard for Incitement

Page 817: Insert at the end of note 4:

In Holder v. Humanitarian Law Project, 130 S. Ct. 2705 (2010), the Court upheld § 2339B's prohibition of providing "training," "expert advice or assistance," "service," or "personnel" to designated terrorist organizations as applied to the respondent's intended speech. The Court concluded that the ban was not unconstitutionally vague and then proceeded to apply strict scrutiny because the statutory prohibition singled out speech on the basis of its content. Only speech to the terrorist organization that constituted specific "training," "expert advice or assistance," or "service" was prohibited; generalized speech or independent advocacy of the aims of the terrorist organization was unaffected by the statutory ban. The Court deferred to congressional findings that "foreign organizations that engage in terrorist activity are so tainted by their criminal conduct that any contribution to such an organization facilitates that conduct." The Court noted that it did not defer because national security was at stake; rather, deference was warranted because "when it comes to collecting evidence and drawing factual inferences in this area, 'the lack of competence on the part of the courts is marked,' and respect for the Government's conclusions is appropriate. One reason for that respect is that national security and foreign policy concerns arise in connection with efforts to confront evolving threats in an area where information can be difficult to obtain and the impact of certain conduct difficult [for courts] to assess." For the same reasons, the Court rejected respondent's claim that its right of expressive association was infringed. Justice Breyer, joined by Justices Ginsburg and Sotomayor, dissented.

Did the Court revert to the *Gitlow* standard, or is the deference in *Holder* both more limited and more warranted than in *Gitlow*?

5. Offensive Speech

a. The General Rule

Page 863: Insert after note 2:

RODRIGUEZ v. MARICOPA COUNTY COMMUNITY COLLEGE DISTRICT
605 F. 3d 703 (9th Cir. 2010)

KOZINSKI, Chief Judge, joined by JUSTICE O'CONNOR, sitting by designation, and IKUTA, Circuit Judge.

We consider the interplay between the First Amendment and the right to be free of workplace harassment on the basis of protected status.

Professor Walter Kehowski sent three racially-charged emails over a distribution list maintained by the Maricopa County Community College District, where he teaches math. Every district employee with an email address received a copy. Plaintiffs, a certified class of the district's Hispanic employees, sued the district, [the college president and district chancellor], . . . claiming that [the] failure to properly respond to Kehowski's emails created a hostile work environment in violation of Title VII and the Equal Protection Clause.

Kehowski's first email had "Dia de la raza" as its subject line and asked, "Why is the district endorsing an explicitly racist event?" Dia de la Raza translates as "Day of the Race" and is celebrated by some Hispanics instead of Columbus Day. Kehowski's next email, sent almost a week later, began, "YES! Today's Columbus Day! It's time to acknowledge and celebrate the superiority of Western Civilization." Kehowski then offered excerpts from a variety of articles. One article quoted Arthur Schlesinger, Jr. as saying that "democracy, human rights and cultural freedom" are "European ideas." Another promoted a theory that "Native Americans actually committed genocide against the original white-skinned inhabitants of North America." Yet another argued that "America did not become the mightiest nation on earth without distinct values and discrimination" and asserted that "[o]ur survival depends on discrimination." Two days later, Kehowski sent a third email [in which he] quoted an email calling his messages "racist" and said: "Boogie-boogie-boo to you too! Racist? Hardly. Realistic is more like it." He quoted an email claiming that "[m]ost thinking people believe that the European, Christian victory over the Moorish, Islamic (and African) culture in Spain is an example of a victory of a 'backward' culture over one that was more civilized." He responded: "[H]istory has answered quite convincingly which cultures were backward." And he warned: "[I]f we don't pull ourselves out of the multicultural stupor, another culture with some pretty unsavory characteristics . . . will dominate. . . . "

This third email linked to a website maintained by Kehowski on the district's web server [in which he] declared that "[t]he only immigration reform imperative is preservation of White majority" and urged visitors to "[r]eport illegal aliens to the INS." Like his emails, Kehowski's website quoted and linked to articles. One critiqued a "shallow and self-contradictory" ideology in which "[r]ace must be held meaningless only by whites." Another expressed concern that "[t]he persistent inflow of Hispanic immigrants threatens to divide the United States into two peoples."

[The college president and the district chancellor] condemned Kehowski's ideas [by email and a press release. Although none of Kehowski's emails had been sent to students, they became aware of them and] the student body president circulated an email to the faculty declaring that Kehowski "did not do anything illegal, but none of us believe [his] actions were ethical or in good taste." Contemporary press accounts describe vocal student protests against Kehowski.

A number of district employees also complained to the administration that Kehowski's statements had created a hostile work environment. No disciplinary action was taken against Kehowski, and no steps were taken to enforce the district's existing anti-harassment policy.

Plaintiffs now seek damages and other relief on the ground that defendants "failed to take immediate or appropriate steps to prevent Mr. Kehowski from sending Plaintiffs harassing emails" and from disseminating harassing speech via his district-hosted website. The district court . . . denied summary judgment to the president and chancellor on plaintiffs' constitutional claim . . . and to the [community college district] on both the constitutional and Title VII claims. The president and chancellor brought this interlocutory appeal, challenging the district court's ruling that they are not entitled to qualified immunity as to the alleged Equal Protection violation.

[In order to dispose of the issue of qualified immunity, we] begin by addressing the precise scope of the district's constitutional obligation. [Pearson v. Callahan, 129 S. Ct. 808, 815-816 (2009).] Plaintiffs may wish that the district had disciplined or dismissed Kehowski, but the district wasn't required to do so. When an employer is made aware of unlawful harassment, employees are entitled to have the employer take reasonable and appropriate steps to investigate and make it stop. . . . Plaintiffs suggest the district should have applied its existing anti-harassment policy to silence Kehowski as soon as the nature of his speech became apparent. . . . It's true that a public employer's refusal to enforce existing policies to stop unlawful harassment may violate the Equal Protection Clause. But Kehowski's speech was not unlawful harassment. Plaintiffs no doubt feel demeaned by Kehowski's speech, as his very thesis can be understood to be that they are less than equal. But that highlights the problem with plaintiffs' suit. Their objection to Kehowski's speech is based entirely on his point of view, and it is axiomatic that the government may not silence speech because the ideas it promotes are thought to be offensive.

Indeed, precisely because Kehowski's ideas fall outside the mainstream, his words sparked intense debate: Colleagues emailed responses, and Kehowski replied; some voiced opinions in the editorial pages of the local paper; the administration issued a press release; and, in the best tradition of higher learning, students protested. The Constitution embraces such a heated exchange of views, even (perhaps especially) when they concern sensitive topics like race, where the risk of conflict and insult is high. Without the right to stand against society's most strongly-held convictions, the marketplace of ideas would decline into a boutique of the banal, as the urge to censor is greatest where debate is most disquieting and orthodoxy most entrenched.

This is particularly so on college campuses. Intellectual advancement has traditionally progressed through discord and dissent, as a diversity of views ensures that ideas survive because they are correct, not because they are popular. Colleges and universities — sheltered from the currents of popular opinion by tradition, geography, tenure and monetary endowments — have historically fostered that exchange. But that role in our society will not survive if certain points of view may be declared beyond the pale. The First Amendment also demands substantial deference to the college's decision not to take action against Kehowski. The academy's freedom to make such decisions without excessive judicial oversight is an "essential" part of academic liberty and a "special concern of the First Amendment." [*Bakke.*] . . . To afford academic speech the breathing room that it requires, courts must defer to colleges' decisions to err on the side of academic freedom. Otherwise, schools will inevitably reassess whether hiring a lightning rod like Kehowski — or, for that matter, Larry Summers or Cornel West — is worth the trouble.

These First Amendment principles must guide our interpretation of the right to be free of purposeful workplace harassment under the Equal Protection Clause. When Congress enacted the Fourteenth Amendment, it enshrined a concept of liberty that has been understood to include the "general principle of free speech.". . . History likewise suggests that the Fourteenth Amendment was intended to extend, and not retract, the freedoms enshrined in the First. In the run up to the Civil War, professors and colleges played a key role in the spread of abolitionist ideas. See Robert Bruce Slater, *The American Colleges That Led the Abolition Movement*, J. Blacks in Higher Educ., Sept. 1995 at 95-97. The South moved to harshly suppress abolitionism as dangerous and incendiary, and Republicans responded by making "demands for free speech a centerpiece of their political program." Michael Kent Curtis, *The 1859 Crisis over Hinton Helper's Book*, The Impending Crisis: *Free Speech, Slavery, and Some Light on the Meaning of the First Section of the Fourteenth Amendment*, 68 Chi.-Kent L. Rev. 1113, 1151 (1993); *see also id.* at 1131, 1134-38. It can hardly be surprising, then, that the Reconstruction Congress sought to protect freedom of speech along with other fundamental liberties when it enacted the Fourteenth Amendment. *See, e.g., id.* at 1172-74. Free speech has been a powerful force for the spread of equality under the law; we must not squelch that freedom because it may also be harnessed by those who promote retrograde or unattractive ways of thought.

We therefore doubt that a college professor's expression on a matter of public concern, directed to the college community, could ever constitute unlawful harassment and justify the judicial intervention that plaintiffs seek. *See* Eugene Volokh, Comment, *Freedom of Speech and Workplace Harassment*, 39 UCLA L. Rev. 1791, 1849-55 (1992). Harassment law generally targets conduct, and it sweeps in speech as harassment only when consistent with the First Amendment. [*R.A.V.*] For instance, racial insults or sexual advances directed at particular individuals in the workplace may be prohibited on the basis of their non-expressive qualities, as they do not "seek to disseminate a message to the general public, but to intrude upon the targeted [listener], and to do so in an especially offensive way." [Frisby v. Schultz, 487 U.S. 474, 486 (1988).] But Kehowski's website and emails were pure speech; they were the effective equivalent of standing on a soap box in a campus quadrangle and speaking to all within earshot. Their offensive quality was based entirely on their meaning, and not on any conduct or implicit threat of conduct that they contained. . . .

We therefore conclude that defendants did not violate plaintiffs' right to be free of workplace harassment. . . .

* * *

It's easy enough to assert that Kehowski's ideas contribute nothing to academic debate, and that the expression of his point of view does more harm than good. But the First Amendment doesn't allow us to weigh the pros and cons of certain types of speech. Those offended by Kehowski's ideas should engage him in debate or hit the "delete" button when they receive his emails. They may not invoke the power of the government to shut him up.

c.   *Indecent Speech, Broadcasting, and Captive Audiences*

Page 873: Insert at the end of Problem 2b, at the end of the section:

In Federal Communications Commission v. Fox, 129 S. Ct. 1800 (2009), the Supreme Court reversed the Second Circuit on the statutory authority issue and remanded for further proceedings, but the Court did not address the constitutional questions.

6.   False Statements of Fact

c.   *The Unresolved Scope of the Exception*

Page 889: Insert at the end of the first problem, "Lies About Oneself":

See United States v. Alvarez, 617 F.3d 1198 (9th Cir. 2010).

7. Tortious Invasion of Emotional and Economic Interests

a. *Intentional Infliction of Emotional Distress*

Page 892: Insert after Notes, just before subsection b:

SNYDER v. PHELPS
131 S. Ct. 1207 (2011)

CHIEF JUSTICE ROBERTS delivered the opinion of the Court.

A jury held members of the Westboro Baptist Church liable for millions of dollars in damages for picketing near a soldier's funeral service. The picket signs reflected the church's view that the United States is overly tolerant of sin and that God kills American soldiers as punishment. The question presented is whether the First Amendment shields the church members from tort liability for their speech in this case.

I. A. Fred Phelps founded the Westboro Baptist Church in Topeka, Kansas, in 1955. The church's congregation believes that God hates and punishes the United States for its tolerance of homosexuality, particularly in America's military. The church frequently communicates its views by picketing, often at military funerals. In the more than 20 years that the members of Westboro Baptist have publicized their message, they have picketed nearly 600 funerals.

Marine Lance Corporal Matthew Snyder was killed in Iraq in the line of duty. Lance Corporal Snyder's father selected the Catholic church in the Snyders' hometown of Westminster, Maryland, as the site for his son's funeral. Local newspapers provided notice of the time and location of the service. Phelps became aware of Matthew Snyder's funeral and decided to travel to Maryland with six other Westboro Baptist parishioners (two of his daughters and four of his grandchildren) to picket. On the day of the memorial service, the Westboro congregation members picketed on public land adjacent to public streets near . . . Matthew Snyder's funeral. The Westboro picketers carried signs that . . . stated, for instance: "God Hates the USA/Thank God for 9/11," "America is Doomed," "Don't Pray for the USA," "Thank God for IEDs," "Thank God for Dead Soldiers," "Pope in Hell," "Priests Rape Boys," "God Hates Fags," "You're Going to Hell," and "God Hates You."

The church had notified the authorities in advance of its intent to picket at the time of the funeral, and the picketers complied with police instructions in staging their demonstration. The picketing took place within a 10- by 25-foot plot of public land adjacent to a public street, behind a temporary fence [that] was approximately 1,000 feet from the church where the funeral was held. . . . The Westboro picketers displayed their signs for about 30 minutes before the funeral began and sang hymns and recited Bible verses. None of the picketers entered church property or went to the cemetery. They did not yell or use profanity, and there was no violence associated with the picketing.

The funeral procession passed within 200 to 300 feet of the picket site. Although Snyder testified that he could see the tops of the picket signs as he drove to the funeral, he did not see what was written on the signs until later that night, while watching a news broadcast covering the event.[1]

B. Snyder filed suit against Phelps, Phelps's daughters, and the Westboro Baptist Church (collectively Westboro or the church) in the United States District Court for the District of Maryland under that court's diversity jurisdiction. [After trial, a jury found for Snyder on state tort law claims of intentional infliction of emotional distress, intrusion upon seclusion, and civil conspiracy. The jury] held Westboro liable for $2.9 million in compensatory damages and $8 million in punitive damages, [later reduced to $2.1 million. The Court of Appeals] reviewed the picket signs and concluded that Westboro's statements were entitled to First Amendment protection because those statements were on matters of public concern, were not provably false, and were expressed solely through hyperbolic rhetoric.

We granted certiorari.

II. To succeed on a claim for intentional infliction of emotional distress in Maryland, a plaintiff must demonstrate that the defendant intentionally or recklessly engaged in extreme and outrageous conduct that caused the plaintiff to suffer severe emotional distress. The Free Speech Clause of the First Amendment . . . can serve as a defense in state tort suits, including suits for intentional infliction of emotional distress. Hustler Magazine, Inc. v. Falwell. . . .

Whether the First Amendment prohibits holding Westboro liable for its speech in this case turns largely on whether that speech is of public or private concern, as determined by all the circumstances of the case. "[S]peech on 'matters of public concern'. . . is 'at the heart of the First Amendment's protection.'" Dun & Bradstreet, Inc. v. Greenmoss Builders, Inc. (opinion of Powell, J.) (quoting First Nat. Bank of Boston v. Bellotti.) The First Amendment reflects "a profound national commitment to the principle that debate on public issues should be uninhibited, robust, and wide-open". . . because "speech concerning public affairs is more than self-expression; it is the essence of self-government." Accordingly, "speech on public issues occupies the highest rung of the hierarchy of First Amendment values, and is entitled to special protection."

" '[N]ot all speech is of equal First Amendment importance,'" however, and where matters of purely private significance are at issue, First Amendment protections are often less rigorous. That is because restricting speech on purely private matters does not implicate the same constitutional concerns as limiting speech on matters of public interest: "[T]here is no threat to the free and robust debate of public issues; there is no potential interference with a meaningful

---

1. A few weeks after the funeral, one of the picketers posted a message on Westboro's Web site discussing the picketing and containing religiously oriented denunciations of the Snyders, interspersed among lengthy Bible quotations. Snyder discovered the posting, referred to by the parties as the "epic," during an Internet search for his son's name. The epic is not properly before us and does not factor in our analysis. . . .

dialogue of ideas"; and the "threat of liability" does not pose the risk of "a reaction of self-censorship" on matters of public import. *Dun & Bradstreet.* . . .

We noted a short time ago . . . that "the boundaries of the public concern test are not well defined." San Diego v. Roe. Although that remains true today, we have articulated some guiding principles, principles that accord broad protection to speech to ensure that courts themselves do not become inadvertent censors. Speech deals with matters of public concern when it can "be fairly considered as relating to any matter of political, social, or other concern to the community," or when it "is a subject of legitimate news interest; that is, a subject of general interest and of value and concern to the public." The arguably "inappropriate or controversial character of a statement is irrelevant to the question whether it deals with a matter of public concern."

[In] *Dun & Bradstreet*, on the other hand, . . . we held, as a general matter, that information about a particular individual's credit report "concerns no public issue" [but] "was speech solely in the individual interest of the speaker and its specific business audience.". . . [We] concluded in *San Diego* v. *Roe* that, in the context of a government employer regulating the speech of its employees, videos of an employee engaging in sexually explicit acts did not address a public concern; the videos "did nothing to inform the public about any aspect of the [employing agency's] functioning or operation."

Deciding whether speech is of public or private concern requires us to examine the " 'content, form, and context' " of that speech, " 'as revealed by the whole record.' ".... In considering content, form, and context, no factor is dispositive, and it is necessary to evaluate all the circumstances of the speech, including what was said, where it was said, and how it was said.

The "content" of Westboro's signs plainly relates to broad issues of interest to society at large, rather than matters of "purely private concern.". . . While [their] messages may fall short of refined social or political commentary, the issues they highlight — the political and moral conduct of the United States and its citizens, the fate of our Nation, homosexuality in the military, and scandals involving the Catholic clergy — are matters of public import. The signs certainly convey Westboro's position on those issues, in a manner designed, unlike the private speech in *Dun & Bradstreet*, to reach as broad a public audience as possible. And even if a few of the signs — such as "You're Going to Hell" and "God Hates You" — were viewed as containing messages related to Matthew Snyder or the Snyders specifically, that would not change the fact that the overall thrust and dominant theme of Westboro's demonstration spoke to broader public issues.

Apart from the content of Westboro's signs, Snyder contends that the "context" of the speech — its connection with his son's funeral — makes the speech a matter of private rather than public concern. The fact that Westboro spoke in connection with a funeral, however, cannot by itself transform the nature of Westboro's speech. Westboro's signs, displayed on public land next to a public street, reflect the fact that the church finds much to condemn in modern society . . . and the funeral setting does not alter [the] conclusion [that their speech is on matters of public concern].

Snyder argues that the church members in fact mounted a personal attack on Snyder and his family, and then attempted to "immunize their conduct by claiming that they were actually protesting the United States' tolerance of homosexuality or the supposed evils of the Catholic Church." We are not concerned in this case that Westboro's speech on public matters was in any way contrived to insulate speech on a private matter from liability. Westboro had been actively engaged in speaking on the subjects addressed in its picketing long before it became aware of Matthew Snyder, and there can be no serious claim that Westboro's picketing did not represent its "honestly believed" views on public issues. There was no pre-existing relationship or conflict between Westboro and Snyder that might suggest Westboro's speech on public matters was intended to mask an attack on Snyder over a private matter. . . .

Snyder goes on to argue that Westboro's speech should be afforded less than full First Amendment protection "not only because of the words" but also because the church members exploited the funeral "as a platform to bring their message to a broader audience." There is no doubt that Westboro chose to stage its picketing at . . . Matthew Snyder's funeral to increase publicity for its views and because . . . Westboro believes that God is killing American soldiers as punishment for the Nation's sinful policies. Westboro's choice to convey its views in conjunction with Matthew Snyder's funeral made the expression of those views particularly hurtful to many, especially to Matthew's father. The record makes clear that the applicable legal term — "emotional distress" — fails to capture fully the anguish Westboro's choice added to Mr. Snyder's already incalculable grief. But Westboro conducted its picketing peacefully on matters of public concern at a public place adjacent to a public street. Such space occupies a "special position in terms of First Amendment protection." "[W]e have repeatedly referred to public streets as the archetype of a traditional public forum," noting that " '[t]ime out of mind' public streets and sidewalks have been used for public assembly and debate."

That said, . . . Westboro's choice of where and when to conduct its picketing is not beyond the Government's regulatory reach — it is "subject to reasonable time, place, or manner restrictions". . . . Maryland now has a law imposing restrictions on funeral picketing, Md. Crim. Law Code Ann. § 10-205 (Lexis Supp. 2010), as do 43 other States and the Federal Government. To the extent these laws are content neutral, they raise very different questions from the tort verdict at issue in this case. Maryland's law, however, was not in effect at the time of the events at issue here, so we have no occasion to consider how it might apply to facts such as those before us, or whether it or other similar regulations are constitutional.[2] . . .

Simply put, the church members had the right to be where they were. . . . The record confirms that any distress occasioned by Westboro's picketing turned on the content and viewpoint of the message conveyed, rather than any interference

---

2. The Maryland law prohibits picketing within 100 feet of a funeral service or funeral procession; Westboro's picketing would have complied with that restriction.

with the funeral itself. A group of parishioners standing at the very spot where Westboro stood, holding signs that said "God Bless America" and "God Loves You," would not have been subjected to liability. It was what Westboro said that exposed it to tort damages. Given that Westboro's speech was at a public place on a matter of public concern, that speech is entitled to "special protection" [and] cannot be restricted simply because it is upsetting or arouses contempt. . . . Indeed, "the point of all speech protection . . . is to shield just those choices of content that in someone's eyes are misguided, or even hurtful.". . .

The jury here was instructed that it could hold Westboro liable for intentional infliction of emotional distress based on a finding that Westboro's picketing was "outrageous." "Outrageousness," however, is a highly malleable standard with "an inherent subjectiveness about it which would allow a jury to impose liability on the basis of the jurors' tastes or views, or perhaps on the basis of their dislike of a particular expression." *Hustler*. . . . Such a risk is unacceptable; in public debate [we] must tolerate insulting, and even outrageous, speech in order to provide adequate 'breathing space' to the freedoms protected by the First Amendment." . . .

III. The jury also found Westboro liable for the state law torts of intrusion upon seclusion and civil conspiracy. . . . Snyder argues that even assuming Westboro's speech is entitled to First Amendment protection generally, the church is not immunized from liability for intrusion upon seclusion because Snyder was a member of a captive audience at his son's funeral. We do not agree. In most circumstances, "the Constitution does not permit the government to decide which types of otherwise protected speech are sufficiently offensive to require protection for the unwilling listener or viewer. Rather, . . . the burden normally falls upon the viewer to avoid further bombardment of [his] sensibilities simply by averting [his] eyes." Erznoznik v. Jacksonville. As a result, "[t]he ability of government, consonant with the Constitution, to shut off discourse solely to protect others from hearing it is . . . dependent upon a showing that substantial privacy interests are being invaded in an essentially intolerable manner." Cohen v. California.

As a general matter, we have applied the captive audience doctrine only sparingly to protect unwilling listeners from protected speech. For example, we have upheld a statute allowing a homeowner to restrict the delivery of offensive mail to his home, [Rowan v. Post Office Dept.], and an ordinance prohibiting picketing "before or about" any individual's residence, [Frisby v. Schultz]. Here, Westboro stayed well away from the memorial service. Snyder could see no more than the tops of the signs when driving to the funeral. And there is no indication that the picketing in any way interfered with the funeral service itself. We decline to expand the captive audience doctrine to the circumstances presented here. . . .

IV. Our holding today is narrow. . . . Westboro believes that America is morally flawed; many Americans might feel the same about Westboro. Westboro's funeral picketing is certainly hurtful and its contribution to public discourse may be negligible. But Westboro addressed matters of public import on public property, in a peaceful manner, in full compliance with the guidance of local officials. The speech was indeed planned to coincide with Matthew Snyder's funeral, but did not itself disrupt that funeral. . . .

Speech is powerful. It can stir people to action, move them to tears of both joy and sorrow, and — as it did here — inflict great pain. On the facts before us, we cannot react to that pain by punishing the speaker. As a Nation we have chosen a different course — to protect even hurtful speech on public issues to ensure that we do not stifle public debate. That choice requires that we shield Westboro from tort liability for its picketing in this case.

[Affirmed.]

JUSTICE BREYER, concurring.

. . . The opinion does not examine in depth the effect of television broadcasting. Nor does it say anything about Internet postings. . . . While I agree with the Court's conclusion that the picketing addressed matters of public concern, I do not believe that our First Amendment analysis can stop at that point. A State can sometimes regulate picketing, even picketing on matters of public concern. . . .

The dissent requires us to ask whether our holding unreasonably limits liability for intentional infliction of emotional distress — to the point where A (in order to draw attention to his views on a public matter) might launch a verbal assault upon B, a private person, publicly revealing the most intimate details of B's private life, while knowing that the revelation will cause B severe emotional harm. Does our decision leave the State powerless to protect the individual against invasions of, *e.g.*, personal privacy, even in the most horrendous of such circumstances? As I understand the Court's opinion, it does not hold or imply that the State is always powerless to provide private individuals with necessary protection. . . .

JUSTICE ALITO, dissenting.

Our profound national commitment to free and open debate is not a license for the vicious verbal assault that occurred in this case.

Petitioner Albert Snyder is not a public figure. He is simply a parent whose son, Marine Lance Corporal Matthew Snyder, was killed in Iraq. Mr. Snyder wanted what is surely the right of any parent who experiences such an incalculable loss: to bury his son in peace. But respondents, members of the Westboro Baptist Church, deprived him of that elementary right. They first issued a press release and thus turned Matthew's funeral into a tumultuous media event. They then appeared at the church, approached as closely as they could without trespassing, and launched a malevolent verbal attack on Matthew and his family at a time of acute emotional vulnerability. As a result, Albert Snyder suffered severe and lasting emotional injury.[1] The Court now holds that the First Amendment protected respondents' right to brutalize Mr. Snyder. I cannot agree. . . .

1. See 580 F. 3d 206, 213-214, 216 (CA4 2009).

[A]lthough this Court has not decided the question, I think it is clear that the First Amendment does not entirely preclude liability for the intentional infliction of emotional distress by means of speech. This Court has recognized that words may "by their very utterance inflict injury" and that the First Amendment does not shield utterances that form "no essential part of any exposition of ideas, and are of such slight social value as a step to truth that any benefit that may be derived from them is clearly outweighed by the social interest in order and morality." Chaplinsky v. New Hampshire.

In this case, respondents brutally attacked Matthew Snyder, and this attack, which was almost certain to inflict injury, was central to respondents' well-practiced strategy for attracting public attention. On the morning of Matthew Snyder's funeral, respondents could have chosen to stage their protest at countless locations. They could have picketed the United States Capitol, the White House, the Supreme Court, the Pentagon, or any of the more than 5,600 military recruiting stations in this country. They could have returned to the Maryland State House or the United States Naval Academy, where they had been the day before. They could have selected any public road where pedestrians are allowed. (There are more than 4,000,000 miles of public roads in the United States.) They could have staged their protest in a public park. (There are more than 20,000 public parks in this country.) They could have chosen any Catholic church where no funeral was taking place. (There are nearly 19,000 Catholic churches in the United States.) But of course, a small group picketing at any of these locations would have probably gone unnoticed.

The Westboro Baptist Church, however, has devised a strategy that remedies this problem. As the Court notes, church members have protested at nearly 600 military funerals. They have also picketed the funerals of police officers, firefighters, and the victims of natural disasters, accidents, and shocking crimes. And in advance of these protests, they issue press releases to ensure that their protests will attract public attention. This strategy works because it is expected that respondents' verbal assaults will wound the family and friends of the deceased and because the media is irresistibly drawn to the sight of persons who are visibly in grief. The more outrageous the funeral protest, the more publicity the Westboro Baptist Church is able to obtain. Thus, when the church recently announced its intention to picket the funeral of a 9-year-old girl killed in the shooting spree in Tucson — proclaiming that she was "better off dead" — their announcement was national news, and the church was able to obtain free air time on the radio in exchange for canceling its protest. Similarly, in 2006, the church got air time on a talk radio show in exchange for canceling its threatened protest at the funeral of five Amish girls killed by a crazed gunman.

In this case, respondents implemented the Westboro Baptist Church's publicity-seeking strategy. . . . On the day of the funeral, [Westboro's] placards . . . stating "God Hates You" and "Thank God for Dead Soldiers" reiterated the message that God had caused Matthew's death in retribution for his sins. Others, stating "You're Going to Hell" and "Not Blessed Just Cursed," conveyed the message that Matthew was "in Hell. . . . " Since respondents chose to stage their protest at Matthew Snyder's funeral and not at any of the other countless available venues, a reasonable person would have assumed that there was a connection between the messages on the placards and the deceased. [Some] of respondents' signs . . . would have likely been interpreted as referring to God's judgment of the deceased. Other signs would most naturally have been understood as suggesting — falsely — that Matthew was gay. Homosexuality was the theme of many of the signs. There were signs reading "God Hates Fags," "Semper Fi Fags," "Fags Doom Nations," and "Fag Troops." Another placard depicted two men engaging in anal intercourse. A reasonable bystander seeing those signs would have likely concluded that they were meant to suggest that the deceased was a homosexual.

After the funeral, the Westboro picketers reaffirmed the meaning of their protest. They posted an online account entitled "The Burden of Marine Lance Cpl. Matthew A. Snyder. The Visit of Westboro Baptist Church to Help the Inhabitants of Maryland Connect the Dots!"[3] Belying any suggestion that they had simply made general comments about homosexuality, the Catholic Church, and the United States military, the "epic" addressed the Snyder family directly:

> God blessed you, Mr. and Mrs. Snyder, with a resource and his name was Matthew. He was an arrow in your quiver! In thanks to God for the comfort the child could bring you, you had a DUTY to prepare that child to serve the LORD his GOD — PERIOD! You did JUST THE OPPOSITE — you raised himfor the devil. . . .
>
> Albert and Julie RIPPED that body apart and taught Matthew to defy his Creator, to divorce, and to commit adultery. They taught him how to support the largest pedophile machine in the history of the entire world, the Roman Catholic monstrosity. Every dime they gave the Roman Catholic monster they condemned their own souls. They also, in supporting satanic Catholicism, taught Matthew to be an idolater. . . .
>
> Then after all that they sent him to fight for the United States of Sodom, a filthy country that is in lock step with his evil, wicked, and sinful manner of life, putting him in the cross hairs of a God that is so mad He has smoke coming from his nostrils and fire from his mouth! How dumb was that?

In light of this evidence, it is abundantly clear that respondents, going far beyond commentary on matters of public concern, specifically attacked Matthew Snyder because (1) he was a Catholic and (2) he was a member of the United States military. Both Matthew and petitioner were private figures, and this attack was not speech on a matter of public concern. While commentary on the Catholic Church or the United States military constitutes speech on matters of public concern, speech regarding Matthew Snyder's purely private conduct does not.

---

3. The Court refuses to consider the epic because it was not discussed in Snyder's petition for certiorari. The epic, however, is not a distinct claim but a piece of evidence that the jury considered in imposing liability for the claims now before this Court. The protest and the epic are parts of a single course of conduct that the jury found to constitute intentional infliction of emotional distress. . . .

. . . The Court concludes that respondents' speech was protected by the First Amendment for essentially three reasons, but none is sound.

First . . . I fail to see why actionable speech should be immunized simply because it is interspersed with speech that is protected. The First Amendment allows recovery for defamatory statements that are interspersed with non-defamatory statements on matters of public concern, and there is no good reason why respondents' attack on Matthew Snyder and his family should be treated differently.

Second, the Court suggests that respondents' personal attack on Matthew Snyder is entitled to First Amendment protection because it was not motivated by a private grudge, but [respondents'] publicity-seeking motivation [did not] soften the sting of their attack. . . . [One] might well think that wounding statements uttered in the heat of a private feud are less, not more, blameworthy than similar statements made as part of a cold and calculated strategy to slash a stranger as a means of attracting public attention.

Third, the Court finds it significant that respondents' protest occurred on a public street, but this fact alone should not be enough to preclude IIED liability. To be sure, statements made on a public street may be less likely to satisfy the elements of the IIED tort than statements made on private property, but there is no reason why a public street in close proximity to the scene of a funeral should be regarded as a free-fire zone in which otherwise actionable verbal attacks are shielded from liability. If the First Amendment permits the States to protect their residents from the harm inflicted by such attacks — and the Court does not hold otherwise — then the location of the tort should not be dispositive. A physical assault may occur without trespassing; it is no defense that the perpetrator had "the right to be where [he was]." . . .

Respondents' outrageous conduct caused petitioner great injury, and the Court now compounds that injury by depriving petitioner of a judgment that acknowledges the wrong he suffered. In order to have a society in which public issues can be openly and vigorously debated, it is not necessary to allow the brutalization of innocent victims like petitioner. I therefore respectfully dissent.

8. Commercial Speech

Page 911: Insert new Note 4 at the end:

4. Regulation of Prescription Drug Information. Vermont requires that pharmacies keep a record of prescriptions authored by each physician. The records do not disclose the patient's identity but do reveal each prescribing physician's choices. A Vermont law forbade the sale or use of this information for marketing purposes but permitted it to be sold, used, or given away for many other uses. Before the law was enacted, so-called "data miners" acquired this information and sold it to pharmaceutical manufacturers, who used it in their sales calls on physicians to explain to physicians why a branded drug offered by the representative's firm was superior to competing drugs that the physician had prescribed in the past. A federal district court upheld the law against a free speech challenge; the Second Circuit reversed and in Sorrell v. IMS Health, Inc., 2011 U.S. Lexis 4794, the Supreme Court, 6-3, affirmed. Justice Kennedy wrote for the Court.

The Court concluded that the law was both content-based (it only applied to information used for marketing purposes) and speaker-based (it only applied to those speakers using the prescriber data for marketing purposes), and that in its application it was also viewpoint based, because it banned the use of the information only to advance the view that branded drugs were better than generic drugs. Thus, heightened scrutiny was warranted, and the Court applied the *Central Hudson* test.

Vermont said its reasons for the ban were to preserve physician privacy and to lower health care costs. While Vermont's objectives were substantial the law did not directly advance the objectives and the fit between the means and ends was so poor that the Court concluded that the law was designed to suppress a disfavored message. The law did almost nothing to protect physician privacy — the data could be shared with just about anyone except pharmaceutical marketers. Vermont also claimed that doctors were harassed and pressured by pharmaceutical salespersons; the Court's reply was that doctors could refuse to see such salespersons. The means selected by Vermont to lower health care costs were impermissible:

> The State seeks to achieve its policy objectives through the indirect means of restraining certain speech by certain speakers — that is, by diminishing detailers' ability to influence prescription decisions. Those who seek to censor or burden free expression often assert that disfavored speech has adverse effects. But the "fear that people would make bad decisions if given truthful information" cannot justify content-based burdens on speech. . . . The State has burdened a form of protected expression that it found too persuasive. At the same time, the State has left unburdened those speakers whose messages are in accord with its own views. This the State cannot do.

Justice Breyer dissented, joined by Justices Ginsburg and Kagan. He thought that the question was "whether Vermont's regulatory provisions work harm to First Amendment interests that is disproportionate to their furtherance of legitimate regulatory objectives." How would a judge measure the "harm to free speech," on the one hand, against the efficacy of regulation, on the other hand? Is there a good reason to use such an open-ended balancing test for commercial speech, but not other forms of speech?

In any case, Justice Breyer thought that *Central Hudson* was satisfied because it directly advanced the goal of reducing health care costs by making it more difficult to sell more expensive branded drugs, and the ban was well tailored to that end. Recall that in *Central Hudson* the Court agreed that the state had a substantial interest in reducing electrical usage and the ban on promotion of electricity usage directly advanced that interest, but the ban was voided because it also prohibited promotion of energy-saving electrical devices and was thus not sufficiently well-tailored to the objective. Thus, *Central Hudson* implicitly approved the idea that honest commercial advertising can be restricted because it will promote something the government thinks is harmful, even though lawful. But that idea has been repudiated in *Virginia Pharmacy* and, more recently, in *Thompson*, where the Court observed that "[w]e have previously rejected the notion that the Government has an interest in preventing the dissemination of truthful commercial information in order to prevent members of the public from making bad decisions with the information." Are there any circumstances in which the government may restrict truthful, non-misleading commercial speech because the speech may cause people to make bad decisions? Promotion of an independently illegal commercial transaction might be one such circumstance. Are there others?

9. The Process of Identifying Categories of Unprotected Speech

Page 911: Insert at the end of Section 8:

UNITED STATES v. STEVENS
130 S. Ct. 1577 (2010)

CHIEF JUSTICE ROBERTS delivered the opinion of the Court.

Congress enacted 18 U.S.C. § 48 to criminalize the commercial creation, sale, or possession of certain depictions of animal cruelty. The statute does not address underlying acts harmful to animals, but only portrayals of such conduct. The question presented is whether the prohibition in the statute is consistent with the freedom of speech guaranteed by the First Amendment.

I. Section 48 establishes a criminal penalty of up to five years in prison for anyone who knowingly "creates, sells, or possesses a depiction of animal cruelty," if done "for commercial gain" in interstate or foreign commerce. A depiction of "animal cruelty" is defined as one "in which a living animal is intentionally maimed, mutilated, tortured, wounded, or killed," if that conduct violates federal or state law where "the creation, sale, or possession takes place." In . . . the "exceptions clause," the law exempts from prohibition any depiction "that has serious religious, political, scientific, educational, journalistic, historical, or artistic value."

[Congress enacted § 48 to eradicate the interstate market for "crush videos," which] feature the intentional torture and killing of helpless animals, including cats, dogs, monkeys, mice, and hamsters. Crush videos often depict women slowly crushing animals to death "with their bare feet or while wearing high heeled shoes," sometimes while "talking to the animals in a kind of dominatrix patter" over "[t]he cries and squeals of the animals, obviously in great pain."

Apparently these depictions "appeal to persons with a very specific sexual fetish who find them sexually arousing or otherwise exciting." The acts depicted in crush videos are typically prohibited by the animal cruelty laws enacted by all 50 States and the District of Columbia. . . .

This case, however, involves an application of § 48 to depictions of animal fighting. Dogfighting, for example, is unlawful in all 50 States and the District of Columbia . . . and has been restricted by federal law since 1976. Respondent Robert J. Stevens ran a business [and Web site,] through which he sold videos of pit bulls engaging in dogfights and attacking other animals. Among these videos were [one showing] contemporary footage of dogfights in Japan (where such conduct is allegedly legal) [and a second one] of American dogfights from the 1960s and 1970s. A third video . . . depicts the use of pit bulls to hunt wild boar, as well as a "gruesome" scene of a pit bull attacking a domestic farm pig. On the basis of these videos, Stevens was indicted on three counts of violating § 48.

Stevens moved to dismiss the indictment, arguing that § 48 is facially invalid under the First Amendment. The District Court denied the motion. It held that the depictions subject to § 48, like obscenity or child pornography, are categorically unprotected by the First Amendment, [and] that § 48 is not substantially overbroad, because the exceptions clause sufficiently narrows the statute to constitutional applications. The jury convicted Stevens on all counts, and the District Court sentenced him to . . . 37 months' imprisonment, followed by three years of supervised release.

The en banc Third Circuit . . . declared § 48 facially unconstitutional and vacated Stevens's conviction. The Court of Appeals first held that § 48 regulates speech that is protected by the First Amendment. The Court declined to recognize a new category of unprotected speech for depictions of animal cruelty, and rejected the Government's analogy between animal cruelty depictions and child pornography. The Court of Appeals then held that § 48 could not survive strict scrutiny as a content-based regulation of protected speech [because] the statute lacked a compelling government interest and was neither narrowly tailored to preventing animal cruelty nor the least restrictive means of doing so. . . . We granted certiorari.

II. The Government's primary submission is that § 48 necessarily complies with the Constitution because the banned depictions of animal cruelty, as a class, are categorically unprotected by the First Amendment. We disagree. . . .

Section 48 explicitly regulates expression based on content[; thus it] is " 'presumptively invalid,' and the Government bears the burden to rebut that presumption" [by surmounting strict scrutiny.] "From 1791 to the present," however, the First Amendment has "permitted restrictions upon the content of speech in a few limited areas," and has never "include[d] a freedom to disregard these traditional limitations." These "historic and traditional categories" [include] obscenity, defamation, fraud, incitement [of crime], and speech integral to criminal conduct. . . . [Additional categories include child pornography, misleading commercial speech, true threats, and so-called fighting words. — Ed.] The Government argues that "depictions of animal cruelty" should be added to the list. . . . The claim is [that] depictions of animal cruelty . . . are outside the reach of [the First] Amendment altogether. . . .

[T]he prohibition of animal cruelty itself has a long history in American law, starting with the early settlement of the Colonies. But we are unaware of any similar tradition excluding *depictions* of animal cruelty from "the freedom of speech" codified in the First Amendment, and the Government points us to none. The Government contends that "historical evidence" about the reach of the First Amendment is not "a necessary prerequisite for regulation today," and that categories of speech may be exempted from the First Amendment's protection without any long-settled tradition of subjecting that speech to regulation. Instead, the Government points to Congress's " 'legislative judgment that . . . depictions of animals being intentionally tortured and killed [are] of such minimal redeeming value as to render [them] unworthy of First Amendment protection,' " and . . . proposes that a claim of categorical exclusion should be considered under a simple balancing test: "Whether a given category of speech enjoys First Amendment protection depends upon a categorical balancing of the value of the speech against its societal costs."

As a free-floating test for First Amendment coverage, that sentence is startling and dangerous. The First Amendment's guarantee of free speech does not extend only to categories of speech that survive an ad hoc balancing of relative social costs and benefits. The First Amendment itself reflects a judgment by the American people that the benefits of its restrictions on the Government outweigh the costs. Our Constitution forecloses any attempt to revise that judgment simply on the basis that some speech is not worth it. The Constitution is not a document "prescribing limits, and declaring that those limits may be passed at pleasure." Marbury v. Madison.

To be fair to the Government, its view did not emerge from a vacuum. As the Government correctly notes, this Court has often *described* historically unprotected categories of speech as being "of such slight social value as a step to truth that any benefit that may be derived from them is clearly outweighed by the social interest in order and morality." [*Chaplinsky.*] In New York v. Ferber, we noted that within these categories of unprotected speech, "the evil to be restricted so overwhelmingly outweighs the expressive interests, if any, at stake, that no process of case-by-case adjudication is required," because "the balance of competing interests is clearly struck." The Government derives its proposed test from these descriptions in our precedents. But such descriptions are just that — descriptive. They do not set forth a test that may be applied as a general matter to permit the Government to imprison any speaker so long as his speech is deemed valueless or unnecessary, or so long as an ad hoc calculus of costs and benefits tilts in a statute's favor.

When we have identified categories of speech as fully outside the protection of the First Amendment, it has not been on the basis of a simple cost-benefit analysis. In *Ferber*, for example, [when] we classified child pornography as such a category, [w]e noted that the State of New York had a compelling interest in protecting children from abuse, and that the value of using children in these works (as opposed to simulated conduct or adult actors) was *de minimis*. But our decision did not rest on this "balance of competing interests" alone. We made clear that *Ferber* presented a special case: The market for child pornography was "intrinsically related" to the underlying abuse, and was therefore "an integral part of the production of such materials, an activity illegal throughout the Nation." As we noted, " '[i]t rarely has been suggested that the constitutional freedom for speech and press extends its immunity to speech or writing used as an integral part of conduct in violation of a valid criminal statute.' " *Ferber* thus grounded its analysis in a previously recognized, long-established category of unprotected speech, and our subsequent decisions have shared this understanding. See Osborne v. Ohio (describing *Ferber* as finding "persuasive" the argument that the advertising and sale of child pornography was "an integral part" of its unlawful production); Ashcroft v. Free Speech Coalition (noting that distribution and sale "were intrinsically related to the sexual abuse of children," giving the speech at issue "a proximate link to the crime from which it came").

Our decisions in *Ferber* and other cases cannot be taken as establishing a freewheeling authority to declare new categories of speech outside the scope of the First Amendment. Maybe there are some categories of speech that have been historically unprotected, but have not yet been specifically identified or discussed as such in our case law. But if so, there is no evidence that "depictions of animal cruelty" is among them. We need not foreclose the future recognition of such additional categories to reject the Government's highly manipulable balancing test as a means of identifying them.

[The Court then concluded that the law was facially invalid. The law was "of alarming breadth" because it applied to any killing of an animal, no matter the reason, if the killing is illegal in the jurisdiction where the depiction is possessed. That meant that hunting videos would be included because hunting, while legal in all states, is illegal in the District of Columbia. The exceptions clause did not sufficiently limit the law's potential application to so-called crush videos, as the Government argued the law should be construed. Thus, § 48 was found to be substantially overbroad and void on its face.]

NOTES AND QUESTIONS

1. History as the Guide to Categorically Excluded Speech. The majority says that the categories of speech that do not receive First Amendment protection are those that have been "historically unprotected." Is resort to history as the guide to decision a useful criterion? Note that several of the historically unprotected categories of speech in 1791 now receive either complete or limited constitutional protection. Blasphemy, for example, was unprotected in 1791 but is surely protected now. Defamation, vulgarity, and commercial speech, each unprotected in 1791, now receive limited protection. Obscenity, while still unprotected, is defined more narrowly than would have been the case in 1791. Much pornography that is protected today would have been unprotected in 1791.

Does this suggest that a historically based approach to categorical exclusion is a one-way street, permitting extension of protection to historically unprotected categories but restricting the creation of new unprotected categories? Perhaps a tradition of no protection is a necessary but insufficient condition for denying protection to a category of speech. But note that the Court included speech that is integral to criminal conduct within the historically unprotected categories of speech, and explained *Ferber*'s conclusion that child pornography was an unprotected category on that basis. The question of the breadth of that category is the subject of the following note.

2. Speech Integral to Criminal Conduct.   The majority says that there has not been any historical protection for "speech integral to criminal conduct," citing Giboney v. Empire Storage & Ice Co., 336 U.S. 490 (1949), in which the Court upheld an injunction against peaceful picketing of a company that was intended to pressure it "to agree to stop selling ice to nonunion peddlers." *Id.* at 492. The injunction did not violate the First Amendment because the agreement it sought to induce would violate Missouri's law forbidding restraints of trade. What is included within the concept of speech integral to criminal conduct?

The category might be limited to speech that causes harms unrelated to the communicative impact of the speech (as is true of the secondary effects doctrine), but the harm in *Giboney* resulted from the communicative impact of the speech. The category might be limited to speech that is evidence of some independent criminal conduct, as is true of racist speech used to help determine whether a person selected his crime victim on the basis of race, but that would not explain *Giboney*. Nor can the category be defined as speech that itself violates a law forbidding such speech, because the idea of free speech is built upon the premise that laws forbidding speech are generally presumed to be invalid. While one might try to limit this category to speech that is part of a broader course of illegal conduct by the speaker or others, this has its problems as well. In *Giboney*, for example, the speakers were not engaging in any illegal conduct of which the speech was a part, and if the speech is regarded as inciting illegal conduct by others the category is bounded by *Brandenburg*'s incitement principle. If the category is regarded as limited to true threats, it adds nothing. In any case, the facts of *Giboney* hardly qualify as a true threat, especially after NAACP v. Claiborne Hardware Co., 458 U.S. 886 (1982). Finally, *Ferber* suggested that child pornography could be denied protection because its advertising and sales provided an economic motive for the underlying criminal conduct of its production, but that might be true of protected speech as well. For example, while the prospect of publication might have been the motive for unlawful disclosure of the Pentagon Papers purloined by Daniel Ellsberg, the Court held that the subsequent publication was protected. See New York Times v. United States, 403 U.S. 713 (1971); Bartnicki v. Vopper, 532 U.S. 514 (2001).

So what is included within the category of speech that is integral to criminal conduct? Are any of the following instances of speech exiled from First Amendment protection under this category? Should they be so exiled?

a. A book that details specifically how to commit murder for hire. See Rice v. Paladin Enterprises, 128 F.3d 233 (4th Cir. 1997).

b. A physician advises his patient to use marijuana, although such use is illegal. See, e.g., Pearson v. McCaffrey, 139 F. Supp. 2d 113, 121 (D.D.C. 2001). But see Conant v. Walters, 309 F.3d 629, 637-638 (9th Cir. 2002).

c. Employees of a business use racially and sexually offensive words to create a hostile work environment. See, e.g., Jarman v. City of Northlake, 950 F. Supp. 1375, 1379 (N.D. Ill. 1997); Robinson v. Jacksonville Shipyards, Inc., 760 F. Supp. 1486, 1535 (M.D. Fla. 1991).

For more on this topic, see Kent Greenawalt, Speech, Crime, and the Uses of Language (1989); Eugene Volokh, Speech as Conduct: Generally Applicable Laws, Course of Conduct, "Situation-Altering Utterances," and the Uncharted Zones, 90 Cornell L. Rev. 1277 (2005).

BROWN v. ENTERTAINMENT MERCHANTS ASSOCIATION
2011 U.S. Lexis 4802

JUSTICE SCALIA delivered the opinion of the Court.

We consider whether a California law imposing restrictions on violent video games comports with the First Amendment.

I. California Assembly Bill 1179 (2005), Cal. Civ. Code Ann. §§ 1746-1746.5 (West 2009) (Act), prohibits the sale or rental of "violent video games" to minors, and requires their packaging to be labeled "18." The Act covers games "in which the range of options available to a player includes killing, maiming, dismembering, or sexually assaulting an image of a human being, if those acts are depicted" in a manner that "[a] reasonable person, considering the game as a whole, would find appeals to a deviant or morbid interest of minors," that is "patently offensive to prevailing standards in the community as to what is suitable for minors," and that "causes the game, as a whole, to lack serious literary, artistic, political, or scientific value for minors." § 1746(d)(1)(A). Violation of the Act is punishable by a civil fine of up to $1,000. § 1746.3.

Respondents, representing the video-game and software industries, brought a pre-enforcement challenge to the Act in the United States District Court for the Northern District of California. That court concluded that the Act violated the First Amendment and permanently enjoined its enforcement. The Court of Appeals affirmed, and we granted certiorari.

II. California correctly acknowledges that video games qualify for First Amendment protection. The Free Speech Clause exists principally to protect discourse on public matters, but we have long recognized that it is difficult to distinguish politics from entertainment, and dangerous to try. "Everyone is familiar with instances of propaganda through fiction. What is one man' amusement, teaches another' doctrine." Winters v. New York, 333 U.S. 507, 510

(1948). Like the protected books, plays, and movies that preceded them, video games communicate ideas — and even social messages — through many familiar literary devices (such as characters, dialogue, plot, and music) and through features distinctive to the medium (such as the player's interaction with the virtual world). That suffices to confer First Amendment protection. . . . And whatever the challenges of applying the Constitution to ever-advancing technology, "the basic principles of freedom of speech and the press, like the First Amendment's command, do not vary" when a new and different medium for communication appears. Joseph Burstyn, Inc. v. Wilson, 343 U.S. 495, 503 (1952).

The most basic of those principles is this: "[A]s a general matter, . . . government has no power to restrict expression because of its message, its ideas, its subject matter, or its content." Ashcroft v. American Civil Liberties Union, 535 U.S. 564, 573 (2002). There are of course exceptions. . . . These limited areas — such as obscenity, incitement, and fighting words — represent "well-defined and narrowly limited classes of speech, the prevention and punishment of which have never been thought to raise any Constitutional problem."

Last Term, in *Stevens*, we held that new categories of unprotected speech may not be added to the list by a legislature that concludes certain speech is too harmful to be tolerated. *Stevens* concerned a federal statute purporting to criminalize the creation, sale, or possession of certain depictions of animal cruelty. . . . A saving clause largely borrowed from our obscenity jurisprudence exempted depictions with "serious religious, political, scientific, educational, journalistic, historical, or artistic value." We held that statute to be an impermissible content-based restriction on speech. There was no American tradition of forbidding the *depiction of* animal cruelty — though States have long had laws against *committing* it. The Government argued in *Stevens* that lack of a historical warrant did not matter; that it could create new categories of unprotected speech by applying a "simple balancing test" that weighs the value of a particular category of speech against its social costs and then punishes that category of speech if it fails the test. We emphatically rejected that "startling and dangerous" proposition. [Without] persuasive evidence that a novel restriction on content is part of a long (if heretofore unrecognized) tradition of proscription, a legislature may not revise the "judgment [of] the American people," embodied in the First Amendment, "that the benefits of its restrictions on the Government outweigh the costs."

That holding controls this case. As in *Stevens*, California has tried to make violent-speech regulation look like obscenity regulation by appending a saving clause required for the latter. That does not suffice. Our cases have been clear that the obscenity exception to the First Amendment does not cover whatever a legislature finds shocking, but only depictions of "sexual conduct.". . .

Stevens was not the first time we have encountered and rejected a State's attempt to shoehorn speech about violence into obscenity. In *Winters*, we considered a New York criminal statute "forbid[ding] the massing of stories of bloodshed and lust in such a way as to incite to crime against the person." The

New York Court of Appeals upheld the provision as a law against obscenity. . . . Our opinion in *Winters* . . . made clear that violence is not part of the
obscenity that the Constitution permits to be regulated. . . . Because speech
about violence is not obscene, it is of no consequence that California's statute
mimics the New York statute regulating obscenity-for-minors that we upheld in
Ginsberg v. New York, 390 U.S. 629 (1968). . . . [B]ecause "obscenity is not
protected expression," the New York statute [in *Ginsberg*] could be sustained so
long as the legislature's judgment that the proscribed materials were harmful to
children "was not irrational."

The California Act is something else entirely. It does not adjust the boundaries
of an existing category of unprotected speech to ensure that a definition designed
for adults is not uncritically applied to children. California does not argue that it
is empowered to prohibit selling offensively violent works *to adults* — and it is
wise not to, since that is but a hair's breadth from the argument rejected in
Stevens. Instead, it wishes to create a wholly new category of content-based
regulation that is permissible only for speech directed at children.

That is unprecedented and mistaken. . . . No doubt a State possesses legitimate power to protect children from harm, but that does not include a free-
floating power to restrict the ideas to which children may be exposed. . . .

California's argument would fare better if there were a longstanding tradition
in this country of specially restricting children's access to depictions of violence,
but there is none. Certainly the *books* we give children to read — or read to them
when they are younger — contain no shortage of gore. Grimm's Fairy Tales, for
example, are grim indeed. As her just deserts for trying to poison Snow White,
the wicked queen is made to dance in red hot slippers "till she fell dead on the
floor, a sad example of envy and jealousy." The Complete Brothers Grimm
Fairy Tales 198 (2006 ed.). Cinderella's evil stepsisters have their eyes pecked
out by doves. *Id.*, at 95. And Hansel and Gretel (children!) kill their captor by
baking her in an oven. *Id.*, at 54.

High-school reading lists are full of similar fare. Homer's Odysseus blinds
Polyphemus the Cyclops by grinding out his eye with a heated stake. The Od-
yssey of Homer, Book IX, p. 125 (S. Butcher & A. Lang transls. 1909) ("Even
so did we seize the fiery-pointed brand and whirled it round in his eye, and the
blood flowed about the heated bar. And the breath of the flame singed his eyelids
and brows all about, as the ball of the eye burnt away, and the roots thereof
crackled in the flame"). In the Inferno, Dante and Virgil watch corrupt politicians struggle to stay submerged beneath a lake of boiling pitch, lest they be
skewered by devils above the surface. Canto XXI, pp. 187-189 (A. Mandelbaum
transl. Bantam Classic ed. 1982). And Golding's Lord of the Flies recounts how
a schoolboy called Piggy is savagely murdered *by other children* while mar-
ooned on an island. W. Golding, Lord of the Flies 208-209 (1997 ed.).[4]

---

4. Justice Alito accuses us of pronouncing that playing violent video games "is not different in
'kind' " from reading violent literature. . . . Well of course it is different in kind, but not in a way
that causes the provision and viewing of violent video games, unlike the provision and reading of

This is not to say that minors' consumption of violent entertainment has never encountered resistance. In the 1800s, dime novels depicting crime and "penny dreadfuls" (named for their price and content) were blamed in some quarters for juvenile delinquency. When motion pictures came along, they became the villains instead. . . . For a time, our Court did permit broad censorship of movies because of their capacity to be "used for evil," but we eventually reversed course. Radio dramas were next, and then came comic books. Many in the late 1940s and early 1950s blamed comic books for fostering a "preoccupation with violence and horror" among the young, leading to a rising juvenile crime rate. See Note, Regulation of Comic Books, 68 Harv. L. Rev. 489, 490 (1955). But efforts to convince Congress to restrict comic books failed. And, of course, after comic books came television and music lyrics.

California claims that video games present special problems because they are "interactive," in that the player participates in the violent action on screen and determines its outcome. The latter feature is nothing new: Since at least the publication of The Adventures of You: Sugarcane Island in 1969, young readers of choose-your-own-adventure stories have been able to make decisions that determine the plot by following instructions about which page to turn to. As for the argument that video games enable participation in the violent action, that seems to us more a matter of degree than of kind. As Judge Posner has observed, all literature is interactive. "[T]he better it is, the more interactive. Literature when it is successful draws the reader into the story, makes him identify with the characters, invites him to judge them and quarrel with them, to experience their joys and sufferings as the reader's own." American Amusement Machine Assn. v. Kendrick, 244 F.3d 572, 577 (CA7 2001) (striking down a similar restriction on violent video games).

Justice Alito has done considerable independent research to identify video games in which "the violence is astounding. Victims are dismembered, decapitated, disemboweled, set on fire, and chopped into little pieces. . . . Blood gushes, splatters, and pools." Justice Alito recounts all these disgusting video games in order to disgust us — but disgust is not a valid basis for restricting expression. And the same is true of Justice Alito's description of those video games he has discovered that have a racial or ethnic motive for their violence — " 'ethnic cleansing' [of] . . . African Americans, Latinos, or Jews." To what end does he relate this? Does it somehow increase the "aggressiveness" that California wishes to suppress? Who knows? But it does arouse the reader's ire, and the reader's desire to put an end to this horrible message. Thus,

---

books, not to be expressive activity and hence not to enjoy First Amendment protection. Reading Dante is unquestionably more cultured and intellectually edifying than playing Mortal Kombat. But these cultural and intellectual differences are not *constitutional* ones. Crudely violent video games, tawdry TV shows, and cheap novels and magazines are no less forms of speech than The Divine Comedy, and restrictions upon them must survive strict scrutiny — a question to which we devote our attention in Part III, *infra*. Even if we can see in them "nothing of any possible value to society . . . , they are as much entitled to the protection of free speech as the best of literature." *Winters v. New York*, 333 U. S. 507, 510 (1948).

ironically, Justice Alito's argument highlights the precise danger posed by the California Act: that the *ideas* expressed by speech — whether it be violence, or gore, or racism — and not its objective effects, may be the real reason for governmental proscription.

III. Because the Act imposes a restriction on the content of protected speech, it is invalid unless California can demonstrate that it passes strict scrutiny — that is, unless it is justified by a compelling government interest and is narrowly drawn to serve that interest. The State must specifically identify an "actual problem" in need of solving, and the curtailment of free speech must be actually necessary to the solution. That is a demanding standard. "It is rare that a regulation restricting speech because of its content will ever be permissible."

California cannot meet that standard. At the outset, it acknowledges that it cannot show a direct causal link between violent video games and harm to minors. Rather, relying upon our decision in Turner Broadcasting System, Inc. v. FCC, 512 U.S. 622 (1994), the State claims that it need not produce such proof because the legislature can make a predictive judgment that such a link exists, based on competing psychological studies. But reliance on *Turner Broadcasting* is misplaced. That decision applied *intermediate scrutiny* to a content-neutral regulation. California's burden is much higher, and because it bears the risk of uncertainty, ambiguous proof will not suffice.

The State's evidence is not compelling. California relies primarily on the research of . . . a few . . . research psychologists whose studies purport to show a connection between exposure to violent video games and harmful effects on children. These studies have been rejected by every court to consider them, and with good reason: They do not prove that violent video games *cause* minors to *act* aggressively (which would at least be a beginning). Instead, "[n]early all of the research is based on correlation, not evidence of causation, and most of the studies suffer from significant, admitted flaws in methodology." They show at best some correlation between exposure to violent entertainment and minuscule real-world effects, such as children's feeling more aggressive or making louder noises in the few minutes after playing a violent game than after playing a nonviolent game.

Even taking for granted . . . that violent video games produce some effect on children's feelings of aggression, those effects are both small and indistinguishable from effects produced by other media. [California's expert psychologist] admitted that the "effect sizes" of children's exposure to violent video games are "about the same" as that produced by their exposure to violence on television. And he admits that the *same* effects have been found when children watch cartoons starring Bugs Bunny or the Road Runner, or when they play video games like Sonic the Hedgehog that are rated "E" (appropriate for all ages), or even when they "vie[w] a picture of a gun.". . . Of course, California has (wisely) declined to restrict Saturday morning cartoons, the sale of games rated for young children, or the distribution of pictures of guns. The consequence is that its regulation is wildly underinclusive when judged against its asserted justification, which in our view is alone enough to defeat it. Underinclusiveness raises serious doubts about whether the government is in fact pursuing the interest it invokes, rather than disfavoring a particular speaker or viewpoint. Here, California has singled out the purveyors of video games for disfavored treatment — at least when compared to booksellers, cartoonists, and movie producers — and has given no persuasive reason why.

The Act is also seriously underinclusive in another respect — and a respect that renders irrelevant the contentions of the concurrence and the dissents that video games are qualitatively different from other portrayals of violence. The California Legislature is perfectly willing to leave this dangerous, mind-altering material in the hands of children so long as one parent (or even an aunt or uncle) says it's OK. And there are not even any requirements as to how this parental or avuncular relationship is to be verified; apparently the child's or putative parent's, aunt's, or uncle's say-so suffices. That is not how one addresses a serious social problem.

California claims that the Act is justified in aid of parental authority: By requiring that the purchase of violent video games can be made only by adults, the Act ensures that parents can decide what games are appropriate. At the outset, we note our doubts that punishing third parties for conveying protected speech to children *just in case* their parents disapprove of that speech is a proper governmental means of aiding parental authority. Accepting that position would largely vitiate the rule that "only in relatively narrow and well-defined circumstances may government bar public dissemination of protected materials to [minors]." But leaving that aside, California cannot show that the Act's restrictions meet a substantial need of parents who wish to restrict their children's access to violent video games but cannot do so. The video-game industry has in place a voluntary rating system designed to inform consumers about the content of games. The system, implemented by the Entertainment Software Rating Board (ESRB), assigns age-specific ratings to each video game submitted: EC (Early Childhood); E (Everyone); E10+ (Everyone 10 and older); T (Teens); M (17 and older); and AO (Adults Only — 18 and older). The Video Software Dealers Association encourages retailers to prominently display information about the ESRB system in their stores; to refrain from renting or selling adults-only games to minors; and to rent or sell "M" rated games to minors only with parental consent. In 2009, the Federal Trade Commission (FTC) found that, as a result of this system, "the video game industry outpaces the movie and music industries" in "(1) restricting target-marketing of mature-rated products to children; (2) clearly and prominently disclosing rating information; and (3) restricting children's access to mature-rated products at retail." FTC, Report to Congress, Marketing Violent Entertainment to Children 30 (Dec. 2009), online at http://www.ftc.gov/os/2009/12/P994511violententertainment.pdf (FTC Report). This system does much to ensure that minors cannot purchase seriously violent games on their own, and that parents who care about the matter can readily evaluate the games their children bring home. Filling the remaining modest gap in concerned-parents' control can hardly be a compelling state interest.

And finally, the Act's purported aid to parental authority is vastly over-inclusive. Not all of the children who are forbidden to purchase violent video games on their own have parents who *care* whether they purchase violent video games. While some of the legislation's effect may indeed be in support of what some parents of the restricted children actually want, its entire effect is only in support of what the State thinks parents *ought* to want. This is not the narrow tailoring to "assisting parents" that restriction of First Amendment rights requires.

                                              * * *

California's effort to regulate violent video games is the latest episode in a long series of failed attempts to censor violent entertainment for minors. While we have pointed out above that some of the evidence brought forward to support the harmfulness of video games is unpersuasive, we do not mean to demean or disparage the concerns that underlie the attempt to regulate them — concerns that may and doubtless do prompt a good deal of parental oversight. We have no business passing judgment on the view of the California Legislature that violent video games (or, for that matter, any other forms of speech) corrupt the young or harm their moral development. Our task is only to say whether or not such works constitute a "well-defined and narrowly limited clas[s] of speech, the prevention and punishment of which have never been thought to raise any Constitutional problem" (the answer plainly is no); and if not, whether the regulation of such works is justified by that high degree of necessity we have described as a compelling state interest (it is not). Even where the protection of children is the object, the constitutional limits on governmental action apply.

California's legislation straddles the fence between (1) addressing a serious social problem and (2) helping concerned parents control their children. Both ends are legitimate, but when they affect First Amendment rights they must be pursued by means that are neither seriously underinclusive nor seriously over-inclusive. As a means of protecting children from portrayals of violence, the legislation is seriously underinclusive, not only because it excludes portrayals other than video games, but also because it permits a parental or avuncular veto. And as a means of assisting concerned parents it is seriously overinclusive because it abridges the First Amendment rights of young people whose parents (and aunts and uncles) think violent video games are a harmless pastime. And the overbreadth in achieving one goal is not cured by the underbreadth in achieving the other. Legislation such as this, which is neither fish nor fowl, cannot survive strict scrutiny.

We affirm the judgment below.

JUSTICE ALITO, with whom THE CHIEF JUSTICE joins, concurring in the judgment.

The California statute that is before us in this case represents a pioneering effort to address what the state legislature and others regard as a potentially serious social problem: the effect of exceptionally violent video games on impressionable minors, who often spend countless hours immersed in the alternative worlds that these games create. Although the California statute is well intentioned, its terms are not framed with the precision that the Constitution demands, and I therefore agree with the Court that this particular law cannot be sustained.

I disagree, however, with the approach taken in the Court's opinion. In considering the application of unchanging constitutional principles to new and rapidly evolving technology, this Court should proceed with caution. . . . We should take into account the possibility that developing technology may have important societal implications that will become apparent only with time. We should not jump to the conclusion that new technology is fundamentally the same as some older thing with which we are familiar. And we should not hastily dismiss the judgment of legislators, who may be in a better position than we are to assess the implications of new technology. The opinion of the Court exhibits none of this caution. . . .

Spending hour upon hour controlling the actions of a character who guns down scores of innocent victims is not different in "kind" from reading a description of violence in a work of literature. The Court is sure of this; I am not. There are reasons to suspect that the experience of playing violent video games just might be very different from reading a book, listening to the radio, or watching a movie or a television show. . . .

[Justice Alito concluded that the California law should be held void for vagueness.]

I will now briefly elaborate on my reasons for questioning the wisdom of the Court's approach. . . . The Court is wrong in saying that the holding in *Stevens* "controls this case.". . . *Stevens* struck down a law that broadly prohibited *any person* from creating, selling, or possessing depictions of animal cruelty for commercial gain. The California law involved here, by contrast, is limited to the sale or rental of violent video games *to minors*. The California law imposes no restriction on the creation of violent video games, or on the possession of such games by anyone, whether above or below the age of 18. The California law does not regulate the sale or rental of violent games by adults. And the California law does not prevent parents and certain other close relatives from buying or renting violent games for their children or other young relatives if they see fit. . . .

I certainly agree with the Court that the government has no "free-floating power to restrict the ideas to which children may be exposed," but the California law does not exercise such a power. If parents want their child to have a violent video game, the California law does not interfere with that parental prerogative. Instead, the California law reinforces parental decisionmaking in exactly the same way as the New York statute upheld in *Ginsberg*. Under both laws, minors are prevented from purchasing certain materials; and under both laws, parents are free to supply their children with these items if that is their wish.

Citing the video-game industry's voluntary rating system, the Court . . . does not mention the fact that the industry adopted this system in response to the threat of federal regulation, a threat that the Court's opinion may now be seen as largely eliminating. Nor does the Court acknowledge that compliance with this system at the time of the enactment of the California law left much to be desired — or that future enforcement may decline if the video-game industry perceives that any threat of government regulation has vanished. Nor does the Court note, as Justice Breyer points out, that many parents today are simply not able to monitor their children's use of computers and gaming devices.

Finally, the Court is far too quick to dismiss the possibility that the experience of playing video games (and the effects on minors of playing violent video games) may be very different from anything that we have seen before. Any assessment of the experience of playing video games must take into account certain characteristics of the video games that are now on the market and those that are likely to be available in the near future. Today's most advanced video games create realistic alternative worlds in which millions of players immerse themselves for hours on end. These games feature visual imagery and sounds that are strikingly realistic, and in the near future video-game graphics may be virtually indistinguishable from actual video footage. Many of the games already on the market can produce high definition images, and it is predicted that it will not be long before video-game images will be seen in three dimensions. It is also forecast that video games will soon provide sensory feedback. By wearing a special vest or other device, a player will be able to experience physical sensations supposedly felt by a character on the screen. Some *amici* who support respondents foresee the day when " 'virtual-reality shoot-'em-ups' " will allow children to " 'actually feel the splatting blood from the blown-off head' " of a victim.

Persons who play video games also have an unprecedented ability to participate in the events that take place in the virtual worlds that these games create. Players can create their own video-game characters and can use photos to produce characters that closely resemble actual people. A person playing a sophisticated game can make a multitude of choices and can thereby alter the course of the action in the game. In addition, the means by which players control the action in video games now bear a closer relationship to the means by which people control action in the real world. While the action in older games was often directed with buttons or a joystick, players dictate the action in newer games by engaging in the same motions that they desire a character in the game to perform. For example, a player who wants a video-game character to swing a baseball bat — either to hit a ball or smash a skull — could bring that about by simulating the motion of actually swinging a bat.

These present-day and emerging characteristics of video games must be considered together with characteristics of the violent games that have already been marketed. In some of these games, the violence is astounding. Victims by the dozens are killed with every imaginable implement, including machine guns, shotguns, clubs, hammers, axes, swords, and chainsaws. Victims are dismembered, decapitated, disemboweled, set on fire, and chopped into little pieces. They cry out in agony and beg for mercy. Blood gushes, splatters, and pools. Severed body parts and gobs of human remains are graphically shown. In some games, points are awarded based, not only on the number of victims killed, but on the killing technique employed. It also appears that there is no antisocial theme too base for some in the video-game industry to exploit. There are games in which a player can take on the identity and reenact the killings carried out by the perpetrators of the murders at Columbine High School and Virginia Tech. The objective of one game is to rape a mother and her daughters; in another, the goal is to rape Native American women. There is a game in which players engage in "ethnic cleansing" and can choose to gun down African-Americans, Latinos, or Jews. In still another game, players attempt to fire a rifle shot into the head of President Kennedy as his motorcade passes by the Texas School Book Depository.

If the technological characteristics of the sophisticated games that are likely to be available in the near future are combined with the characteristics of the most violent games already marketed, the result will be games that allow troubled teens to experience in an extraordinarily personal and vivid way what it would be like to carry out unspeakable acts of violence.

The Court is untroubled by this possibility. According to the Court, the "interactive" nature of video games is "nothing new" because "all literature is interactive.". . . But only an extraordinarily imaginative reader who reads a description of a killing in a literary work will experience that event as vividly as he might if he played the role of the killer in a video game. To take an example, think of a person who reads the passage in Crime and Punishment in which Raskolnikov kills the old pawn broker with an axe. See F. Dostoyevsky, Crime and Punishment 78 (Modern Library ed. 1950). Compare that reader with a video-game player who creates an avatar that bears his own image; who sees a realistic image of the victim and the scene of the killing in high definition and in three dimensions; who is forced to decide whether or not to kill the victim and decides to do so; who then pretends to grasp an axe, to raise it above the head of the victim, and then to bring it down; who hears the thud of the axe hitting her head and her cry of pain; who sees her split skull and feels the sensation of blood on his face and hands. For most people, the two experiences will not be the same.

When all of the characteristics of video games are taken into account, there is certainly a reasonable basis for thinking that the experience of playing a video game may be quite different from the experience of reading a book, listening to a radio broadcast, or viewing a movie. And if this is so, then for at least some minors, the effects of playing violent video games may also be quite different. The Court acts prematurely in dismissing this possibility out of hand.

* * *

For all these reasons, I would hold only that the particular law at issue here fails to provide the clear notice that the Constitution requires. I would not squelch legislative efforts to deal with what is perceived by some to be a significant and developing social problem. If differently framed statutes are enacted by the States or by the Federal Government, we can consider the constitutionality of those laws when cases challenging them are presented to us.

JUSTICE THOMAS, dissenting.

The Court's decision today does not comport with the original public understanding of the First Amendment. . . . The practices and beliefs of the founding generation establish that "the freedom of speech," as originally understood, does not include a right to speak to minors (or a right of minors to access speech) without going through the minors' parents or guardians. I would hold that the law at issue is not facially unconstitutional under the First Amendment, and reverse and remand for further proceedings. . . .

The historical evidence shows that the founding generation believed parents had absolute authority over their minor children and expected parents to use that authority to direct the proper development of their children. . . . The founding generation would not have considered it an abridgment of "the freedom of speech" to support parental authority by restricting speech that bypasses minors' parents. . . .

In the Puritan tradition common in the New England Colonies, fathers ruled families with absolute authority. . . . Part of the father's absolute power was the right and duty "to fill his children's minds with knowledge and . . . make them apply their knowledge in right action." E. Morgan, The Puritan Family 97 (rev. ed. 1966). Puritans thought children were "innately sinful and that parents' primary task was to suppress their children's natural depravity." S. Mintz & S. Kellogg, Domestic Revolutions 2 (1988). . . . Accordingly, parents were not to let their children read "vain Books, profane Ballads, and filthy Songs" or "fond and amorous Romances, . . . fabulous Histories of Giants, the bombast Achievements of Knight Errantry, and the like." The History of Genesis, pp. vi-vii (3d ed. corrected 1708). This conception of parental authority was reflected in laws at that time. In the Massachusetts Colony, for example, it was unlawful for tavern keepers (or anyone else) to entertain children without their parents' consent. . . .

In the decades leading up to and following the Revolution, attitudes towards children changed. Children came to be seen less as innately sinful and more as blank slates requiring careful and deliberate development. But the same overarching principles remained. Parents continued to have both the right and duty to ensure the proper development of their children. They exercised significant authority over their children, including control over the books that children read. And laws at the time continued to reflect strong support for parental authority and the sense that children were not fit to govern themselves. . . .

The works of John Locke and Jean-Jacques Rousseau were a driving force behind the changed understanding of children and childhood. Locke taught that children's minds were blank slates and that parents therefore had to be careful and deliberate about what their children were told and observed. . . . Rousseau disagreed with Locke in important respects, but his philosophy was similarly premised on parental control over a child's development. Although Rousseau advocated that children should be allowed to develop naturally, he instructed that the environment be directed by "a tutor who is given total control over the child and who removes him from society, from all competing sources of authority and influence." These writings received considerable attention in America. . . .

Locke's and Rousseau's writings fostered a new conception of childhood. . . . Children were increasingly viewed as malleable creatures, and childhood came to be seen as an important period of growth, development, and preparation for adulthood. . . . Children lacked reason and decisionmaking ability. . . . This conception of childhood led to great concern about influences on children. . . . As a result, it was widely accepted that children needed close monitoring and carefully planned development. . . . In an essay on the education of youth in America, Noah Webster . . . advocated sheltering children from "every low-bred, drunken, immoral character" and keeping their minds "untainted till their reasoning faculties have acquired strength and the good principles which may be planted in their minds have taken deep root.". . .

The Revolution only amplified these concerns. The Republic would require virtuous citizens, which necessitated proper training from childhood. . . .

Based on these views of childhood, the founding generation understood parents to have a right and duty to govern their children's growth. Parents were expected to direct the development and education of their children and ensure that bad habits did not take root. They were responsible for instilling "moral prohibitions, behavioral standards, and a capacity for self-government that would prepare a child for the outside world.". . .

Society's concern with children's development extended to the books they read. . . . Stories written for children were dedicated to moral instruction and were relatively austere, lacking details that might titillate children's minds. . . . Parents had total authority over what their children read. . . .

The law at the time reflected the founding generation's understanding of parent-child relations. According to Sir William Blackstone, parents were responsible for maintaining, protecting, and education their children, and therefore had "power" over their children. 1 Commentaries on the Laws of England 434, 440 (1765). . . . Chancellor James Kent agreed. 2 Commentaries on American Law *189-*207. The law entitled parents to "the custody of their [children]," "the value of th[e] [children's] labor and services," and the "right to the exercise of such discipline as may be requisite for the discharge of their sacred trust." Id., at *193, *203. Children, in turn, were charged with "obedience and assistance during their own minority, and gratitude and reverance during the rest of their lives." Id., at *207. . . .

The history clearly shows a founding generation that believed parents to have complete authority over their minor children and expected parents to direct the development of those children. . . . In light of this history, the Framers could not possibly have understood "the freedom of speech" to include an unqualified right to speak to minors . . . without going through their parents. As a consequence, I do not believe that laws limiting such speech—for example, by requiring parental consent to speak to a minor—"abridg[e] the freedom of speech" within the original meaning of the First Amendment. . . .

Admittedly, the original public understanding of a constitutional provision does not always comport with modern sensibilities. . . . This, however, is not such a case. Although much has changed in this country since the Revolution, the notion that parents have authority over their children and that the law can support that authority persists today. For example, at least some States make it a crime to lure or entice a minor away from the minor's parent. See, *e.g.,* Cal. Penal Code Ann. § 272(b)(1) (West 2008); Fla. Stat. § 787.03 (2010). Every State in the Union still establishes a minimum age for marriage without parental or judicial consent. Individuals less than 18 years old cannot enlist in the military without parental consent. 10 U.S.C. § 505(a). And minors remain subject to curfew laws across the country and cannot unilaterally consent to most medical procedures. Moreover, there are many things minors today cannot do at all, whether they have parental consent or not. State laws set minimum ages for voting and jury duty. In California . . . minors cannot drive for hire or drive a school bus, Cal. Veh. Code Ann. §§ 12515, 12516 (West 2010), purchase tobacco, Cal. Penal Code Ann. § 308(b) (West 2008), play bingo for money, § 326.5(e), or execute a will, Cal. Probate Code Ann. § 6220 (West 2009). . . .

[Under the California law at issue here,] the only speech affected is speech that bypasses a minor's parent or guardian. Because such speech does not fall within "the freedom of speech" as originally understood, California's law does not ordinarily implicate the First Amendment and is not facially unconstitutional. . . .

I respectfully dissent.

JUSTICE BREYER, dissenting.

. . . California's statute provides "fair notice of what is prohibited," and consequently it is not impermissibly vague. . . .

Video games combine physical action with expression. . . . But because video games also embody important expressive and artistic elements, I agree with the Court that the First Amendment significantly limits the State's power to regulate. . . . Like the majority, I believe that the California law must be "narrowly tailored" to further a "compelling interest," without there being a "less restrictive" alternative that would be "at least as effective." [In applying this standard] I would evaluate the degree to which the statute injures speech-related interests, the nature of the potentially-justifying "compelling interests," the degree to which the statute furthers that interest, the nature and effectiveness of possible alternatives, and, in light of this evaluation, whether, overall, "the statute works speech-related harm . . . out of proportion to the benefits that the statute seeks to provide." . . .

California's law imposes no more than a modest restriction on expression. The statute prevents no one from playing a video game, it prevents no adult from buying a video game, and it prevents no child or adolescent from obtaining a game provided a parent is willing to help. All it prevents is a child or adolescent from buying, without a parent's assistance, a gruesomely violent video game of a kind that the industry *itself* tells us it wants to keep out of the hands of those under the age of 17. Nor is the statute, if upheld, likely to create a precedent that would adversely affect other media, say films, or videos, or books. A typical video game involves a significant amount of physical activity. And pushing buttons that achieve an interactive, virtual form of target practice (using images of human beings as targets), while containing an expressive component, is not just like watching a typical movie.

The interest that California advances in support of the statute is compelling. [It] consists of both (1) the "basic" parental claim "to authority in their own household to direct the rearing of their children," which makes it proper to enact "laws designed to aid discharge of [parental] responsibility," and (2) the State's "independent interest in the well-being of its youth.". . . And where these interests work in tandem, it is not fatally "underinclusive" for a State to advance its interests in protecting children against the special harms present in an interactive video game medium through a default rule that still allows parents to provide their children with what their parents wish. . . .

At the same time, there is considerable evidence that California's statute significantly furthers this compelling interest. [V]ideo games are excellent teaching tools. Learning a practical task often means developing habits, becoming accustomed to performing the task, and receiving positive reinforcement when performing that task well. Video games can help develop habits, accustom the player to performance of the task, and reward the player for performing that task well. Why else would the Armed Forces incorporate video games into its training? . . .

When the military uses video games to help soldiers train for missions, it is using this medium for a beneficial purpose. But California argues that when the teaching features of video games are put to less desirable ends, harm can ensue. In particular, extremely violent games can harm children by rewarding them for being violently aggressive in play, and thereby often teaching them to be violently aggressive in life. And video games can cause more harm in this respect than can typically passive media, such as books or films or television programs.

There are many scientific studies that support California's views. Social scientists, for example, have found *causal* evidence that playing these games results in harm. Longitudinal studies, which measure changes over time, have found that increased exposure to violent video games causes an increase in aggression over the same period. See Moller & Krahe, Exposure to Violent Video Games and Aggression in German Adolescents: A Longitudinal Analysis, 35 Aggressive Behavior 75 (2009); Gentile & Gentile, Violent Video Games as Exemplary Teachers: A Conceptual Analysis, 37 J. Youth & Adolescence 127 (2008); Anderson et al., Longitudinal Effects of Violent Video Games on Aggression in Japan and the United States, 122 Pediatrics e1067 (2008); Wallenius & Punamaki, Digital Game Violence and Direct Aggression in Adolescence: A Longitudinal Study of the Roles of Sex, Age, and Parent-Child Communication, 29 J. Applied Developmental Psychology 286 (2008).

Experimental studies in laboratories have found that subjects randomly assigned to play a violent video game subsequently displayed more characteristics of aggression than those who played nonviolent games. See, *e.g.*, Anderson et al., Violent Video Games: Specific Effects of Violent Content on Aggressive Thoughts and Behavior, 36 Advances in Experimental Soc. Psychology 199 (2004).

Surveys of 8th and 9th grade students have found a correlation between playing violent video games and aggression. See, *e.g.*, Gentile, Lynch, Linder, &

Walsh, The Effects of Violent Video Game Habits On Adolescent Hostility, Aggressive Behaviors, and School Performance, 27 J. Adolescence 5 (2004). Cutting-edge neuroscience has shown that "virtual violence in video game playing results in those neural patterns that are considered characteristic for aggressive cognition and behavior." Weber, Ritterfeld, & Mathiak, Does Playing Violent Video Games Induce Aggression? Empirical Evidence of a Functional Magnetic Resonance Imaging Study, 8 Media Psychology 39, 51 (2006). . . .

Some of these studies take care to explain in a common-sense way why video games are potentially more harmful than, say, films or books or television. In essence, they say that the closer a child's behavior comes, not to watching, but to *acting* out horrific violence, the greater the potential psychological harm. See Bushman & Huesmann, Aggression, in 2 Handbook of Social Pscyhology 833, 851 (S. Fiske, D. Gilbert, & G. Lindzey eds., 5th ed. 2010). . . .

Experts debate the conclusions of all these studies. . . . I, like most judges, lack the social science expertise to say definitively who is right. But associations of public health professionals who do possess that expertise have reviewed many of these studies and found a significant risk that violent video games, when compared with more passive media, are particularly likely to cause children harm. . . .

Unlike the majority, I would find sufficient grounds in these studies and expert opinions for this Court to defer to an elected legislature's conclusion that the video games in question are particularly likely to harm children. This Court has always thought it owed an elected legislature some degree of deference in respect to legislative facts of this kind, particularly when they involve technical matters that are beyond our competence, and even in First Amendment cases. . . . The majority . . . grants the legislature no deference at all. . . .

I can find no "less restrictive alternative to California's law that would be at least as effective." The majority points to a voluntary alternative. . . . But this voluntary system has serious enforcement gaps. When California enacted its law, a Federal Trade Commission (FTC) study had found that nearly 70% of unaccompanied 13- to 16-year-olds were able to buy M-rated video games. . . . Subsequently the voluntary program has become more effective. But as of the FTC's most recent update to Congress, 20% of those under 17 are still able to buy M-rated video games, and, breaking down sales by store, one finds that this number rises to nearly 50% in the case of one large national chain. . . .

I add that the majority's different conclusion creates a serious anomaly in First Amendment law. *Ginsberg* makes clear that a State can prohibit the sale to minors of depictions of nudity; today the Court makes clear that a State cannot prohibit the sale to minors of the most violent interactive video games. But what sense does it make to forbid selling to a 13-year-old boy a magazine with an image of a nude woman, while protecting a sale to that 13-year-old of an interactive video game in which he actively, but virtually, binds and gags the woman, then tortures and kills her? What kind of First Amendment would permit the government to protect children by restricting sales of that extremely violent video game *only* when the woman — bound, gagged, tortured, and killed — is also topless?

This anomaly is not compelled by the First Amendment. It disappears once one recognizes that extreme violence, where interactive, and *without literary, artistic, or similar justification*, can prove at least as, if not more, harmful to children as photographs of nudity. And the record here is more than adequate to support such a view. That is why I believe that *Ginsberg* controls the outcome here *a fortiori*. And it is why I believe California's law is constitutional on its face.

This case is ultimately less about censorship than it is about education. Our Constitution cannot succeed in securing the liberties it seeks to protect unless we can raise future generations committed cooperatively to making our system of government work. Education, however, is about choices. Sometimes, children need to learn by making choices for themselves. Other times, choices are made for children — by their parents, by their teachers, and by the people acting democratically through their governments. In my view, the First Amendment does not disable government from helping parents make such a choice here — a choice not to have their children buy extremely violent, interactive video games, which they more than reasonably fear pose only the risk of harm to those children.

For these reasons, I respectfully dissent.

D. Regulation of Speech When the Government Is Both Sovereign and Proprietor

1. Public Forum

Page 942: Insert at the end of note 1:

In Christian Legal Society v. Martinez, 130 S. Ct. 2971 (2010), the Court (5-4) upheld a public law school's policy of conditioning recognition as a student group (and thus access to school facilities and modest funding) on the willingness of a group to accept any student as a member. The "all-comers" policy was challenged by the Christian Legal Society, a group that required its members to adhere to a statement of faith that included the pledge that they abstain from sexual intimacies outside of a traditional marriage. The Court reasoned that the law school had created a limited public forum and concluded that the all-comers condition was reasonable and viewpoint-neutral. It was reasonable, said the majority, because it furthered the school's desire to support student groups in order to (1) make available to all students the leadership, educational, and social opportunities afforded by student organizations, (2) bring together individuals with diverse backgrounds and beliefs in the hope of encouraging tolerance, cooperation, and learning among students, and (3) signal the school's support of state nondiscrimination mandates. The Court thought that the all-comers policy was viewpoint-neutral because it made no distinction between groups based on their message or perspective. The dissent charged that the all-comers policy was devised as a pretext to mask the school's selective enforcement of the policy, and that the alleged selective enforcement targeted the viewpoint of the Christian Legal Society.

4. Public Sponsorship of Speech

Page 972: Insert the following at the end of note 3:

3a. Subsequent Developments: *Pleasant Grove.* Pleasant Grove, Utah's Pioneer Park is a public park that sports at least 15 permanent displays, 11 of which were donated by private entities. Among the displays are "an historic granary, a wishing well, the City's first fire station, a September 11 monument, and a Ten Commandments monument donated by the Fraternal Order of Eagles in 1971." The Summum Church requested that the city accept its donation of a stone monument, similar in size and shape to the Ten Commandments monument, on which would be inscribed the Seven Aphorisms of Summum.[1] The City refused and the Summum Church sued, contending that the City had violated the free speech guarantee. The Tenth Circuit concluded that the proposed display was speech of the Summum sect, that the park was a traditional public forum, and that the City had failed to justify its content-based exclusion of the Summum Church's speech. In Pleasant Grove v. Summum, 555 U.S. 460 (2009), the Supreme Court reversed.

The Court concluded that Pleasant Grove was not affording a public forum for private speech by displaying monuments in its park. Rather, the city was delivering its own message by accepting donated monuments for display in Pioneer Park. Citing Johanns v. Livestock Marketing Association, 544 U.S. 550 (2005), the Court repeated that "the Government's own speech . . . is exempt from First Amendment scrutiny." While government speech is limited by the establishment clause, the question of whether the City's display of the Ten Commandments violated the establishment clause had not been briefed or argued to either the Tenth Circuit or the Supreme Court, and thus the Court did not rule on this issue. The Court ruled that "[p]ermanent monuments displayed on public property

---

1. Summum is a religion that incorporates elements of Gnostic Christianity, specifically the belief "that spiritual knowledge is experiential and that through devotion comes revelation, which 'modifies human perception, and transfigures the individual.'" Summum holds that the Seven Aphorisms, or Seven Principles of Creation, were inscribed on the original stone tablets given to Moses by God. The Biblical account is that when Moses brought the first set of tablets down from Mount Sinai and witnessed his people worshipping a golden calf, "his anger burned and he threw the tablets out of his hands, breaking them to pieces at the foot of the mountain." Exodus 32:19 (New International Version). After the Israelites repented God wrote the Ten Commandments on a second set of tablets, which Moses brought to his people. Exodus 34. Summum adherents believe that the Seven Aphorisms were on the first tablets, but because the people were not ready to receive them, the Aphorisms, though shared with a few believers, were destroyed. See also http://www.summum.us/philosophy/tencommandments.shtml.

typically represent government speech," reasoning that "[g]overnments have long used monuments to speak to the public," and that there was no distinction between governmentally funded monuments and those accepted from private donors. "[P]ersons who observe donated monuments routinely — and reasonably — interpret them as conveying some message on the property owner's behalf. . . . This is true whether the monument is located on private property or on public property, such as national, state, or city park land." The conclusion that such monuments constitute governmental speech was reinforced by the fact that "throughout our Nation's history, the general government practice with respect to donated monuments has been one of selective receptivity." In short, by accepting or rejecting donations, governments choose what they wish to say.

The message conveyed, however, is not necessarily unitary. The Court noted a number of monuments that might send multiple or mixed messages. New York's Central Park contains a donated mosaic in memory of John Lennon, which features the word "Imagine." What the viewer may imagine is up to the viewer, whether it be "the musical contributions that John Lennon would have made if he had not been killed, . . . the lyrics of the Lennon song that obviously inspired the mosaic," or something else. Fayetteville, Arkansas has a large bronze statue on which the word "peace" is inscribed in many of the world's languages. Tucson, Arizona accepted the Mexican government's donation of a statue of Pancho Villa. The Statue of Liberty was originally intended as an expression of "republican solidarity and friendship" between France and the United States, but has "come to be viewed as a beacon welcoming immigrants to a land of freedom."

Public forum doctrine did not apply to the exclusion of the Summum monument because that "doctrine has been applied in situations in which government-owned property or a government program was capable of accommodating a large number of public speakers without defeating the essential function of the land or the program." While "a park can accommodate many speakers and, over time, many parades and demonstrations," they "can accommodate only a limited number of permanent monuments. . . . Speakers, no matter how long-winded, eventually come to the end of their remarks; persons distributing leaflets and carrying signs at some point tire and go home; monuments, however, endure. They monopolize the use of the land on which they stand and interfere permanently with other uses of public space." Because parks have traditionally served to facilitate assembly, communication of thoughts between citizens, and discussion of public issues, they "can provide a soapbox for a very large number of orators . . . but it is hard to imagine how a public park could be opened up for the installation of permanent monuments by every person or group wishing to engage in that form of expression." While the Court noted that "there are limited circumstances in which the forum doctrine might properly be applied to a permanent monument — for example, if a town created a monument on which all of its residents (or all those meeting some other criterion) could place . . . some . . . private message," it repeated that "as a general matter, forum analysis simply does not apply to the installation of permanent monuments on public property."

F. Expression Rights Implicit in the Free Speech Guarantee

1. Freedom of Association

Page 996: Insert at the end of note 4:

Ysursa v. Pocatello Education Association, 555 U.S. 353 (2009), presented the question of whether a state could bar public employees from consenting to payroll deductions for labor union political activities. Idaho law permitted payroll deductions for union dues, but prohibited such deductions for union political activities, even when the employee had consented to the deduction. The Court upheld the validity of the ban. Because Idaho had no obligation to permit any payroll deductions for public employees its refusal to permit such deductions for political purposes was a refusal to subsidize speech. Governments are "not required to assist others in funding the expression of particular ideas, including political ones. . . . While publicly administered payroll deductions for political purposes can enhance the unions' exercise of First Amendment rights, Idaho is under no obligation to aid the unions in their political activities. [Idaho's] decision not to do so is not an abridgment of the unions' speech; they are free to engage in such speech as they see fit. They simply are barred from enlisting the State in support of that endeavor." Accordingly, the Court applied minimal scrutiny and concluded that the ban was rationally related to Idaho's legitimate "interest in avoiding the reality or appearance of government favoritism or entanglement with partisan politics."

Page 1010: Insert new note 1a:

1a. Compelled Disclosure of Internal Campaign Strategies.   After California voters adopted initiative Proposition 8, which amended the state constitution to prohibit same-sex marriage, the constitutional validity of Proposition 8 was challenged in federal court. When proponents of Prop. 8 intervened to defend its validity, the challengers sought discovery of internal campaign strategy memoranda of the proponents. The District Judge granted the request and the Ninth Circuit reversed in Perry v. Schwarzenegger, 591 F.3d 1147 (9th Cir. 2010). A panel of the Court of Appeals ruled that disclosure of campaign strategies and the identity of campaign strategists and volunteers would deter participation in political campaigns and the free flow of ideas essential to political persuasion. Taken together, these deterrents operated to chill protected political association. The challengers failed to demonstrate a compelling interest in disclosure. The Supreme Court denied certiorari. Hollingsworth v. Perry, 130 S. Ct. 2432 (2010).

Consider two Supreme Court precedents that bear on this issue. In EEOC v. University of Pennsylvania, 493 U.S. 182 (1990), the Court rejected a claim of academic freedom to shield peer review materials in a tenure denial case from discovery. In Herbert v. Lando, 441 U.S. 153 (1979), the Court denied a claim of a press exemption from discovery of editorial communications in a defamation case. Are these cases distinguishable from *Perry* on the grounds that neither involved an inquiry into the effect of disclosure on political association nor consideration of the First Amendment interests involved in association to influence electoral outcomes?

Page 1010: Insert before the problems in "Anonymous Speech":

In Doe v. Reed, 130 S. Ct. 2811 (2010), the Court rejected a facial challenge to a Washington law that required disclosure of the names and addresses of signatories to initiative or referendum petitions. Because the act of signing such a petition expresses either the view that the subject of the petition should be adopted or that the public ought to vote on the matter, disclosure implicates free expression. For mandated disclosure to be valid the state must prove that there is a substantial relationship between disclosure and a "sufficiently important" governmental interest. In making this assessment courts must consider the strength of the interest asserted in light of the seriousness of the burden on expression imposed by disclosure. The Court thought that the government's interest in detecting fraud by public revelation of the identities of purported signatories was sufficiently important and substantially related to the disclosure requirement to uphold the requirement on its face. However, the plaintiffs objecting to disclosure remained free to prove that, as applied to them, disclosure would lead to threats, harassment, and reprisals. Citing *Buckley* and *Citizens United*, the Court noted that evidence of a reasonable probability that disclosure will produce these harms is enough to establish that disclosure would violate free expression rights.

Justice Thomas, the sole dissenter, contended that mandated disclosure of the identity of petition signatories should be subject to strict scrutiny because of the inherently chilling effect of disclosure upon citizen participation in the electoral process. Justice Thomas thought that Washington had several less restrictive alternatives to vindicate its interest in preventing and detecting fraudulent signatures and, thus, that the disclosure requirement was not narrowly tailored to its asserted interests in maintaining the integrity of the electoral process.

G. Free Expression and the Political Process

1. Money as Speech: Political Contributions and Expenditures

Page 1020: Insert the following at the end of note 6, prior to McConnell:

But *Austin* was overruled in Citizens United v. Federal Elections Commission, 130 S. Ct. 876 (2010), excerpted following *McConnell*. The Court ruled that the

First Amendment barred limitations on political expenditures by corporations and unions.

Page 1036: Insert the following at the end of the section:

4. Judicial Elections and Due Process. A.T. Massey Coal Co. and its affiliates were found by a West Virginia jury to have committed fraud and tortious interference with contract. The jury awarded plaintiff Hugh Caperton and his affiliated entities $50 million in compensatory and punitive damages. Before the judgment was appealed to the West Virginia Supreme Court of Appeals the state held its 2004 judicial elections. In that election Don Blankenship, the Chief Executive Officer of Massey Coal, donated the maximum permissible amount ($1,000) to the campaign of Brett Benjamin, who was seeking election to the West Virginia Supreme Court of Appeals. Blankenship also donated $2.5 million to a political organization formed under 26 U.S.C. § 527 that supported Benjamin, and spend an additional $500,000 on independent expenditures such as direct mailings and media advertisements in support of Benjamin. The total of Blankenship's contributions and expenditures "were more than the total amount spent by all other Benjamin supporters and three times the amount spent by Benjamin's own committee." Benjamin won the election, garnering 53.3% of the vote. When Massey Coal's appeal came before the West Virginia Supreme Court of Appeals, Caperton requested Justice Benjamin to recuse himself. Benjamin refused. By a 3-2 vote, with Justice Benjamin in the majority, the Supreme Court of Appeals reversed the jury verdict.

Caperton contended that due process required Justice Benjamin to recuse himself. In Caperton v. A.T. Massey Coal Company, 129 S. Ct. 2252 (2009), the Supreme Court, 5-4, agreed. Although an earlier Court had held, in Tumey v. Ohio, 273 U.S. 510 (1927), that due process required judicial recusal only when a judge has a "direct, personal, substantial, pecuniary interest" in a case, the Court in *Caperton* broadened the constitutional requirement for recusal. "We conclude that there is a serious risk of actual bias — based on objective and reasonable perceptions — when a person with a personal stake in a particular case had a significant and disproportionate influence in placing the judge on the case by raising funds or directing the judge's election campaign when the case was pending or imminent. The inquiry centers on the contribution's relative size in comparison to the total amount of money contributed to the campaign, the total amount spent in the election, and the apparent effect such contribution had on the outcome of the election." The Court emphasized that this was an "exceptional case," pointing to the relative size of Blankenship's contributions and expenditures, and the "temporal relationship between the campaign contributions, the justice's election, and the pendency of the case. . . . It was reasonably foreseeable, when the campaign contributions were made, that the pending case would be before the newly elected justice. . . . Blankenship's extraordinary contributions were made at a time when he had a vested stake in the outcome. Just as no man is allowed to be a judge in his own cause, similar fears of bias can arise when — without the consent of the other parties — a man chooses the judge in his own cause. And applying this principle to the judicial election process, there was here a serious, objective risk of actual bias that required Justice Benjamin's recusal."

Chief Justice Roberts, in dissent, noted over 40 questions that the majority had left unanswered by its broadening of due process in connection with contributions and expenditures on judicial elections.

How much money is too much money? . . . How do we determine whether a given expenditure is "disproportionate"? Disproportionate *to what?* . . . Are independent, non-coordinated expenditures treated the same as direct contributions to a candidate's campaign? . . . Does it matter whether the litigant has contributed to other candidates or made large expenditures in connection with other elections? . . . Does the amount at issue in the case matter? . . . How long does the probability of bias last? Does the probability of bias diminish over time as the election recedes? Does it matter whether the judge plans to run for reelection? What if the "disproportionately" large expenditure is made by an industry association, trade union, physicians' group, or the plaintiffs' bar? Must the judge recuse in all cases that affect the association's interests? . . . What if the case involves a social or ideological issue rather than a financial one? Must a judge recuse from cases involving, say, abortion rights if he has received "disproportionate" support from individuals who feel strongly about either side of that issue? . . . What if the candidate draws "disproportionate" support from a particular racial, religious, ethnic, or other group, and the case involves an issue of particular importance to that group? What if the supporter is not a party to the pending or imminent case, but his interests will be affected by the decision? Does the Court's analysis apply if the supporter "chooses the judge" not in *his* case, but in someone else's? What if the case implicates a regulatory issue that is of great importance to the party making the expenditures, even though he has no direct financial interest in the outcome . . . ? Must the judge's vote be outcome determinative in order for his nonrecusal to constitute a due process violation? . . . Does it matter whether the decision is clearly right (or wrong) as a matter of state law? . . . What if the judge voted against the supporter in many other cases? . . . What if the judge expressly *disclaims* the support of this person? . . . Must the judge recuse in cases involving individuals or groups who spent large amounts of money trying unsuccessfully to defeat him? . . . Does close personal friendship between a judge and a party or lawyer now give rise to a probability of bias? . . . [D]o we analyze the due process issue through the lens of a reasonable person, a reasonable lawyer, or a reasonable judge? . . . What role does causation play in this analysis? . . . If causation is a pertinent factor, how do we know whether the contribution or expenditure had any effect on the outcome of the election? What if the judge won in a landslide? What if the judge won primarily because of his opponent's missteps? . . . How final must the pending case be with respect to the contributor's interest? What if, for example, the only issue on appeal is whether the court should certify a class of plaintiffs? Is recusal required just as if the issue in the pending case were ultimate liability? . . . Which cases are implicated by this doctrine? Must the case be pending at the time of the election? Reasonably likely to be brought? What about an important but unanticipated case filed shortly after the election? . . . When do we impute a

probability of bias from one party to another? Does a contribution from a corporation get imputed to its executives, and vice-versa? Does a contribution or expenditure by one family member get imputed to other family members? . . . What
if the election is nonpartisan? What if the election is just a yes-or-no vote about
whether to retain an incumbent? . . . What if the supporter's expenditures are used
to fund voter registration or get-out-the-vote efforts rather than television advertisements? . . . Are contributions or expenditures in connection with a primary
aggregated with those in the general election? What if the contributor supported a
different candidate in the primary? . . . May *Caperton* claims only be raised on
direct review? Or may such claims also be brought in federal district court under 42
U.S.C. § 1983, which allows a person deprived of a federal right by a state official
to sue for damages? If § 1983 claims are available, who are the proper defendants?
The judge? The whole court? The clerk of court? . . . What about state-court cases
that are already closed? Can the losing parties in those cases now seek collateral
relief in federal district court under § 1983? What statutes of limitation should be
applied to such suits? . . . Are the parties entitled to discovery with respect to the
judge's recusal decision? . . . If a judge erroneously fails to recuse, do we apply
harmless-error review? . . . Does the *judge* get to respond to the allegation that he
is probably biased, or is his reputation solely in the hands of the parties to the case?
What if the parties settle a *Caperton* claim as part of a broader settlement of the
case? Does that leave the judge with no way to salvage his reputation?

What implications, if any, does *Caperton* have with respect to campaign
finance issues? If independent expenditures can create a probability of bias on
the part of a judicial candidate who is the beneficiary of such expenditures, do
such expenditures create a similar probability of bias on the part of legislative or
executive candidates who are benefitted by such expenditures? Is the probability
of bias more constitutionally significant in the case of judicial elections? If
so, why?

CITIZENS UNITED v. FEDERAL ELECTION COMMISSION
130 S. Ct. 876 (2010)

JUSTICE KENNEDY delivered the opinion of the Court.
Federal law prohibits corporations and unions from using their general treasury funds to make independent expenditures for speech defined as an "electioneering communication" or for speech expressly advocating the election or
defeat of a candidate. 2 U.S.C. § 441b. Limits on electioneering communications
were upheld in McConnell v. Federal Election Comm'n, 540 U.S. 93, 203-209
(2003). The holding of *McConnell* rested to a large extent on . . . Austin v.
Michigan Chamber of Commerce, 494 U.S. 652 (1990). *Austin* had held that
political speech may be banned based on the speaker's corporate identity.
In this case we are asked to reconsider *Austin* and, in effect, *McConnell*.
[Because] "*Austin* was a significant departure from ancient First Amendment
principles," [we] hold that *stare decisis* does not compel the continued acceptance of *Austin*. The Government may regulate corporate political speech

through disclaimer and disclosure requirements, but it may not suppress that speech altogether. We turn to the case now before us.

I. A. Citizens United is a nonprofit corporation [which] has an annual budget of about $12 million. Most of its funds are from donations by individuals; but, in addition, it accepts a small portion of its funds from for-profit corporations. In January 2008, Citizens United released a film entitled *Hillary: The Movie*. We refer to the film as *Hillary*. It is a 90-minute documentary about then-Senator Hillary Clinton, who was a candidate in the Democratic Party's 2008 Presidential primary elections. *Hillary* mentions Senator Clinton by name and depicts interviews with political commentators and other persons, most of them quite critical of Senator Clinton. *Hillary* was released in theaters and on DVD, but Citizens United wanted to increase distribution by making it available through video-on-demand. . . . In December 2007, a cable company offered . . . to make *Hillary* available on a video-on-demand channel called "Elections '08." [To] promote the film [Citizens United] produced two 10-second ads and one 30-second ad for *Hillary*. Each ad includes a short (and, in our view, pejorative) statement about Senator Clinton, followed by the name of the movie and the movie's Website address. Citizens United desired to promote the video-on-demand offering by running advertisements on broadcast and cable television.

B. Before the Bipartisan Campaign Reform Act of 2002 (BCRA), federal law prohibited — and still does prohibit — corporations and unions from using general treasury funds to make direct contributions to candidates or independent expenditures that expressly advocate the election or defeat of a candidate, through any form of media, in connection with certain qualified federal elections. 2 U.S.C. § 441b. BCRA § 203 amended § 441b to prohibit any "electioneering communication" as well. 2 U.S.C. § 441b(b)(2). An electioneering communication is defined as "any broadcast, cable, or satellite communication" that "refers to a clearly identified candidate for Federal office" and is made within 30 days of a primary or 60 days of a general election. The Federal Election Commission's (FEC) regulations further define an electioneering communication as a communication that is "publicly distributed." "In the case of a candidate for nomination for President . . . *publicly distributed* means" that the communication "[c]an be received by 50,000 or more persons in a State where a primary election . . . is being held within 30 days." Corporations and unions are barred from using their general treasury funds for express advocacy or electioneering communications. They may establish, however, a "separate segregated fund" (known as a political action committee, or PAC) for these purposes. 2 U.S.C. § 441b(b)(2). The moneys received by the segregated fund are limited to donations from stockholders and employees of the corporation or, in the case of unions, members of the union.

C. Citizens United . . . feared . . . that both the film and the ads would be covered by § 441b's ban on corporate-funded independent expenditures, thus subjecting the corporation to civil and criminal penalties. . . . Citizens United sought declaratory and injunctive relief against the FEC. It argued that (1) § 441b is unconstitutional as applied to *Hillary;* and (2) BCRA's disclaimer and disclosure requirements, BCRA §§ 201 and 311, are unconstitutional as applied to *Hillary* and to the three ads for the movie. [A three-judge] District Court denied Citizens United's motion for a preliminary injunction, and then granted the FEC's motion for summary judgment. . . . We noted probable jurisdiction. The case was reargued in this Court after the Court asked the parties to file supplemental briefs addressing whether we should overrule either or both *Austin* and the part of *McConnell* which addresses the facial validity of 2 U.S.C. § 441b.

II. [The Court considered and rejected the claim that *Hillary* was not an electioneering communication. The Court then rejected the claim that *Hillary* was exempt from the BCRA's limits because it was not "express advocacy": a communication "susceptible of no reasonable interpretation other than as an appeal to vote for or against a specific candidate." Federal Election Comm'n v. Wisconsin Right to Life, Inc., 551 U.S. 449, 469-470 (2007) (*WRTL*).] Under this test, *Hillary* is equivalent to express advocacy. The movie, in essence, is a feature-length negative advertisement that urges viewers to vote against Senator Clinton for President. [The Court then rejected Citizens United's claim] that § 441b should be invalidated as applied to movies shown through video-on-demand, [because] this delivery system has a lower risk of distorting the political process than do television ads. [But we] decline to draw, and then redraw, constitutional lines based on the particular media or technology used to disseminate political speech from a particular speaker. . . .

Citizens United also asks us to carve out an exception to § 441b's expenditure ban for nonprofit corporate political speech funded overwhelmingly by individuals. As an alternative to reconsidering *Austin*, the Government also seems to prefer this approach. [In Federal Election Comm'n v. Massachusetts Citizens for Life, Inc., 479 U.S. 238, 263-264 (1986) (*MCFL*),] the Court found unconstitutional § 441b's restrictions on corporate expenditures as applied to nonprofit corporations that were formed for the sole purpose of promoting political ideas, did not engage in business activities, and did not accept contributions from for-profit corporations or labor unions. BCRA's so-called Wellstone Amendment applied § 441b's expenditure ban to all nonprofit corporations. *McConnell* then interpreted the Wellstone Amendment to retain the *MCFL* exemption to § 441b's expenditure prohibition. Citizens United does not qualify for the *MCFL* exemption, however, since some funds used to make the movie were donations from for-profit corporations. The Government suggests we could find BCRA's Wellstone Amendment unconstitutional, sever it from the statute, and hold that Citizens United's speech is exempt from § 441b's ban under BCRA's Snowe-Jeffords Amendment, [which] operates as a backup provision that only takes effect if the Wellstone Amendment is invalidated. The Snowe-Jeffords Amendment would exempt from § 441b's expenditure ban the political speech of certain nonprofit corporations if the speech were funded "exclusively" by individual donors and the funds were maintained in a segregated account. Citizens United would not qualify for the Snowe-Jeffords exemption . . . because *Hillary* was funded in part with donations from for-profit corporations. Consequently, to hold for Citizens United on this argument, the Court would be required to revise the text of *MCFL*, sever BCRA's Wellstone Amendment, and ignore the plain text of BCRA's Snowe-Jeffords Amendment. Though it is true that the Court should construe statutes as necessary to avoid constitutional questions, the series of steps suggested would be difficult to take in view of the language of the statute. [Although the Government suggests that the statute could be interpreted to imply a *de minimis* standard with respect to funding from for-profit corporations, but] this standard would . . . require case-by-case determinations [and] archetypical political speech would be chilled in the meantime. . . . [The] Court cannot resolve this case on a narrower ground without chilling political speech, speech that is central to the meaning and purpose of the First Amendment. It is not judicial restraint to accept an unsound, narrow argument just so the Court can avoid another argument with broader implications. Indeed, a court would be remiss in performing its duties were it to accept an unsound principle merely to avoid the necessity of making a broader ruling. Here, the lack of a valid basis for an alternative ruling requires full consideration of the continuing effect of the speech suppression upheld in *Austin.* . . .

III. . . . Laws enacted to control or suppress speech may operate at different points in the speech process. . . . The law before us is an outright ban, backed by criminal sanctions. Section 441b makes it a felony for all corporations — including nonprofit advocacy corporations — either to expressly advocate the election or defeat of candidates or to broadcast electioneering communications within 30 days of a primary election and 60 days of a general election. Thus, the following acts would all be felonies under § 441b: The Sierra Club runs an ad, within the crucial phase of 60 days before the general election, that exhorts the public to disapprove of a Congressman who favors logging in national forests; the National Rifle Association publishes a book urging the public to vote for the challenger because the incumbent U.S. Senator supports a handgun ban; and the American Civil Liberties Union creates a Web site telling the public to vote for a Presidential candidate in light of that candidate's defense of free speech. These prohibitions are classic examples of censorship.

Section 441b is a ban on corporate speech notwithstanding the fact that a PAC created by a corporation can still speak. A PAC is a separate association from the corporation. So the PAC exemption from § 441b's expenditure ban does not allow corporations to speak. . . .

Section 441b's prohibition on corporate independent expenditures is thus a ban on speech. As a "restriction on the amount of money a person or group can spend on political communication during a campaign," that statute "necessarily reduces the quantity of expression by restricting the number of issues discussed, the depth of their exploration, and the size of the audience reached." Buckley v. Valeo, 424 U.S. 1, 19 (1976) (*per curiam*). Were the Court to uphold these restrictions, the Government could repress speech by silencing certain voices at any of the various points in the speech process. . . . If § 441b applied to individuals, no one would believe that it is merely a time, place, or manner restriction on speech. Its purpose and effect are to silence entities whose voices the Government deems to be suspect.

Speech is an essential mechanism of democracy, for it is the means to hold officials accountable to the people. . . . The right of citizens to inquire, to hear, to speak, and to use information to reach consensus is a precondition to enlightened self-government and a necessary means to protect it. The First Amendment " 'has its fullest and most urgent application' to speech uttered during a campaign for political office." Eu v. San Francisco County Democratic Central Comm., 489 U.S. 214, 223 (1989) (quoting Monitor Patriot Co. v. Roy, 401 U.S. 265, 272 (1971)). . . . For these reasons, political speech must prevail against laws that would suppress it, whether by design or inadvertence. Laws that burden political speech are "subject to strict scrutiny," which requires the Government to prove that the restriction "furthers a compelling interest and is narrowly tailored to achieve that interest.". . .

Premised on mistrust of governmental power, the First Amendment stands against attempts to disfavor certain subjects or viewpoints. Prohibited, too, are restrictions distinguishing among different speakers, allowing speech by some but not others. See First Nat. Bank of Boston v. Bellotti, 435 U.S. 765, 784 (1978). As instruments to censor, these categories are interrelated: Speech restrictions based on the identity of the speaker are all too often simply a means to control content.

Quite apart from the purpose or effect of regulating content, moreover, the Government may commit a constitutional wrong when by law it identifies certain preferred speakers. By taking the right to speak from some and giving it to others, the Government deprives the disadvantaged person or class of the right to use speech to strive to establish worth, standing, and respect for the speaker's voice. The Government may not by these means deprive the public of the right and privilege to determine for itself what speech and speakers are worthy of consideration. The First Amendment protects speech and speaker, and the ideas that flow from each.

The Court has upheld a narrow class of speech restrictions that operate to the disadvantage of certain persons, but these rulings were based on an interest in allowing governmental entities to perform their functions. See, e.g., Bethel School Dist. No. 403 v. Fraser, 478 U.S. 675, 683 (1986) (protecting the "function of public school education"); Jones v. North Carolina Prisoners' Labor Union, Inc., 433 U.S. 119, 129 (1977) (furthering "the legitimate penological objectives of the corrections system". . .); Parker v. Levy, 417 U.S. 733, 759 (1974) (ensuring "the capacity of the Government to discharge its [military] responsibilities". . .); Civil Service Comm'n v. Letter Carriers, 413 U.S. 548, 557 (1973) ("[F]ederal service should depend upon meritorious performance rather than political service"). The corporate independent expenditures at issue in this case, however, would not interfere with governmental functions, so these cases are inapposite. These precedents stand only for the proposition that there are certain governmental functions that cannot operate without some restrictions on particular kinds of speech. By contrast, it is inherent in the nature of the political process that voters must be free to obtain information from diverse sources in order to determine how to cast their votes. At least before *Austin*, the Court had not allowed the exclusion of a class of speakers from the general public dialogue.

We find no basis for the proposition that, in the context of political speech, the Government may impose restrictions on certain disfavored speakers. Both history and logic lead us to this conclusion.

A. The Court has recognized that First Amendment protection extends to corporations. [The Court cited a long string of cases in which corporate speech in a nonelectoral context received constitutional protection.] This protection has been extended by explicit holdings to the context of political speech. See, e.g., . . . Grosjean v. American Press Co., 297 U.S. 233, 244 (1936). [P]olitical speech does not lose First Amendment protection "simply because its source is a corporation.". . . "The identity of the speaker is not decisive in determining whether speech is protected. Corporations and other associations, like individuals, contribute to the 'discussion, debate, and the dissemination of information and ideas' that the First Amendment seeks to foster." The Court has thus rejected the argument that political speech of corporations or other associations should be treated differently under the First Amendment simply because such associations are not "natural persons."

At least since the latter part of the 19th century, the laws of some States and of the United States imposed a ban on corporate direct contributions to candidates. Yet not until 1947 did Congress first prohibit independent expenditures by corporations and labor unions in § 304 of the Labor Management Relations Act 1947. In passing this Act Congress overrode the veto of President Truman, who warned that the expenditure ban was a "dangerous intrusion on free speech." For almost three decades thereafter, the Court did not reach the question whether restrictions on corporate and union expenditures are constitutional. [The Court described the intervening cases challenging the 1947 ban, codified at 18 U.S.C. § 610, all of which were decided on nonconstitutional grounds.]

In Buckley [v. Valeo], 424 U.S. 1 [(1976)], the Court addressed various challenges to the Federal Election Campaign Act of 1971 (FECA) as amended in 1974. These amendments created 18 U.S.C. § 608(e), an independent expenditure ban separate from § 610 that applied to individuals as well as corporations and labor unions. [The Court in *Buckley* upheld FECA's limits on contributions to candidates because of the risk of actual or perceived *quid pro quo* corruption, but] *Buckley* invalidated § 608(e)'s restrictions on independent expenditures [because] "the independent expenditure ceiling . . . fails to serve any substantial governmental interest in stemming the reality or appearance of corruption in the electoral process," [due to the fact that the] "absence of prearrangement and coordination . . . alleviates the danger that expenditures will be given as a *quid pro quo* for improper commitments from the candidate.". . .

Buckley did not consider § 610's separate ban on corporate and union independent expenditures. . . . Had § 610 been challenged in the wake of *Buckley*, however, it could not have been squared with the reasoning and analysis of that precedent [because the] expenditure ban invalidated in *Buckley*, § 608(e), applied to corporations and unions, and some of the prevailing plaintiffs in *Buckley* were corporations. . . . Notwithstanding this precedent, Congress recodified § 610's corporate and union expenditure ban at 2 U.S.C. § 441b four months after *Buckley* was decided. Section 441b is the independent expenditure restriction challenged here.

Less than two years after *Buckley*, [the Court in] *Bellotti*, 435 U.S. 765, reaffirmed the First Amendment principle that the Government cannot restrict political speech based on the speaker's corporate identity. *Bellotti* could not have been clearer when it struck down a state-law prohibition on corporate independent expenditures related to referenda issues:

> We thus find no support in the First . . . Amendment, or in the decisions of this Court, for the proposition that speech that otherwise would be within the protection of the First Amendment loses that protection simply because its source is a corporation that cannot prove, to the satisfaction of a court, a material effect on its business or property. . . . [That proposition] amounts to an impermissible legislative prohibition of speech based on the identity of the interests that spokesmen may represent in public debate over controversial issues and a requirement that the speaker have a sufficiently great interest in the subject to justify communication.
>
> . . .
>
> In the realm of protected speech, the legislature is constitutionally disqualified from dictating the subjects about which persons may speak and the speakers who may address a public issue.

. . . *Bellotti* did not address the constitutionality of the State's ban on corporate independent expenditures to support candidates [but] that restriction would have been unconstitutional under *Bellotti*'s central principle: that the First Amendment does not allow political speech restrictions based on a speaker's corporate identity.

Thus the law stood until *Austin*. . . . [The] Michigan Chamber of Commerce sought to use general treasury funds to run a newspaper ad supporting a specific candidate. Michigan law, however, prohibited corporate independent expenditures that supported or opposed any candidate for state office. A violation of the law was punishable as a felony. The Court sustained the speech prohibition. To bypass *Buckley* and *Bellotti*, the *Austin* Court identified a new governmental interest in limiting political speech: an anti-distortion interest. *Austin* found a compelling governmental interest in preventing "the corrosive and distorting effects of immense aggregations of wealth that are accumulated with the help of the corporate form and that have little or no correlation to the public's support for the corporation's political ideas."

B. The Court is thus confronted with conflicting lines of precedent: a pre-*Austin* line that forbids restrictions on political speech based on the speaker's corporate identity and a post-*Austin* line that permits them. No case before *Austin* had held that Congress could prohibit independent expenditures for political speech based on the speaker's corporate identity. . . . In its defense of the corporate-speech restrictions in § 441b, the Government notes the anti-distortion rationale on which *Austin* [rests], yet it all but abandons reliance upon it. It argues instead that two other compelling interests support *Austin*'s holding that corporate expenditure restrictions are constitutional: an anti-corruption interest and a shareholder-protection interest. We consider the three points in turn.

1. As for *Austin*'s anti-distortion rationale, the Government does little to defend it. And with good reason, for the rationale cannot support § 441b. If the First Amendment has any force, it prohibits Congress from fining or jailing citizens, or associations of citizens, for simply engaging in political speech. If the anti-distortion rationale were to be accepted, however, it would permit Government to ban political speech simply because the speaker is an association that has taken on the corporate form. The Government contends that *Austin* permits it to ban corporate expenditures for almost all forms of communication stemming from a corporation. If *Austin* were correct, the Government could prohibit a corporation from expressing political views in media beyond those presented here, such as by printing books.

Political speech is "indispensable to decision-making in a democracy, and this is no less true because the speech comes from a corporation rather than an individual.". . . "[T]he concept that government may restrict the speech of some elements of our society in order to enhance the relative voice of others is wholly foreign to the First Amendment," *Automobile Workers*, 352 U.S., at 597 (Douglas, J., dissenting). . . . *Austin* sought to defend the anti-distortion rationale as a means to prevent corporations from obtaining "an unfair advantage in the political marketplace" by using "resources amassed in the economic marketplace." But *Buckley* rejected the premise that the Government has an interest "in equalizing the relative ability of individuals and groups to influence the outcome of elections.". . .

[In Davis v. Federal Election Commission, 128 S. Ct. 2759 (2008), the Court] invalidated the BCRA provision that increased the cap on contributions to one candidate if the opponent made certain expenditures from personal funds. . . . The rule that political speech cannot be limited based on a speaker's wealth is a necessary consequence of the premise that the First Amendment generally prohibits the suppression of political speech based on the speaker's identity.

[*Austin*] distinguish[ed] wealthy individuals from corporations on the ground that "[s]tate law grants corporations special advantages — such as limited liability, perpetual life, and favorable treatment of the accumulation and distribution of assets," [but it] "is rudimentary that the State cannot exact as the price of those special advantages the forfeiture of First Amendment rights."

It is irrelevant for purposes of the First Amendment that corporate funds may "have little or no correlation to the public's support for the corporation's political ideas." All speakers, including individuals and the media, use money amassed from the economic marketplace to fund their speech. The First Amendment protects the resulting speech, even if it was enabled by economic transactions with persons or entities who disagree with the speaker's ideas. . . .

Austin's anti-distortion rationale would produce the dangerous, and unacceptable, consequence that Congress could ban political speech of media corporations. . . . Media corporations are now exempt from § 441b's ban on corporate expenditures. Yet media corporations accumulate wealth with the help of the corporate form, the largest media corporations have "immense aggregations of wealth," and the views expressed by media corporations often "have little or no correlation to the public's support" for those views. . . . There is no precedent supporting laws that attempt to distinguish between corporations which are deemed to be exempt as media corporations and those which are not. "We have consistently rejected the proposition that the institutional press has any constitutional privilege beyond that of other speakers.". . . With the advent of the Internet and the decline of print and broadcast media, moreover, the line between the media and others who wish to comment on political and social issues becomes far more blurred. . . . [The media] exemption results in a further, separate reason for finding this law invalid: [B]y its own terms, the law exempts some corporations but covers others, even though both have the need or the motive to communicate their views. The exemption applies to media corporations owned or controlled by corporations that have diverse and substantial investments and participate in endeavors other than news. So even assuming the most doubtful proposition that a news organization has a right to speak when others do not, the exemption would allow a conglomerate that owns both a media business and an unrelated business to influence or control the media in order to advance its overall business interest. At the same time, some other corporation, with an identical business interest but no media outlet in its ownership structure, would be forbidden to speak or inform the public about the same issue. This differential treatment cannot be squared with the First Amendment. . . .

Austin interferes with the "open marketplace" of ideas protected by the First Amendment. It permits the Government to ban the political speech of millions of associations of citizens. [About 5.8 million for-profit corporations filed 2006 tax returns.] Most of these are small corporations without large amounts of wealth. This fact belies the Government's argument that the statute is justified on the ground that it prevents the "distorting effects of immense aggregations of wealth." It is not even aimed at amassed wealth.

The censorship we now confront is vast in its reach. . . . By suppressing the speech of manifold corporations, both for-profit and nonprofit, the Government prevents their voices and viewpoints from reaching the public and advising voters on which persons or entities are hostile to their interests. Factions will necessarily form in our Republic, but the remedy of "destroying the liberty" of some factions is "worse than the disease." The Federalist No. 10, (J. Madison). Factions should be checked by permitting them all to speak, and by entrusting the people to judge what is true and what is false. . . .

When Government seeks to use its full power, including the criminal law, to command where a person may get his or her information or what distrusted source he or she may not hear, it uses censorship to control thought. This is unlawful. The First Amendment confirms the freedom to think for ourselves.

2. [The Government argues] that corporate political speech can be banned in order to prevent corruption or its appearance. [While] *Buckley* . . . sustained limits on direct contributions in order to ensure against the reality or appearance of corruption, [it] did not extend this rationale to independent expenditures, and the Court does not do so here.

Limits on independent expenditures, such as § 441b, have a chilling effect extending well beyond the Government's interest in preventing *quid pro quo* corruption. . . . Indeed, 26 States do not restrict independent expenditures by for-profit corporations. The Government does not claim that these expenditures have corrupted the political process in those States. . . .

When *Buckley* identified a sufficiently important governmental interest in preventing corruption or the appearance of corruption, that interest was limited to *quid pro quo* corruption. The fact that speakers may have influence over or access to elected officials does not mean that these officials are corrupt: "It is in the nature of an elected representative to favor certain policies, and, by necessary corollary, to favor the voters and contributors who support those policies. It is well understood that a substantial and legitimate reason, if not the only reason, to cast a vote for, or to make a contribution to, one candidate over another is that the candidate will respond by producing those political outcomes the supporter favors.". . .

The *McConnell* record was "over 100,000 pages" long, yet it "does not have any direct examples of votes being exchanged for . . . expenditures." This confirms *Buckley*'s reasoning that independent expenditures do not lead to, or create the appearance of, *quid pro quo* corruption. In fact, there is only scant evidence that independent expenditures even ingratiate. Ingratiation and access, in any event, are not corruption. . . .

3. The Government contends further that corporate independent expenditures can be limited because of its interest in protecting dissenting shareholders from being compelled to fund corporate political speech. This asserted interest, like Austin's anti-distortion rationale, would allow the Government to ban the political speech even of media corporations. Assume, for example, that a shareholder of a corporation that owns a newspaper disagrees with the political views the newspaper expresses. Under the Government's view, that potential disagreement could give the Government the authority to restrict the media corporation's political speech. The First Amendment does not allow that power. There is, furthermore, little evidence of abuse that cannot be corrected by shareholders "through the procedures of corporate democracy."

Those reasons are sufficient to reject this shareholder-protection interest; and, moreover, the statute is both underinclusive and overinclusive. As to the first, if Congress had been seeking to protect dissenting shareholders, it would not have banned corporate speech in only certain media within 30 or 60 days before an election. A dissenting shareholder's interests would be implicated by speech in any media at any time. As to the second, the statute is overinclusive because it covers all corporations, including nonprofit corporations and for-profit corporations with only single shareholders. . . .

4. We need not reach the question whether the Government has a compelling interest in preventing foreign individuals or associations from influencing our Nation's political process. [2 U.S.C. § 441e bans contributions from and political expenditures by "foreign national[s]," including corporations chartered abroad or that have their principal place of business outside of the United States.] Section 441b is not limited to corporations or associations that were created in foreign countries or funded predominately by foreign shareholders. Section 441b therefore would be overbroad even if we assumed, *arguendo,* that the Government has a compelling interest in limiting foreign influence over our political process.

C. [The Court explained why *stare decisis* did not preclude overturning *Austin.* The decision was not well reasoned, a point underscored by the fact that the Government did not defend *Austin*'s antidistortion rationale in *Citizens United. Austin* has been] undermined by experience. . . . Political speech is so ingrained in our culture that speakers find ways to circumvent campaign finance laws. . . . Corporations, like individuals, do not have monolithic views. On certain topics corporations may possess valuable expertise, leaving them the best equipped to point out errors or fallacies in speech of all sorts, including the speech of candidates and elected officials. Rapid changes in technology — and the creative dynamic inherent in the concept of free expression — counsel against upholding a law that restricts political speech in certain media or by certain speakers. Today, 30-second television ads may be the most effective way to convey a political message. Soon, however, it may be that Internet sources, such as blogs and social networking Web sites, will provide citizens with significant information about political candidates and issues. Yet, § 441b would seem to ban a blog post expressly advocating the election or defeat of a candidate if that blog were created with corporate funds. . . . No serious reliance interests are at stake. . . .

Austin should be and now is overruled. We return to the principle established in *Buckley* and *Bellotti* that the Government may not suppress political speech on the basis of the speaker's corporate identity. No sufficient governmental interest justifies limits on the political speech of nonprofit or for-profit corporations.

D. [Because *Austin* is overruled] Section 441b's restrictions on corporate independent expenditures are therefore invalid and cannot be applied to *Hillary.* [We] are further required to overrule the part of *McConnell* that upheld BCRA § 203's extension of § 441b's restrictions on corporate independent expenditures. . . .

IV. A. Citizens United next challenges BCRA's disclaimer and disclosure provisions as applied to *Hillary* and the three advertisements for the movie. Under BCRA § 311, televised electioneering communications funded by anyone other than a candidate must include a disclaimer that " ' _____ is responsible for the content of this advertising.' " 2 U.S.C. § 441d(d)(2). [The statement must be "clearly spoken" and "clearly readable" on screen for four seconds, must be accompanied by a disclaimer that the communication is not authorized by a candidate, and must reveal the funder's name and address. Anybody who spends

$10,000 or more in any calendar year on electioneering communications must disclose to the FEC his or her identity, the amount spent, the relevant election(s), and the identity of certain contributors.]

Disclaimer and disclosure requirements may burden the ability to speak, but they "impose no ceiling on campaign-related activities" and "do not prevent anyone from speaking." [Such requirements are valid if there is] a "substantial relation" between the disclosure requirement and a "sufficiently important" governmental interest. [The facial validity of forced disclosure is] justified [by the] governmental interest in "provid[ing] the electorate with information" about the sources of election-related spending, [but] as-applied challenges would be available if a group could show a " 'reasonable probability' " that disclosure of its contributors' names " 'will subject them to threats, harassment, or reprisals from either Government officials or private parties.' " [*Buckley; McConnell.*] [W]e find the statute valid as applied to the ads for the movie and to the movie itself. . . .

V. . . . Some members of the public might consider *Hillary* to be insightful and instructive; some might find it to be neither high art nor a fair discussion on how to set the Nation's course; still others simply might suspend judgment on these points but decide to think more about issues and candidates. Those choices and assessments, however, are not for the Government to make. "The First Amendment underwrites the freedom to experiment and to create in the realm of thought and speech. Citizens must be free to use new forms, and new forums, for the expression of ideas. The civic discourse belongs to the people, and the Government may not prescribe the means used to conduct it." The judgment of the District Court is reversed with respect to the constitutionality of 2 U.S.C. § 441b's restrictions on corporate independent expenditures. The judgment is affirmed with respect to BCRA's disclaimer and disclosure requirements. The case is remanded for further proceedings consistent with this opinion.

CHIEF JUSTICE ROBERTS, joined by JUSTICE ALITO, concurring.

The Government urges us in this case to uphold a direct prohibition on political speech. It asks us to embrace a theory of the First Amendment that would allow censorship not only of television and radio broadcasts, but of pamphlets, posters, the Internet, and virtually any other medium that corporations and unions might find useful in expressing their views on matters of public concern. Its theory, if accepted, would empower the Government to prohibit newspapers from running editorials or opinion pieces supporting or opposing candidates for office, so long as the newspapers were owned by corporations—as the major ones are. First Amendment rights could be confined to individuals, subverting the vibrant public discourse that is at the foundation of our democracy. The Court properly rejects that theory, and I join its opinion in full. . . .

If taken seriously, *Austin*'s logic would apply most directly to newspapers and other media corporations. They have a more profound impact on public discourse than most other speakers. These corporate entities are, for the time being, not subject to § 441b's otherwise generally applicable prohibitions on corporate political speech. But this is simply a matter of legislative grace. . . .

[A concurring opinion by Justice Scalia, in which Justice Alito joined, and in which Justice Thomas joined in part, is omitted.]

JUSTICE STEVENS, with whom JUSTICE GINSBURG, JUSTICE BREYER, and JUSTICE SOTOMAYOR join, concurring in part and dissenting in part.

The real issue in this case concerns how, not if, the appellant may finance its electioneering. Citizens United is a wealthy nonprofit corporation that runs a political action committee (PAC) with millions of dollars in assets. Under the Bipartisan Campaign Reform Act of 2002 (BCRA), it could have used those assets to televise and promote *Hillary: The Movie* wherever and whenever it wanted to. It also could have spent unrestricted sums to broadcast *Hillary* at any time other than the 30 days before the last primary election. Neither Citizens United's nor any other corporation's speech has been "banned." All that the parties dispute is whether Citizens United had a right to use the funds in its general treasury to pay for broadcasts during the 30-day period. The notion that the First Amendment dictates an affirmative answer to that question is, in my judgment, profoundly misguided. . . .

The basic premise underlying the Court's ruling is . . . the proposition that the First Amendment bars regulatory distinctions based on a speaker's identity, including its "identity" as a corporation. . . . The conceit that corporations must be treated identically to natural persons in the political sphere is not only inaccurate but also inadequate to justify the Court's disposition of this case. In the context of election to public office, the distinction between corporate and human speakers is significant. Although they make enormous contributions to our society, corporations are not actually members of it. They cannot vote or run for office. Because they may be managed and controlled by nonresidents, their interests may conflict in fundamental respects with the interests of eligible voters. The financial resources, legal structure, and instrumental orientation of corporations raise legitimate concerns about their role in the electoral process. . . .

Although I concur in the Court's decision to sustain BCRA's disclosure provisions and join Part IV of its opinion, I emphatically dissent from its principal holding. . . .

The [Court's] ruling rests on several premises. First, the Court claims that *Austin* and *McConnell* have "banned" corporate speech. Second, it claims that the First Amendment precludes regulatory distinctions based on speaker identity, including the speaker's identity as a corporation. Third, it claims that *Austin* and *McConnell* were radical outliers in our First Amendment tradition and our campaign finance jurisprudence. Each of these claims is wrong.

The So-Called "Ban." [The] statutes upheld in *Austin* and *McConnell* do "not impose an *absolute* ban on all forms of corporate political spending." [B]oth statutes provide exemptions for PACs, separate segregated funds established by a corporation for political purposes. . . . Administering a PAC entails some administrative burden, but so does complying with the disclaimer, disclosure, and reporting requirements that the Court today upholds. . . . Like all other natural persons, every shareholder of every corporation remains entirely free under *Austin* and *McConnell* to do however much electioneering she pleases outside of the corporate form. The owners of a "mom & pop" store can simply place ads in their own names, rather than the store's. If ideologically aligned individuals wish to make unlimited expenditures through the corporate form, they may utilize an *MCFL* organization that has policies in place to avoid becoming a conduit for business or union interests. The laws upheld in *Austin* and *McConnell* leave open . . . genuine issue advertising — a category of corporate speech Congress found to be far more substantial than election-related advertising — or to Internet, telephone, and print advocacy. . . . [The law at issue here] functions as a source restriction or a time, place, and manner restriction. It applies in a viewpoint-neutral fashion to a narrow subset of advocacy messages about clearly identified candidates for federal office, made during discrete time periods through discrete channels. . . . Neither *Austin* nor *McConnell* held or implied that corporations may be silenced. . . . Laws such as [those at issue here] target a class of communications that is especially likely to corrupt the political process, that is at least one degree removed from the views of individual citizens, and that may not even reflect the views of those who pay for it. Such laws burden political speech, and that is always a serious matter, demanding careful scrutiny. But the majority's incessant talk of a "ban" aims at a straw man.

Identity-Based Distinctions. [In] a variety of contexts, we have held that speech can be regulated differentially on account of the speaker's identity, when identity is understood in categorical or institutional terms. The Government routinely places special restrictions on the speech rights of students, prisoners, members of the Armed Forces, foreigners, and its own employees. When such restrictions are justified by a legitimate governmental interest, they do not necessarily raise constitutional problems. . . . It is fair to say that our First Amendment doctrine has "frowned on" certain identity-based distinctions, particularly those that may reflect invidious discrimination or preferential treatment of a politically powerful group.

The election context is distinctive in many ways, and the Court . . . is right that the First Amendment closely guards political speech. But in this context, too, the authority of legislatures to enact viewpoint-neutral regulations based on content and identity is well settled. We have, for example, allowed state-run broadcasters to exclude independent candidates from televised debates. Arkansas Ed. Television Comm'n v. Forbes, 523 U.S. 666 (1998). We have upheld statutes that prohibit the distribution or display of campaign materials near a polling place. Burson v. Freeman, 504 U.S. 191 (1992). Although we have not reviewed them directly, we have never cast doubt on laws that place special restrictions on campaign spending by foreign nationals. See, e.g., 2 U.S.C. § 441e(a)(1). And we have consistently approved laws that bar Government employees, but not others, from contributing to or participating in political activities. . . .

Not only has the distinctive potential of corporations to corrupt the electoral process long been recognized, but . . . campaign finance . . . distinctions based on corporate identity tend to be less worrisome . . . because the "speakers" are not natural persons, much less members of our political community, and the governmental interests are of the highest order. . . . If taken seriously, our colleagues' assumption that the identity of a speaker has *no* relevance to the Government's ability to regulate political speech would lead to some remarkable conclusions. Such an assumption would have accorded the propaganda broadcasts to our troops by "Tokyo Rose" during World War II the same protection as speech by Allied commanders. More pertinently, it would appear to afford the same protection to multinational corporations controlled by foreigners as to individual Americans: To do otherwise, after all, could "enhance the relative voice" of some (*i.e.*, humans) over others (*i.e.*, non-humans). Under the majority's view, I suppose it may be a First Amendment problem that corporations are not permitted to vote, given that voting is, among other things, a form of speech. . . .

Our First Amendment Tradition. A third fulcrum of the Court's opinion is the idea that *Austin* and *McConnell* are radical outliers, "aberration[s]" in our First Amendment tradition. The Court has it exactly backwards. . . . At the federal level, the express distinction between corporate and individual political spending on elections stretches back to 1907, when Congress passed the Tillman Act, banning all corporate contributions to candidates. [The Tillman] Act was primarily driven by two pressing concerns: first, the enormous power corporations had come to wield in federal elections, with the accompanying threat of both actual corruption and a public perception of corruption; and second, a respect for the interest of shareholders and members in preventing the use of their money to support candidates they opposed. Over the years, the limitations on corporate political spending have been modified in a number of ways, as Congress responded to changes in the American economy and political practices that threatened to displace the commonweal. The Taft-Hartley Act of 1947 . . . extended the prohibition on corporate support of candidates to cover not only direct contributions, but independent expenditures as well [because the] bar on contributions "was being so narrowly construed" that corporations were easily able to defeat the purposes of the Act by supporting candidates through other means. . . . *Buckley* famously (or infamously) distinguished direct contributions from independent expenditures, but its silence on corporations only reinforced the understanding that corporate expenditures could be treated differently from individual expenditures. . . . Thus, it was unremarkable, in a 1982 case holding that Congress could bar nonprofit corporations from soliciting nonmembers for PAC funds, that . . . a unanimous Court [declared] that Congress'[s] "careful legislative adjustment of the federal electoral laws, in a cautious advance, step by step, to account for the particular legal and economic attributes of corporations . . . warrants considerable deference," and "reflects a permissible assessment of the dangers posed by those entities to the electoral process." [Federal Election Commission v. National Right to Work Committee, 459 U.S. 197, 209 (1982).] "The governmental interest in preventing both actual corruption and the appearance of corruption of elected representatives has long been recognized . . . and there is no reason why it may not . . . be accomplished by treating . . . corporations . . . differently from individuals." *Id.*, at 210-211. . . . When we asked in *McConnell* "whether a compelling governmental interest justifie[d]" [the statute at issue here], we found the question "easily answered": "We have repeatedly sustained legislation aimed at 'the corrosive and distorting effects of immense aggregations of wealth that are accumulated with the help of the corporate form and that have little or no correlation to the public's support for the corporation's political ideas.' " [quoting *Austin.*] . . .

[The majority's view is] that the only "sufficiently important governmental interest in preventing corruption or the appearance of corruption" is one that is "limited to *quid pro quo* corruption.". . . While it is true that we have not always spoken about corruption in a clear or consistent voice, the approach taken by the majority . . . disregards . . . the fundamental demands of a democratic society. . . . Corruption can take many forms. Bribery may be the paradigm case. But the difference between selling a vote and selling access is a matter of degree, not kind. And selling access is not qualitatively different from giving special preference to those who spent money on one's behalf. Corruption operates along a spectrum, and the majority's apparent belief that *quid pro quo* arrangements can be neatly demarcated from other improper influences does not accord with the theory or reality of politics. [The trial court record in *McConnell* established that unions and corporation make members of Congress aware of their advertisements, the members are grateful and appreciative, members seek to have unions and corporations run these ads, and that most of the American people think that corporations and unions that engage in electioneering communications receive special considerations from the members that they backed. This] shows the great difficulty in delimiting the precise scope of the *quid pro quo* category, as well as the adverse consequences that *all* such arrangements may have. There are threats of corruption that are far more destructive to a democratic society than the odd bribe. Yet the majority's understanding of corruption would leave lawmakers impotent to address all but the most discrete abuses. . . . At stake in the legislative efforts to address this threat is . . . not only the legitimacy and quality of Government but also the public's faith therein. . . .

Even under the majority's "crabbed view of corruption" the Government should not lose this case. . . . Even in the cases that have construed the anticorruption interest most narrowly, we have never suggested that such *quid pro quo* debts must take the form of outright vote buying or bribes, which have long been distinct crimes. Rather, they encompass the myriad ways in which outside parties may induce an officeholder to confer a legislative benefit in direct response to, or anticipation of, some outlay of money the parties have made or will make on behalf of the officeholder. . . . It has likewise never been doubted that "[o]f almost equal concern as the danger of actual *quid pro quo* arrangements is the impact of the appearance of corruption.". . . A democracy cannot function effectively when its constituent members believe laws are being bought and sold. . . .

The *Austin* Court did not rest its holding on *quid pro quo* corruption, as it found the broader corruption implicated by the anti-distortion and shareholder protection rationales a sufficient basis for Michigan's restriction on corporate electioneering. . . . Corporations, as a class, tend to be more attuned to the complexities of the legislative process and more directly affected by tax and appropriations measures that receive little public scrutiny; they also have vastly more money with which to try to buy access and votes. Business corporations must engage the political process in instrumental terms if they are to maximize shareholder value. The unparalleled resources, professional lobbyists, and single-minded focus they bring to this effort . . . make *quid pro quo* corruption and its appearance inherently more likely when they (or their conduits or trade groups) spend unrestricted sums on elections. . . . [E]ven if "[i]ngratiation and access. . . . are not corruption" themselves, they are necessary prerequisites to it; they can create both the opportunity for, and the appearance of, *quid pro quo* arrangements. The influx of unlimited corporate money into the electoral realm also creates new opportunities for the mirror image of *quid pro quo* deals: threats, both explicit and implicit. Starting today, corporations with large war chests to deploy on electioneering may find democratically elected bodies becoming much more attuned to their interests. . . .

[T]he consequences of today's holding will not be limited to the legislative or executive context. The majority of the States select their judges through popular elections. At a time when concerns about the conduct of judicial elections have reached a fever pitch, the Court today unleashes the floodgates of corporate and union general treasury spending in these races. . . .

[We should acknowledge] that "Congress surely has both wisdom and experience in these matters that is far superior to ours." [But such] deference would [not] be appropriate if there were a solid basis for believing that a legislative action was motivated by the desire to protect incumbents or that it will degrade the competitiveness of the electoral process. [There is] no record evidence from which to conclude that [the federal electioneering ban], or any of the dozens of state laws that the Court today calls into question, reflects or fosters such invidious discrimination. Our colleagues have opined that "*any* restriction upon a type of campaign speech that is equally available to challengers and incumbents tends to favor incumbents." This kind of airy speculation could easily be turned on its head. The electioneering prohibited [here] might well tend to favor incumbents, because incumbents have pre-existing relationships with corporations and unions, and groups that wish to procure legislative benefits may tend to support the candidate who, as a sitting officeholder, is already in a position to dispense benefits and is statistically likely to retain office. If a corporation's goal is to induce officeholders to do its bidding, the corporation would do well to cultivate stable, long-term relationships of dependency.

. . . The fact that corporations are different from human beings might seem to need no elaboration, except that the majority opinion almost completely elides it. . . . Unlike natural persons, corporations have "limited liability" for their owners and managers, "perpetual life," separation of ownership and control, "and favorable treatment of the accumulation and distribution of assets . . . that enhance their ability to attract capital and to deploy their resources in ways that maximize the return on their shareholders' investments.". . . It might also be added that corporations have no consciences, no beliefs, no feelings, no thoughts, no desires. Corporations help structure and facilitate the activities of human beings, to be sure, and their "personhood" often serves as a useful legal fiction. But they are not themselves members of "We the People" by whom and for whom our Constitution was established. . . . It is an interesting question "who" is even speaking when a business corporation places an advertisement that endorses or attacks a particular candidate. Presumably it is not the customers or employees, who typically have no say in such matters. It cannot realistically be said to be the shareholders, who tend to be far removed from the day-to-day decisions of the firm and whose political preferences may be opaque to management. Perhaps the officers or directors of the corporation have the best claim to be the ones speaking, except their fiduciary duties generally prohibit them from using corporate funds for personal ends. . . .

Recognizing the weakness of a speaker-based critique of *Austin*, the Court places primary emphasis not on the corporation's right to electioneer, but rather on the listener's interest in hearing what every possible speaker may have to say. . . . It is only certain Members of this Court, not the listeners themselves, who have agitated for more corporate electioneering. . . . [T]here are substantial reasons why a legislature might conclude that unregulated general treasury expenditures will . . . distort public debate in ways that undermine rather than advance the interests of listeners. . . . In a state election . . . , the interests of nonresident corporations may be fundamentally adverse to the interests of local voters. . . . [C]orporations [can] grab up the prime broadcasting slots on the eve of an election, [and] flood the market with advocacy. . . . The opinions of real people may be marginalized. . . . Corporate "domination" of electioneering can generate the impression that corporations dominate our democracy [with the result that citizens] may lose faith in their capacity . . . to influence public policy. A Government captured by corporate interests, they may . . . believe, will be neither responsive to their needs nor willing to give their views a fair hearing. The predictable result is cynicism and disenchantment. . . . Politicians who fear that a certain corporation can make or break their reelection chances may be cowed into silence about that corporation. . . . At the least, . . . a legislature is entitled to credit these concerns and to take tailored measures in response. . . .

When large numbers of citizens have a common stake in a measure that is under consideration, it may be very difficult for them to coordinate resources on behalf of their position. [Corporations, however,] are uniquely equipped to seek laws that favor their owners, not simply because they have a lot of money but because of their legal and organizational structure. Remove all restrictions on their electioneering, and the door may be opened to a type of rent seeking that is "far more destructive" than what noncorporations are capable of. . . .

All of the majority's theoretical arguments turn on a proposition with undeniable surface appeal but little grounding in evidence or experience, "that there is no such thing as too much speech." If individuals in our society had infinite free time to listen to and contemplate every last bit of speech uttered by anyone, anywhere; and if broadcast advertisements had no special ability to influence elections apart from the merits of their arguments (to the extent they make any); and if legislators always operated with nothing less than perfect virtue; then I suppose the majority's premise would be sound. . . .

[*Austin* also embodies] a concern to protect the rights of shareholders from a kind of coerced speech: electioneering expenditures that do not "reflec[t] [their] support." [S]hareholders who disagree with the corporation's electoral message may find their financial investments being used to undermine their political convictions. The PAC mechanism, by contrast, helps assure that those who pay for an electioneering communication actually support its content and that managers do not use general treasuries to advance personal agendas. . . . The Court dismisses this interest on the ground that abuses of shareholder money can be corrected "through the procedures of corporate democracy. . . . " [But] the rights of shareholders to vote and to bring derivative suits for breach of fiduciary duty . . . "are so limited as to be almost nonexistent," given the internal authority wielded by boards and managers and the expansive protections afforded by the business judgment rule. . . . [Though shareholders can divest,] this solution is only partial. The injury to the shareholders' expressive rights has already occurred; they might have preferred to keep that corporation's stock in their portfolio for any number of economic reasons; and they may incur a capital gains tax or other penalty from selling their shares, changing their pension plan, or the like. [While it is true] that corporations also spend money on lobbying and charitable contributions in ways that any particular shareholder might disapprove[,] those expenditures do not implicate the selection of public officials, an area in which "the interests of unwilling . . . corporate shareholders [in not being] forced to subsidize that speech . . . are at their zenith."

At bottom, the Court's opinion is . . . a rejection of the common sense of the American people, who have . . . fought against the distinctive corrupting potential of corporate electioneering since the days of Theodore Roosevelt. It is a strange time to repudiate that common sense. While American democracy is imperfect, few outside the majority of this Court would have thought its flaws included a dearth of corporate money in politics.

ARIZONA FREE ENTERPRISE CLUB'S FREEDOM CLUB PAC v. BENNETT
2011 U.S. Lexis 4992

CHIEF JUSTICE ROBERTS delivered the opinion of the Court.

Under Arizona law, candidates for state office who accept public financing can receive additional money from the State in direct response to the campaign activities of privately financed candidates and independent expenditure groups. Once a set spending limit is exceeded, a publicly financed candidate receives roughly one dollar for every dollar spent by an opposing privately financed candidate. The publicly financed candidate also receives roughly one dollar for every dollar spent by independent expenditure groups to support the privately financed candidate, or to oppose the publicly financed candidate. We hold that Arizona's matching funds scheme substantially burdens protected political speech without serving a compelling state interest and therefore violates the First Amendment.

I. A. The Arizona Citizens Clean Elections Act . . . created a voluntary public financing system to fund the primary and general election campaigns of candidates for state office. . . . Eligibility is contingent on the collection of a specified number of five-dollar contributions from Arizona voters and the acceptance of certain campaign restrictions and obligations. Publicly funded candidates must agree, among other things, to limit their expenditure of personal funds to $500, participate in at least one public debate, adhere to an overall expenditure cap, and return all unspent public moneys to the State.

In exchange for accepting these conditions, participating candidates are granted public funds to conduct their campaigns. In many cases, this initial allotment may be the whole of the State's financial backing of a publicly funded candidate. But when certain conditions are met, publicly funded candidates are granted additional "equalizing" or matching funds. Matching funds are available in both primary and general elections. In a primary, matching funds are triggered when a privately financed candidate's expenditures, combined with the expenditures of independent groups made in support of the privately financed candidate or in opposition to a publicly financed candidate, exceed the primary election allotment of state funds to the publicly financed candidate. During the general election, matching funds are triggered when the amount of money a privately financed candidate receives in contributions, combined with the expenditures of independent groups made in support of the privately financed candidate or in opposition to a publicly financed candidate, exceed the general election allotment of state funds to the publicly financed candidate. A privately financed candidate's expenditures of his personal funds are counted as contributions for purposes of calculating matching funds during a general election.

Once matching funds are triggered, each additional dollar that a privately financed candidate spends during the primary results in one dollar in additional state funding to his publicly financed opponent (less a 6% reduction meant to account for fundraising expenses). During a general election, every dollar that a candidate receives in contributions — which includes any money of his own that a candidate spends on his campaign — results in roughly one dollar in additional state funding to his publicly financed opponent. In an election where a privately funded candidate faces multiple publicly financed candidates, one dollar raised or spent by the privately financed candidate results in an almost one dollar increase in public funding to each of the publicly financed candidates.

Once the public financing cap is exceeded, additional expenditures by independent groups can result in dollar-for-dollar matching funds as well. Spending by independent groups on behalf of a privately funded candidate, or in opposition to a publicly funded candidate, results in matching funds. Independent expenditures made in support of a publicly financed candidate can result in matching funds for other publicly financed candidates in a race. The matching funds provision is not activated, however, when independent expenditures are made in opposition to a privately financed candidate. Matching funds top out at two times the initial authorized grant of public funding to the publicly financed candidate.

Under Arizona law, a privately financed candidate may raise and spend unlimited funds, subject to state-imposed contribution limits and disclosure requirements. Contributions to candidates for statewide office are limited to $840 per contributor per election cycle and contributions to legislative candidates are limited to $410 per contributor per election cycle.

An example may help clarify how the Arizona matching funds provision operates. Arizona is divided into 30 districts for purposes of electing members to the State's House of Representatives. Each district elects two representatives to the House biannually. In the last general election, the number of candidates competing for the two available seats in each district ranged from two to seven. Arizona's Fourth District had three candidates for its two available House seats. Two of those candidates opted to accept public funding; one candidate chose to operate his campaign with private funds. In that election, if the total funds contributed to the privately funded candidate, added to that candidate's expenditure of personal funds and the expenditures of supportive independent groups, exceeded $21,479 — the allocation of public funds for the general election in a contested State House race — the matching funds provision would be triggered. At that point, a number of different political activities could result in the distribution of matching funds. For example:

If the privately funded candidate spent $ 1,000 of his own money to conduct a direct mailing, each of his publicly funded opponents would receive $940 ($1,000 less the 6% offset).

If the privately funded candidate held a fundraiser that generated $1,000 in contributions, each of his publicly funded opponents would receive $940.

If an independent expenditure group spent $1,000 on a brochure expressing its support for the privately financed candidate, each of the publicly financed candidates would receive $940 directly.

If an independent expenditure group spent $1,000 on a brochure opposing one of the publicly financed candidates, but saying nothing about the privately financed candidate, the publicly financed candidates would receive $ 940 directly.

If an independent expenditure group spent $1,000 on a brochure supporting one of the publicly financed candidates, the other publicly financed candidate would receive $940 directly, but the privately financed candidate would receive nothing.

If an independent expenditure group spent $1,000 on a brochure opposing the privately financed candidate, no matching funds would be issued.

A publicly financed candidate would continue to receive additional state money in response to fundraising and spending by the privately financed candidate and independent expenditure groups until that publicly financed candidate received a total of $64,437 in state funds (three times the initial allocation for a State House race).[1]

B. Petitioners in this case, plaintiffs below, are five past and future candidates for Arizona state office . . . and two independent groups that spend money to support and oppose Arizona candidates. They filed suit challenging the constitutionality of the matching funds provision. The candidates and independent expenditure groups argued that the matching funds provision unconstitutionally penalized their speech and burdened their ability to fully exercise their First Amendment rights. The District Court agreed that this provision "constitute[d] a substantial burden" on the speech of privately financed candidates because it "award[s] funds to a [privately financed] candidate's opponent" based on the privately financed candidate's speech [and] "no compelling interest [was] served by the" provision that might justify the burden imposed. The District Court entered a permanent injunction against the enforcement of the matching funds provision, but stayed implementation of that injunction. . . . The Court of Appeals for the Ninth Circuit . . . reversed the District Court. The Court of Appeals concluded that the matching funds provision "imposes only a minimal burden on First Amendment rights" because it "does not actually prevent anyone from speaking in the first place or cap campaign expenditures." In that court's view, any burden imposed by the matching funds provision was justified because the provision "bears a substantial relation to the State's important interest in reducing *quid pro quo* political corruption." We stayed the Court of Appeals' decision, vacated the stay of the District Court's injunction, and later granted certiorari.

II. "Discussion of public issues and debate on the qualifications of candidates are integral to the operation" of our system of government. Buckley v. Valeo, 424 U.S. 1, 14 (1976). As a result, the First Amendment " 'has its fullest and most urgent application' to speech uttered during a campaign for political office." Eu v. San Francisco County Democratic Central Comm., 489 U.S. 214, 223 (1989) (quoting Monitor Patriot Co. v. Roy, 401 U.S. 265, 272 (1971)). "Laws that burden political speech are" accordingly "subject to strict scrutiny, which requires the Government to prove that the restriction furthers a compelling interest and is narrowly tailored to achieve that interest." *Citizens United.* . . .

Although the speech of the candidates and independent expenditure groups that brought this suit is not directly capped by Arizona's matching funds provision, those parties contend that their political speech is substantially burdened by the state law in the same way that speech was burdened by the law we recently found invalid in Davis v. Federal Election Comm'n, 554 U.S. 724

---

1. Maine and North Carolina have both passed matching funds statutes that resemble Arizona's law. See Me. Rev. Stat. Ann., Tit. 21-A, §§ 1125(8), (9) (2008); N. C. Gen. Stat. Ann. § 163-278.67 (Lexis 2009). Minnesota, Connecticut, and Florida have also adopted matching funds provisions, but courts have enjoined the enforcement of those schemes after concluding that their operation violates the First Amendment. . . .

(2008). In *Davis*, we considered a First Amendment challenge to the so-called "Millionaire's Amendment" of the Bipartisan Campaign Reform Act of 2002, 2 U.S.C. § 441a-1(a). Under that Amendment, if a candidate for the United States House of Representatives spent more than $350,000 of his personal funds, "a new, asymmetrical regulatory scheme [came] into play." The opponent of the candidate who exceeded that limit was permitted to collect individual contributions up to $6,900 per contributor—three times the normal contribution limit of $2,300. The candidate who spent more than the personal funds limit remained subject to the original contribution cap. Davis argued that this scheme "burden[ed] his exercise of his First Amendment right to make unlimited expenditures of his personal funds because" doing so had "the effect of enabling his opponent to raise more money and to use that money to finance speech that counteract[ed] and thus diminishe[d] the effectiveness of Davis'[s] own speech." [We] acknowledged that the provision did not impose an outright cap on a candidate's personal expenditures [but we] nonetheless concluded that the Amendment was unconstitutional because it forced a candidate "to choose between the First Amendment right to engage in unfettered political speech and subjection to discriminatory fundraising limitations." Any candidate who chose to spend more than $350,000 of his own money was forced to "shoulder a special and potentially significant burden" because that choice gave fundraising advantages to the candidate's adversary. We determined that this constituted an "unprecedented penalty" and "impose[d] a substantial burden on the exercise of the First Amendment right to use personal funds for campaign speech," and concluded that the Government had failed to advance any compelling interest that would justify such a burden.

A. The logic of *Davis* largely controls our approach to this case. Much like the burden placed on speech in *Davis*, the matching funds provision "imposes an unprecedented penalty on any candidate who robustly exercises [his] First Amendment right[s]." Under that provision, "the vigorous exercise of the right to use personal funds to finance campaign speech" leads to "advantages for opponents in the competitive context of electoral politics." Once a privately financed candidate has raised or spent more than the State's initial grant to a publicly financed candidate, each personal dollar spent by the privately financed candidate results in an award of almost one additional dollar to his opponent. That plainly forces the privately financed candidate to "shoulder a special and potentially significant burden" when choosing to exercise his First Amendment right to spend funds on behalf of his candidacy. If the law at issue in *Davis* imposed a burden on candidate speech, the Arizona law unquestionably does so as well.

The penalty imposed by Arizona's matching funds provision is different in some respects from the penalty imposed by the law we struck down in *Davis*. But those differences make the Arizona law *more* constitutionally problematic, not less. First, the penalty in *Davis* consisted of raising the contribution limits for one of the candidates. The candidate who benefited from the increased limits still had to go out and raise the funds. He may or may not have been able to do so. The other candidate, therefore, faced merely the possibility that his opponent would be able to raise additional funds, through contribution limits that remained subject to a cap. And still the Court held that this was an "unprecedented penalty," a "special and potentially significant burden" that had to be justified by a compelling state interest. . . . Here the benefit to the publicly financed candidate is the direct and automatic release of public money. That is a far heavier burden than in *Davis*.

Second, . . . the matching funds provision can create a multiplier effect. In the Arizona Fourth District House election previously discussed, if the spending cap were exceeded, each dollar spent by the privately funded candidate would result in an additional dollar of campaign funding to each of that candidate's publicly financed opponents. In such a situation, the matching funds provision forces privately funded candidates to fight a political hydra of sorts. Each dollar they spend generates two adversarial dollars in response. Again, a markedly more significant burden than in *Davis*.

Third, unlike the law at issue in *Davis*, all of this is to some extent out of the privately financed candidate's hands. Even if that candidate opted to spend less than the initial public financing cap, any spending by independent expenditure groups to promote the privately financed candidate's election — regardless whether such support was welcome or helpful — could trigger matching funds. What is more, that state money would go directly to the publicly funded candidate to use as he saw fit. That disparity in control — giving money directly to a publicly financed candidate, in response to independent expenditures that cannot be coordinated with the privately funded candidate — is a substantial advantage for the publicly funded candidate. That candidate can allocate the money according to his own campaign strategy, which the privately financed candidate could not do with the independent group expenditures that triggered the matching funds.

The burdens that this regime places on independent expenditure groups are akin to those imposed on the privately financed candidates themselves. Just as with the candidate the independent group supports, the more money spent on that candidate's behalf or in opposition to a publicly funded candidate, the more money the publicly funded candidate receives from the State. And just as with the privately financed candidate, the effect of a dollar spent on election speech is a guaranteed financial payout to the publicly funded candidate the group opposes. Moreover, spending one dollar can result in the flow of dollars to multiple candidates the group disapproves of, dollars directly controlled by the publicly funded candidate or candidates.

In some ways, the burden the Arizona law imposes on independent expenditure groups is worse than the burden it imposes on privately financed candidates, and thus substantially worse than the burden we found constitutionally impermissible in *Davis*. If a candidate contemplating an electoral run in Arizona surveys the campaign landscape and decides that the burdens imposed by the matching funds regime make a privately funded campaign unattractive, he at least has the option of taking public financing. Independent expenditure groups, of course, do not.

Once the spending cap is reached, an independent expenditure group that wants to support a particular candidate — because of that candidate's stand on an issue of concern to the group — can only avoid triggering matching funds in one of two ways. The group can either opt to change its message from one addressing the merits of the candidates to one addressing the merits of an issue, or refrain from speaking altogether. Presenting independent expenditure groups with such a choice makes the matching funds provision particularly burdensome to those groups. And forcing that choice — trigger matching funds, change your message, or do not speak — certainly contravenes "the fundamental rule of protection under the First Amendment, that a speaker has the autonomy to choose the content of his own message."...

Arizona . . . argues that the matching funds provision actually results in more speech by "increas[ing] debate about issues of public concern" in Arizona elections and "promot[ing] the free and open debate that the First Amendment was intended to foster." In the State's view, this promotion of First Amendment ideals offsets any burden the law might impose on some speakers. Not so. Any increase in speech resulting from the Arizona law is of one kind and one kind only — that of publicly financed candidates. The burden imposed on privately financed candidates and independent expenditure groups reduces their speech; "restriction[s] on the amount of money a person or group can spend on political communication during a campaign necessarily reduces the quantity of expression." *Buckley.* Thus, even if the matching funds provision did result in more speech by publicly financed candidates and more speech in general, it would do so at the expense of impermissibly burdening (and thus reducing) the speech of privately financed candidates and independent expenditure groups. This sort of "beggar thy neighbor" approach to free speech — "restrict[ing] the speech of some elements of our society in order to enhance the relative voice of others" — is "wholly foreign to the First Amendment." *Id.*

We have rejected government efforts to increase the speech of some at the expense of others outside the campaign finance context. In Miami Herald Publishing Co. v. Tornillo, 418 U.S. 241, 244, 258 (1974), we held unconstitutional a Florida law that required any newspaper assailing a political candidate's character to allow that candidate to print a reply. We have explained that while the statute in that case "purported to advance free discussion, . . . its effect was to deter newspapers from speaking out in the first instance" because it "penalized the newspaper's own expression." Such a penalty, we concluded, could not survive First Amendment scrutiny. The Arizona law imposes a similar penalty: The State grants funds to publicly financed candidates as a direct result of the speech of privately financed candidates and independent expenditure groups. The argument that this sort of burden promotes free and robust discussion is no more persuasive here than it was in *Tornillo.*

Arizona asserts that no "candidate or independent expenditure group is 'obliged personally to express a message he disagrees with' "or " 'required by the government to subsidize a message he disagrees with.' " True enough. But that does not mean that the matching funds provision does not burden speech. The direct result of the speech of privately financed candidates and independent expenditure groups is a state-provided monetary subsidy to a political rival. That cash subsidy, conferred in response to political speech, penalizes speech to a greater extent and more directly than the Millionaire's Amendment in *Davis*. The fact that this may result in more speech by the other candidates is no more adequate a justification here than it was in *Davis*.

In disagreeing with our conclusion, the dissent relies on cases in which we have upheld government subsidies against First Amendment challenge, and asserts that "[w]e have never, not once, understood a viewpoint-neutral subsidy given to one speaker to constitute a First Amendment burden on another." But none of those cases — not one — involved a subsidy given in direct response to the political speech of another, to allow the recipient to counter that speech. And nothing in the analysis we employed in those cases suggests that the challenged subsidies would have survived First Amendment scrutiny if they were triggered by someone else's political speech. . . .

The State contends that if the matching funds provision truly burdened the speech of privately financed candidates and independent expenditure groups, spending on behalf of privately financed candidates would cluster just below the triggering level, but no such phenomenon has been observed. That should come as no surprise. The hypothesis presupposes a privately funded candidate who would spend his own money just up to the matching funds threshold, when he could have simply taken matching funds in the first place. Furthermore, the Arizona law takes into account all manner of uncoordinated political activity in awarding matching funds. If a privately funded candidate wanted to hover just below the triggering level, he would have to make guesses about how much he will receive in the form of contributions and supportive independent expenditures. He might well guess wrong. In addition, some candidates may be willing to bear the burden of spending above the cap. That a candidate is willing to do so does not make the law any less burdensome. . . .

It is not the amount of funding that the State provides to publicly financed candidates that is constitutionally problematic in this case. It is the manner in which that funding is provided — in direct response to the political speech of privately financed candidates and independent expenditure groups. And the fact that the State's matching mechanism may be more efficient than other alternatives . . . is of no moment; "the First Amendment does not permit the State to sacrifice speech for efficiency." Riley v. National Federation of Blind of N. C., Inc., 487 U.S. 781, 795 (1988). . . .

B. Because the Arizona matching funds provision imposes a substantial burden on the speech of privately financed candidates and independent expenditure groups, "that provision cannot stand unless it is 'justified by a compelling state interest.' ". . . The privately financed candidates and independent expenditure groups contend that the provision works to "level[ ] electoral opportunities" by equalizing candidate "resources and influence." The State and the

Clean Elections Institute counter that the provision "furthers Arizona's interest in preventing corruption and the appearance of corruption.". . .

There is ample support for the argument that the matching funds provision seeks to "level the playing field" in terms of candidate resources. The clearest evidence is of course the very operation of the provision: It ensures that campaign funding is equal, up to three times the initial public funding allotment. The text of the Citizens Clean Elections Act itself confirms this purpose. The statutory provision setting up the matching funds regime is titled "Equal funding of candidates." The Act refers to the funds doled out after the Act's matching mechanism is triggered as "equalizing funds." And the regulations implementing the matching funds provision refer to those funds as "equalizing funds"as well.

Other features of the Arizona law reinforce this understanding of the matching funds provision. If the Citizens Clean Election Commission cannot provide publicly financed candidates with the moneys that the matching funds provision envisions because of a shortage of funds, the statute allows a publicly financed candidate to "accept private contributions to bring the total monies received by the candidate" up to the matching funds amount. Limiting contributions, of course, is the primary means we have upheld to combat corruption. *Buckley.* Indeed the State argues that one of the principal ways that the matching funds provision combats corruption is by eliminating the possibility of any *quid pro quo* between private interests and publicly funded candidates by eliminating contributions to those candidates altogether. But when confronted with a choice between fighting corruption and equalizing speech, the drafters of the matching funds provision chose the latter. That significantly undermines any notion that the "Equal funding of candidates" provision is meant to serve some interest other than an interest in equalizing funds.

We have repeatedly rejected the argument that the government has a compelling state interest in "leveling the playing field" that can justify undue burdens on political speech. *Citizens United.* In *Davis,* we stated that discriminatory contribution limits meant to "level electoral opportunities for candidates of different personal wealth" did not serve "a legitimate government objective," let alone a compelling one. And in *Buckley,* we held that limits on overall campaign expenditures could not be justified by a purported government "interest in equalizing the financial resources of candidates.". . . "Leveling electoral opportunities means making and implementing judgments about which strengths should be permitted to contribute to the outcome of an election" — a dangerous enterprise and one that cannot justify burdening protected speech. The dissent essentially dismisses this concern, but it needs to be taken seriously. . . . [Such] basic intrusion by the government into the debate over who should govern goes to the heart of First Amendment values.

"Leveling the playing field" can sound like a good thing. But in a democracy, campaigning for office is not a game. It is a critically important form of speech. The First Amendment embodies our choice as a Nation that, when it comes to such speech, the guiding principle is freedom — the "unfettered interchange of ideas" — not whatever the State may view as fair. . . .

[Arizona] and the Clean Elections Institute . . . assert that the [law] serves the State's compelling interest in combating corruption and the appearance of corruption. But even if the ultimate objective of the matching funds provision is to combat corruption — and not "level the playing field" — the burdens that the matching funds provision imposes on protected political speech are not justified.

Burdening a candidate's expenditure of his own funds on his own campaign does not further the State's anti-corruption interest. Indeed, we have said that "reliance on personal funds *reduces* the threat of corruption" and that "discouraging [the] use of personal funds[ ] disserves the anticorruption interest." *Davis.* That is because "the use of personal funds reduces the candidate's dependence on outside contributions and thereby counteracts the coercive pressures and attendant risks of abuse" of money in politics. *Buckley.* . . .

We have also held that "independent expenditures . . . do not give rise to corruption or the appearance of corruption." *Citizens United.* The candidate-funding circuit is broken. The separation between candidates and independent expenditure groups negates the possibility that independent expenditures will result in the sort of *quid pro quo* corruption with which our case law is concerned. Including independent expenditures in the matching funds provision cannot be supported by any anti-corruption interest.

We have observed in the past that "[t]he interest in alleviating the corrupting influence of large contributions is served by . . . contribution limitations." Arizona already has some of the most austere contribution limits [and disclosure requirements] in the United States. . . . In the face of such ascetic contribution limits, strict disclosure requirements, and the general availability of public funding, it is hard to imagine what marginal corruption deterrence could be generated by the matching funds provision. . . .

III. We do not today call into question the wisdom of public financing as a means of funding political candidacy. That is not our business. But determining whether laws governing campaign finance violate the First Amendment is very much our business. . . . [The] goal of creating a viable public financing scheme can only be pursued in a manner consistent with the First Amendment. The dissent criticizes the Court for standing in the way of what the people of Arizona want. But the whole point of the First Amendment is to protect speakers against unjustified government restrictions on speech, even when those restrictions reflect the will of the majority. When it comes to protected speech, the speaker is sovereign.

Arizona's program gives money to a candidate in direct response to the campaign speech of an opposing candidate or an independent group. It does this when the opposing candidate has chosen not to accept public financing, and has engaged in political speech above a level set by the State. The professed purpose of the state law is to cause a sufficient number of candidates to sign up for public financing, which subjects them to the various restrictions on speech that go along with that program. This goes too far; Arizona's matching funds provision substantially burdens the speech of privately financed candidates and independent expenditure groups without serving a compelling state interest. . . . Laws like Arizona's matching funds provision that inhibit robust and wide-open political debate without sufficient justification cannot stand.

The judgment of the Court of Appeals for the Ninth Circuit is reversed. . . .

JUSTICE KAGAN, with whom JUSTICE GINSBURG, JUSTICE BREYER, and JUSTICE SOTOMAYOR join, dissenting.

. . . The First Amendment's core purpose is to foster a healthy, vibrant political system full of robust discussion and debate. Nothing in Arizona's anticorruption statute . . . violates this constitutional protection. To the contrary, the Act promotes the values underlying both the First Amendment and our entire Constitution by enhancing the "opportunity for free political discussion to the end that government may be responsive to the will of the people." I therefore respectfully dissent.

Campaign finance reform over the last century has focused on one key question: how to prevent massive pools of private money from corrupting our political system. If an officeholder owes his election to wealthy contributors, he may act for their benefit alone, rather than on behalf of all the people. . . . And even if these contributions are not converted into corrupt bargains, they still may weaken confidence in our political system because the public perceives "the opportunities for abuse[s]." To prevent both corruption and the appearance of corruption — and so to protect our democratic system of governance — citizens have implemented reforms designed to curb the power of special interests. Among these measures, public financing of elections has emerged as a potentially potent mechanism to preserve elected officials' independence. . . . The idea was — and remains — straightforward. Candidates who rely on public, rather than private, moneys are "beholden [to] no person and, if elected, should feel no post-election obligation toward any contributor." By supplanting private cash in elections, public financing eliminates the source of political corruption. . . .

For this reason, public financing systems today dot the national landscape. Almost one-third of the States have adopted some form of public financing, and so too has the Federal Government for presidential elections. . . . But this model, which distributes a lump-sum grant at the beginning of an election cycle, has a significant weakness: It lacks a mechanism for setting the subsidy at a level that will give candidates sufficient incentive to participate, while also conserving public resources. Public financing can achieve its goals only if a meaningful number of candidates receive the state subsidy, rather than raise private funds. But a public funding program must be voluntary to pass constitutional muster, because of its restrictions on contributions and expenditures. And candidates will choose to sign up only if the subsidy provided enables them to run competitive races. If the grant is pegged too low, it puts the participating candidate at a disadvantage: Because he has agreed to spend no more than the amount of the subsidy, he will lack the means to respond if his privately funded opponent spends over that threshold. So when lump-sum grants do not keep up with campaign expenditures, more and more candidates will choose not to participate. But if the subsidy is set too high, it may impose an unsustainable burden on the public fisc. . . .

The difficulty, then, is in finding the Goldilocks solution — not too large, not too small, but just right. And this in a world of countless variables — where the amount of money needed to run a viable campaign against a privately funded candidate depends on, among other things, the district, the office, and the election cycle. . . . In short, the dynamic nature of our electoral system makes *ex ante* predictions about campaign expenditures almost impossible. And that creates a chronic problem for lump-sum public financing programs, because inaccurate estimates produce subsidies that either dissuade candidates from participating or waste taxpayer money. And so States have made adjustments to the lump-sum scheme that we approved in *Buckley*, in attempts to more effectively reduce corruption. . . .

The hallmark of Arizona's program is its inventive approach to the challenge that bedevils all public financing schemes: fixing the amount of the subsidy. For each electoral contest, the system calibrates the size of the grant automatically to provide sufficient — but no more than sufficient — funds to induce voluntary participation. In effect, the program's designers found the Goldilocks solution, which produces the "just right" grant to ensure that a participant in the system has the funds needed to run a competitive race. . . . Arizona's . . . arrangement, like the lump-sum model, makes use of a pre-set amount to provide financial support to participants. . . . And they can in no circumstances receive more than three times that amount . . . ; after that, their privately funded competitors hold a marked advantage. But the Arizona system improves on the lump-sum model in a crucial respect. By tying public funding to private spending, the State can afford to set a more generous upper limit — because it knows that in each campaign it will only have to disburse what is necessary to keep a participating candidate reasonably competitive. Arizona can therefore assure candidates that, if they accept public funds, they will have the resources to run a viable race against those who rely on private money. And at the same time, Arizona avoids wasting taxpayers' dollars. In this way, the Clean Elections Act creates an effective and sustainable public financing system. . . .

The majority contends that the matching funds provision "substantially burdens protected political speech" and does not "serv[e] a compelling state interest." But the Court is wrong on both counts.

Arizona's statute . . . subsidizes and so produces *more* political speech. . . . Arizona's . . . law "impose[s] no ceiling on [speech] and do[es] not prevent anyone from speaking." The statute does not tell candidates or their supporters how much money they can spend to convey their message, when they can spend it, or what they can spend it on. . . . What the law does — all the law does — is fund more speech.

And under the First Amendment, that makes all the difference. In case after case, year upon year, we have distinguished between speech restrictions and

speech subsidies. . . . Government subsidies of speech, designed "to stimu-
late . . . expression[,] . . . [are] consistent with the First Amendment," so long
as they do not discriminate on the basis of viewpoint. Board of Regents of Univ.
of Wis. System v. Southworth, 529 U.S. 217, 234 (2000). That is because
subsidies, by definition and contra the majority, do not restrict any speech.

No one can claim that Arizona's law discriminates against particular ideas,
and so violates the First Amendment's sole limitation on speech subsidies. The
State throws open the doors of its public financing program to all candidates who
meet minimal eligibility requirements and agree not to raise private funds.
Republicans and Democrats, conservatives and liberals may participate; so too,
the law applies equally to independent expenditure groups across the political
spectrum. Arizona disburses funds based not on a candidate's (or supporter's)
ideas, but on the candidate's decision to sign up for public funding. So . . .
Arizona's subsidy statute should easily survive First Amendment scrutiny.[2] . . .

[What] petitioners demand is essentially a right to quash others' speech
through the prohibition of a (universally available) subsidy program. Petitioners
are able to convey their ideas without public financing — and they would prefer
the field to themselves, so that they can speak free from response. To attain that
goal, they ask this Court to prevent Arizona from funding electoral speech —
even though that assistance is offered to every state candidate, on the same
(entirely unobjectionable) basis. And this Court gladly obliges.

If an ordinary citizen, without the hindrance of a law degree, thought this
result an upending of First Amendment values, he would be correct. That
Amendment protects no person's, nor any candidate's, "right to be free from
vigorous debate.". . . So to invalidate a statute that restricts no one's speech and
discriminates against no idea — that only provides more voices, wider discussion, and greater competition in elections — is to undermine, rather than to
enforce, the First Amendment. . . .

The majority . . . is wrong to see a substantial burden on expression. . . .
[The] very notion that additional speech constitutes a "burden" is odd and
unsettling. Here is a simple fact: Arizona imposes nothing remotely resembling a
coercive penalty on privately funded candidates. The State does not jail them,
fine them, or subject them to any kind of lesser disability. . . . The only "burden"
in this case comes from the grant of a subsidy to another person, and the
opportunity that subsidy allows for responsive speech. . . . We have never, not
once, understood a viewpoint-neutral subsidy given to one speaker to constitute
a First Amendment burden on another. . . . Yet in this case, the majority says
that the prospect of more speech — responsive speech, competitive speech, the
kind of speech that drives public debate — counts as a constitutional injury. . . .

2. The majority claims that none of our subsidy cases involved the funding of "respons[ive]"
expression. But the majority does not explain why this distinction, created to fit the facts of this case,
should matter so long as the government is not discriminating on the basis of viewpoint. Indeed, the
difference the majority highlights should cut in the opposite direction, because facilitating responsive
speech fosters "uninhibited, robust, and wide-open" public debate.

But put to one side this most fundamental objection to the majority's argument; even then, has the majority shown that the burden resulting from the Arizona statute is "substantial"? I will not quarrel with the majority's assertion that responsive speech by one candidate may make another candidate's speech less effective; that, after all, is the whole idea of the First Amendment, and a *benefit* of having more responsive speech. See Abrams v. United States, 250 U.S. 616, 630 (1919) (Holmes., J., dissenting) ("[T]he best test of truth is the power of the thought to get itself accepted in the competition of the market"). And I will assume that the operation of this statute may on occasion deter a privately funded candidate from spending money, and conveying ideas by that means. My guess is that this does not happen often: Most political candidates, I suspect, have enough faith in the power of their ideas to prefer speech on both sides of an issue to speech on neither. But I will take on faith that the matching funds provision may lead one or another privately funded candidate to stop spending at one or another moment in an election. Still, does that effect count as a severe burden on expression? By the measure of our prior decisions — which have upheld campaign reforms with an equal or greater impact on speech — the answer is no.

Number one: *Any* system of public financing, including the lump-sum model upheld in *Buckley*, imposes a similar burden on privately funded candidates. . . . Indeed, privately funded candidates may well find the lump-sum system *more* burdensome than Arizona's (assuming the lump is big enough). Pretend you are financing your campaign through private donations. Would you prefer that your opponent receive a guaranteed, upfront payment of $150,000, or that he receive only $50,000, with the *possibility* — a possibility that you mostly get to control — of collecting another $100,000 somewhere down the road? . . .

Number two: Our decisions about disclosure and disclaimer requirements show the Court is wrong. Starting in *Buckley* and continuing through last Term, the Court has repeatedly declined to view these requirements as a substantial First Amendment burden, even though they discourage some campaign speech. . . . Like a disclosure rule, the matching funds provision may occasionally deter, but "impose[s] no ceiling on electoral expression. . . . The majority strikes down the matching funds provision because . . . it may deter a person from spending money in an election. But this Court has acknowledged time and again that disclosure obligations have the selfsame effect. If that consequence does not trigger the most stringent judicial review in the one case, it should not do so in the other.

Number three: Any burden that the Arizona law imposes does not exceed the burden associated with contribution limits, which we have also repeatedly upheld. Contribution limits, we have stated, "impose *direct quantity restrictions* on political communication and association," thus " 'significant[ly] interfer[ing]' " with First Amendment interests. Yet we have never subjected these restrictions to the most stringent review. . . .

Under the First Amendment, the similarity between *Davis* and this case matters far less than the differences. Here is the similarity: In both cases, one candidate's campaign expenditure triggered . . . something. Now here are the differences: In *Davis*, the candidate's expenditure triggered a discriminatory speech restriction, which Congress could not otherwise have imposed consistent with the First Amendment; by contrast, in this case, the candidate's expenditure triggers a non-discriminatory speech subsidy. . . . [T]hat difference makes a difference — indeed, it makes *all* the difference. As I have indicated before, two great fault lines run through our First Amendment doctrine: one, between speech restrictions and speech subsidies, and the other, between discriminatory and neutral government action. The Millionaire's Amendment fell on the disfavored side of both divides: To reiterate, it imposed a discriminatory speech restriction. The Arizona Clean Elections Act lands on the opposite side of both: It grants a non-discriminatory speech subsidy. So to say that *Davis* "largely controls" this case is to decline to take our First Amendment doctrine seriously. . . .

[The Court claims] the burden on speech is "greater in this case than in *Davis*." But for reasons already stated, that is not so. The burden on speech in *Davis* — the penalty that campaign spending triggered — *was* the discriminatory contribution restriction, which Congress could not otherwise have imposed. By contrast, the thing triggered here is a non-discriminatory subsidy, of a kind this Court has approved for almost four decades. . . .

For all these reasons, the Court errs in holding that the government action in this case substantially burdens speech and so requires the State to offer a compelling interest. But in any event, Arizona has come forward with just such an interest, explaining that the Clean Elections Act attacks corruption and the appearance of corruption in the State's political system. . . .

Preventing corruption or the appearance of corruption is a compelling government interest. . . . Public financing of elections serves this interest. . . . When private contributions fuel the political system, candidates may make corrupt bargains to gain the money needed to win election. And voters, seeing the dependence of candidates on large contributors (or on bundlers of smaller contributions), may lose faith that their representatives will serve the public's interest. . . . Public financing addresses these dangers by minimizing the importance of private donors in elections. . . .

This compelling interest . . . justifies the matching funds provision at issue because it is a critical facet of Arizona's public financing program. The provision is no more than a disbursement mechanism; but it is also the thing that makes the whole Clean Elections Act work. As described earlier, public financing has an Achilles heel — the difficulty of setting the subsidy at the right amount. Too small, and the grant will not attract candidates to the program; and with no participating candidates, the program can hardly decrease corruption. Too large, and the system becomes unsustainable, or at the least an unnecessary drain on public resources. But finding the sweet-spot is near impossible because of variation, across districts and over time, in the political system. Enter the matching funds provision, which takes an ordinary lump-sum amount, divides it into thirds, and disburses the last two of these (to the extent necessary) via a self-calibrating mechanism. That provision is just a fine-tuning of the lump-sum program approved in *Buckley* — a fine-tuning, it bears repeating, that prevents no one from speaking and discriminates against no message. But that fine-tuning can make the difference between a wholly ineffectual program and one that removes corruption from the political system. If public financing furthers a compelling interest — and according to this Court, it does — then so too does the disbursement formula that Arizona uses to make public financing effective. The one conclusion follows directly from the other. . . .

This case arose because Arizonans wanted their government to work on behalf of all the State's people. On the heels of a political scandal involving the near-routine purchase of legislators' votes, Arizonans passed a law de-signed to sever political candidates' dependence on large contributors. They wished . . . to stop corrupt dealing. . . . The legislation that Arizona's voters enacted . . . put into effect a public financing system that attracted large numbers of candidates at a sustainable cost to the State's taxpayers. The system discriminated against no ideas and prevented no speech. Indeed, by increasing electoral competition and enabling a wide range of candidates to express their views, the system "further[ed] . . . First Amendment values." Less corruption, more speech. . . . The people of Arizona might have expected a decent respect for those objectives.

Today, they do not get it. . . . No fundamental principle of our Constitution backs the Court's ruling; to the contrary, it is the law struck down today that fostered both the vigorous competition of ideas and its ultimate object — a government responsive to the will of the people. Arizonans deserve better. . . . Truly, democracy is not a game. I respectfully dissent.

2. Government Regulation of Elections

Page 1044: Insert after note 3:

4. The Implications of *Caperton*.   After *White* voided Minnesota's "an-nounce clause" the case was remanded for consideration of the validity of Minnesota's rules forbidding judicial candidates from political activities or soliciting campaign contributions or "publicly stated support." The political activities ban prohibited judicial candidates from identifying themselves as part of a political organization; attending "political gatherings"; or seeking, accepting, or using endorsements from a "political organization." In Republican Party v. White ("White II"), 416 F.3d 738 (8th Cir. 2005), the Eighth Circuit applied strict scrutiny and struck down both rules. In Weaver v. Bonner, 309 F.3d 1312 (11th Cir. 2002), the court of appeals voided a Georgia ban on the solicitation of campaign contributions by judicial candidates, as well as a Georgia prohibition of negligent false statements and misleading or deceptive true statements made by judicial candidates. Caperton v. A.T. Massey Coal Company, 129 S. Ct. 2252 (2009), held that judicial recusal is constitutionally required when a judge seeking election has been the beneficiary of "significant and disproportionate" campaign expenditures or contributions by a person or entity with a personal stake in a case that is pending or imminent before the successfully elected judge. Does *Caperton* suggest that prohibitions upon the solicitation of campaign funds or public support by judicial candidates are valid? If not, may judicial candidates solicit funds at the cost of recusal in any case in which a "disproportionate" supporter has a personal interest?

Page 1050: Insert new note 3:

3. Legislative Recusal for Conflicts of Interest. In Nevada Commission on Ethics v. Carrigan, 2011 U.S. Lexis 4379, the Supreme Court unanimously upheld the validity of a Nevada law requiring a legislator to abstain from voting upon or advocating in legislative debate the passage or defeat of any measure in which the legislator has a personal interest or has a commitment to the interests of others. The Court reasoned that a legislator's vote "is not personal to the legislator but belongs to the people" Unlike flag-burning, for example, "the act of voting symbolizes nothing. It *discloses*, to be sure, that the legislator wishes (for whatever reason) that the proposition on the floor be adopted, just as a physical assault discloses that the attacker dislikes the victim. But neither the one nor the other is an act of communication. . . . It is one thing to say that an inherently expressive act remains so despite its having governmental effect, but it is altogether another thing to say that a governmental act becomes expressive simply because the governmental actor wishes it to be so. We have never said the latter is true."

Chapter 11
State Action and the Power to Enforce Constitutional Rights

B. Congressional Power to Enforce Constitutional Rights

2. The Scope of Enforcement Power: Remedial or Substantive?

Page 1191: Insert after note 3:

4. The Fifteenth Amendment and the Voting Rights Act. The Fifteenth Amendment ensures that neither the federal government nor the states may deny or abridge the vote on account of "race, color or previous condition of servitude." Section 2 of the Fifteenth Amendment provides that "Congress shall have power to enforce this article by appropriate legislation." In order to address persistent practices used by states to deny blacks the right to vote, Congress enacted the Voting Rights Act of 1965. Section 2 of the Act forbids any "standard, practice, or procedure" that "results in a denial or abridgment of the right of any citizen of the United States to vote on account of race or color." Section 5 of the Act, codified at 42 U.S.C. § 1973c(a), prohibits "covered jurisdictions" from making any changes in their electoral laws without obtaining permission to do so from the Attorney General. "Covered jurisdictions" were initially defined to include only those states or political subdivisions that in 1964 used certain voter eligibility tests and had less than 50% voter registration or turnout in the 1964 Presidential election. As originally enacted, the Act would expire in 1970, but its life was extended to 1975, then to 1982, then to 2007, and finally to 2032. The validity of the original Act was upheld in South Carolina v. Katzenbach, 383 U.S. 301 (1966), in which the Court concluded that the historical experience of deliberate use of facially race-neutral devices to exclude blacks from voting, coupled with the fact that § 5 only applied to jurisdictions selected by criteria calculated to identify the most flagrant racially based denials of the vote, justified what would otherwise be an extraordinary intervention in the autonomy of states to make their own laws. Each of the subsequent extensions was also upheld, on the ground that the factual circumstances justified the extension. Georgia v. United States, 411 U.S. 526 (1973); City of Rome v.

United States, 446 U.S. 156 (1980); Lopez v. Monterey County, 525 U.S. 266 (1999). The 1970 extension moved the date for assessing the criteria for determining covered jurisdictions to 1968 and the 1975 extension moved that date to 1972. Significantly, however, neither the 1982 extension (to 2007) nor the 2006 extension (to 2032) advanced the date beyond 1972. Because Congress recognized that its formula for defining covered jurisdictions might include jurisdictions that had never engaged in illegal racially discriminatory voting practices, each permutation of the Act provided an opportunity for covered jurisdictions to "bail out" of § 5 by persuading a special court that it had passed a series of stringent statutory tests designed to ensure that the covered jurisdiction was not guilty of racial discrimination in voting.

A Texas municipal utility district with an elected governing board, a covered jurisdiction, contended that it was entitled to bail out of § 5 and, if not, that the latest extension of § 5 to 2032 was unconstitutional. A federal district court ruled that the utility district was not entitled to seek to bail out because it did not register its own voters and concluded that the extension of § 5 was constitutionally valid because it was a prophylactic remedy that was congruent with and proportional to the constitutional violation of racial discrimination in voting. On appeal, in Northwest Austin Municipal Utility District No. 1 v. Holder, 129 S. Ct. 2504 (2009), the Court, 8-1, construed the Act to permit the utility district to seek bail out and, applying the principle of constitutional avoidance, did not reach the constitutional question. Even so, the Court devoted considerable dicta to what it described as the "serious constitutional questions" raised by § 5's pre-clearance requirement.

The historic accomplishments of the Voting Rights Act are undeniable. When it was first passed, unconstitutional discrimination was rampant. . . . Things have changed in the South. Voter turnout and registration rates now approach parity. Blatantly discriminatory evasions of federal decrees are rare. And minority candidates hold office at unprecedented levels. . . . It may be that these improvements are insufficient and that conditions continue to warrant preclearance under the Act. But the Act imposes current burdens and must be justified by current needs. The Act also differentiates between the States, despite our historic tradition that all the States enjoy "equal sovereignty." [A] departure from the fundamental principle of equal sovereignty requires a showing that a statute's disparate geographic coverage is sufficiently related to the problem that it targets. . . . These federalism concerns are underscored by the argument that the preclearance requirements in one State would be unconstitutional in another, [because] "considerations of race that would doom a redistricting plan under the Fourteenth Amendment or § 2 [of the Act] seem to be what save it under § 5.". . . The evil that § 5 is meant to address may no longer be concentrated in the jurisdictions singled out for preclearance. The statute's coverage formula is based on data that is now more than 35 years old, and there is considerable evidence that it fails to account for current political conditions. For example, the racial gap in voter registration and turnout is lower in the States originally covered by § 5 than it is nationwide. . . .

The parties do not agree on the standard to apply in deciding whether, in light of the foregoing concerns, Congress exceeded its Fifteenth Amendment enforcement power in extending the preclearance requirements. The district argues that "[t]here must be a congruence and proportionality between the injury to be prevented or remedied and the means adopted to that end" [City of Boerne v. Flores]; the Federal Government asserts that it is enough that the legislation be a "'rational means' to effectuate the constitutional prohibition." [South Carolina v. Katzenbach.] That question has been extensively briefed in this case, but we need not resolve it. The Act's preclearance requirements and its coverage formula raise serious constitutional questions under either test.

In assessing those questions, we are keenly mindful of our institutional role. . . . The Fifteenth Amendment empowers "Congress," not the Court, to determine in the first instance what legislation is needed to enforce it. [While we] will not shrink from our duty "as the bulwar[k] of a limited constitution against legislative encroachments," The Federalist No. 78, . . . "[i]t is a well-established principle governing the prudent exercise of this Court's jurisdiction that normally the Court will not decide a constitutional question if there is some other ground upon which to dispose of the case."

Justice Thomas was the sole justice to reach the constitutional issue. After noting that the majority "quite properly alerts Congress that § 5 tests the outer boundaries of its Fifteenth Amendment enforcement authority and may not be constitutional," he argued that because the statutory construction adopted by the Court failed to provide the relief sought by the utility district it was proper to decide the constitutional claim. On that point, Justice Thomas noted that § 5 was enacted "to prevent covered jurisdictions from circumventing the direct prohibitions" of § 2. Because "rebellion against the enfranchisement of blacks in the wake of ratification of the Fifteenth Amendment" was violent, determined and, at times, subtle, "by 1965, Congress had every reason to conclude that States with a history of disenfranchising voters based on race would continue to do all they could to evade the constitutional ban on voting discrimination. . . . It was against this backdrop of 'historical experience' that § 5 was first enacted and upheld against a constitutional challenge." Yet, in

upholding § 5 in *Katzenbach*, the Court . . . noted that [it] was an "uncommon exercise of congressional power" that would not have been "appropriate" absent the "exceptional conditions" and "unique circumstances" present in the targeted jurisdictions at that particular time. [The Court] refused to simply accept Congress'[s] representation that the extreme measure was necessary to enforce the Fifteenth Amendment; rather, it closely reviewed the record compiled by Congress to ensure that § 5 was "appropriate" antievasion legislation. In so doing, the Court highlighted evidence showing that black voter registration rates ran approximately 50 percentage points lower than white voter registration in several States [and] observed that voter turnout levels in covered jurisdictions had been at least 12% below the national average in the 1964 Presidential election. The statistical evidence confirmed Congress'[s] judgment that "the extraordinary stratagem of contriving new rules of various kinds for the sole purpose of perpetuating voting discrimination in the face of adverse federal court decrees" was working and could not be defeated through case-by-case enforcement of the Fifteenth Amendment.

This record also clearly supported Congress'[s] predictive judgment that such "States might try similar maneuvers in the future in order to evade the remedies for voting discrimination contained in the Act itself."

Because § 5's pre-clearance requirement "sweeps more broadly than the substantive command of the Fifteenth Amendment" and is a "'substantial departure . . . from ordinary concepts of our federal system'" close scrutiny is required. Section 5's "'encroachment on state sovereignty is significant and undeniable.'" It "'is especially troubling because it destroys local control of the means of self-government, one of the central values of our polity.'" Thus, "the constitutionality of § 5 has always depended on the proven existence of intentional discrimination so extensive that elimination of it through case-by-case enforcement would be impossible. . . . As a result, for § 5 to withstand renewed constitutional scrutiny, there must be a demonstrated connection between the 'remedial measures' chosen and the 'evil presented' in the record made by Congress when it renewed the Act." But this connection had not been demonstrated:

> The extensive pattern of discrimination that led the Court to previously uphold § 5 as enforcing the Fifteenth Amendment no longer exists. Covered jurisdictions are not now engaged in a systematic campaign to deny black citizens access to the ballot through intimidation and violence. . . . The lack of sufficient evidence that the covered jurisdictions currently engage in the type of discrimination that underlay the enactment of § 5 undermines any basis for retaining it. Punishment for long past sins is not a legitimate basis for imposing a forward-looking preventative measure that has already served its purpose. . . . [T]here is no evidence that public officials stand ready, if given the chance, to again engage in concerted acts of violence, terror, and subterfuge in order to keep minorities from voting. Without such evidence, the charge [that covered jurisdictions are eager to return to such methods] can only be premised on outdated assumptions about racial attitudes in the covered jurisdictions. Admitting that a prophylactic law as broad as § 5 is no longer constitutionally justified based on current evidence of discrimination is not a sign of defeat. It is an acknowledgment of victory. The current statistical evidence confirms that the emergency that prompted the enactment of § 5 has long since passed.

Justice Thomas noted that in covered jurisdictions there was no longer any significant disparity between the percentages of blacks and whites registered to vote, that voter turnout among black voters was often higher than among whites, and that both voter registration and turnout rates in covered jurisdictions were the same as the nation as a whole.

Even though the Court avoided deciding the constitutional validity of the latest extension of § 5, *Northwest Austin Municipal Utility District* suggests that the extension is of doubtful validity. This raises the question of what alterations, if any, Congress could make to § 5 in order to preserve its validity. Would moving the date for assessing the coverage criteria forward from 1972 to 2009 be adequate? Note that if Congress were to do so, most of the covered jurisdictions would no longer be covered because they no longer engage in either overt or covert racial discrimination in voting. Does this suggest that the Voting Rights Act has succeeded and that, as a result, there is no longer any warrant for draconian intervention into local governance autonomy? See, e.g., Samuel Issacharoff, Is Section 5 of the Voting Rights Act a Victim of Its Own Success?, 104 Colum. L. Rev. 1710 (2004).

Chapter 12
The Right to Keep and Bear Arms

Page 1214: Insert at the end of note 3:

In McDonald v. City of Chicago, 130 S. Ct. 3020 (2010), the Supreme Court, by a margin of 5 to 4, ruled that the Second Amendment right to possession of a firearm for purposes of self-defense was "fundamental to *our* scheme of ordered liberty" and "deeply rooted in this Nation's history and tradition." Thus, the Fourteenth Amendment made the Second Amendment right applicable to the states. But the justices could not agree on the rationale. Justice Alito, joined by Chief Justice Roberts and Justices Scalia and Kennedy, concluded that the Second Amendment right is one of the fundamental rights that are made applicable to the states via the due process guarantee.

Self-defense is a basic right [and] individual self-defense is the *"central component"* of the Second Amendment right. [By] 1765 Blackstone was able to assert that the right to keep and bear arms was "one of the fundamental rights of Englishmen," [and his] assessment was shared by the American colonists. King George III's attempt to disarm the colonists in the 1760s and 1770s "provoked polemical reactions by Americans invoking their rights as Englishmen to keep arms." . . . The right to keep and bear arms was considered no less fundamental by those who drafted and ratified the Bill of Rights. . . . This understanding persisted in the years immediately following the ratification of the Bill of Rights. By the 1850s . . . the right to keep and bear arms was highly valued for purposes of self-defense. Abolitionist authors wrote in support of the right. And when attempts were made to disarm "Free-Soilers" in "Bloody Kansas," Senator Charles Sumner, who later played a leading role in the adoption of the Fourteenth Amendment, proclaimed that "[n]ever was [the rifle] more needed in just self-defense than now in Kansas." Indeed, the 1856 Republican Party Platform protested that in Kansas the constitutional rights of the people had been "fraudulently and violently taken from them" and the "right of the people to keep and bear arms" had been "infringed." . . . Abolitionists and Republicans were not alone in believing that the right to keep and bear arms was a fundamental right. The 1864 Democratic Party Platform complained that the confiscation of firearms by Union troops occupying parts of the South constituted "[a] denial of the right of the people to bear arms in their defense."

After the Civil War, [in reaction to] systematic efforts [by southern states to disarm freed blacks, Congress enacted] § 14 of the Freedmen's Bureau Act of 1866, which provided that "the . . . *constitutional right to bear arms* shall be secured to

159

and enjoyed by all the citizens . . . without respect to race or color, or previous condition of slavery." . . . The Civil Rights Act of 1866 . . . similarly sought to protect the right of all citizens to keep and bear arms. . . . Congress, however, ultimately deemed these legislative remedies insufficient [and concluded] that a constitutional amendment was necessary to provide full protection for the rights of blacks. Today, it is generally accepted that the Fourteenth Amendment was understood to provide a constitutional basis for protecting the rights set out in the Civil Rights Act of 1866. . . . Evidence from the period immediately following the ratification of the Fourteenth Amendment only confirms that the right to keep and bear arms was considered fundamental. . . . [In] debating the Civil Rights Act of 1871, Congress routinely referred to the right to keep and bear arms and decried the continued disarmament of blacks in the South. Finally, legal commentators from the period emphasized the fundamental nature of the right.

The right to keep and bear arms was also widely protected by state constitutions at the time when the Fourteenth Amendment was ratified. [It] is clear that the Framers and ratifiers of the Fourteenth Amendment counted the right to keep and bear arms among those fundamental rights necessary to our system of ordered liberty. . . .

Under our precedents, if a Bill of Rights guarantee is fundamental from an American perspective, then . . . that guarantee is fully binding on the States and thus *limits* (but by no means eliminates) their ability to devise solutions to social problems that suit local needs and values. . . . We therefore hold that the Due Process Clause of the Fourteenth Amendment incorporates the Second Amendment right recognized in *Heller*.

Page 1214: Insert at the end of note 4:

Justice Thomas concurred in the judgment in *McDonald*, but contended that the Second Amendment right was a privilege of national citizenship encompassed in the Fourteenth Amendment's command that no state may "abridge the privileges or immunities of citizens of the United States."

At the time of Reconstruction, the terms "privileges" and "immunities" had an established meaning as synonyms for "rights." The two words, standing alone or paired together, were used interchangeably with the words "rights," "liberties," and "freedoms," and had been since the time of Blackstone. . . . By the time of Reconstruction, it had long been established that both the States and the Federal Government existed to preserve their citizens' inalienable rights, and that these rights were considered "privileges" or "immunities" of citizenship. . . . As English subjects, the colonists considered themselves to be vested with the same fundamental rights as other Englishmen. They consistently claimed the rights of English citizenship in their founding documents, repeatedly referring to these rights as "privileges" and "immunities." . . . Consistent with their English heritage, the founding generation generally did not consider many of the rights identified in [the Bill of Rights] as new entitlements, but as inalienable rights of all men, given legal effect by their codification in the Constitution's text. . . . Section 1 [of the Fourteenth Amendment] protects the rights of citizens "of the United States" specifically. The evidence overwhelmingly demonstrates that the privileges and immunities of such citizens included individual rights enumerated in the Constitution, including the right to keep and bear arms. . . . Evidence from the political branches in the years leading to the Fourteenth Amendment's adoption demonstrates broad public understanding that the privileges and immunities of United States citizenship included rights set forth in the Constitution. . . . Records from the 39th Congress further support this understanding. . . . Before considering that record here, it is important to clarify its relevance. When interpreting constitutional text, the goal is to discern the most likely public understanding of a particular provision at the time it was adopted. Statements by legislators can assist in this process to the extent they demonstrate the manner in which the public used or understood a particular word or phrase. They can further assist to the extent there is evidence that these statements were disseminated to the public. In other words, this evidence is useful not because it demonstrates what the draftsmen of the text may have been thinking, but only insofar as it illuminates what the public understood the words chosen by the draftsmen to mean.

Representative John Bingham, the principal draftsman of § 1 [of the Fourteenth Amendment], delivered a speech on the floor of the House in February 1866 introducing his first draft of the provision. Bingham began by discussing *Barron* and its holding that the Bill of Rights did not apply to the States. . . . Bingham emphasized that § 1 was designed "to arm the Congress of the United States . . . with the power to enforce the bill of rights as it stands in the Constitution to-day." . . . Bingham's speech was printed in pamphlet form and broadly distributed in 1866 under the title, "One Country, One Constitution, and One People," and the subtitle, "In Support of the Proposed Amendment to Enforce the Bill of Rights." . . .

Bingham . . . amended his draft of § 1 to include the text of the Privileges or Immunities Clause that was ultimately adopted. Senator Jacob Howard introduced the new draft on the floor of the Senate, [explaining] that the Constitution recognized "a mass of privileges, immunities, and rights, some of them secured by . . . the first eight amendments of the Constitution," and that "there is no power given in the Constitution to enforce and to carry out any of these guarantees" against the States. Howard then stated that "the great object" of § 1 was to "restrain the power of the States and compel them at all times to respect these great fundamental guarantees." Section 1, he indicated, imposed "a general prohibition upon all the States, as such, from abridging the privileges and immunities of the citizens of the United States." In describing these rights, Howard explained that they included . . . "*the personal rights guaranteed by the first eight amendments of the Constitution*; such as freedom of speech . . . and *the right to keep and bear arms.*" News of Howard's speech was carried in major newspapers across the country, including the New York Herald, which was the best-selling paper in the Nation at that time. . . . As a whole, these well-circulated speeches indicate that § 1 was understood to enforce constitutionally declared rights against the States, and they provide no suggestion that any language in the section other than the Privileges or Immunities Clause would accomplish that task. When read against this backdrop, the civil rights legislation adopted by the 39th Congress in 1866 further supports this view.

Interpretations of the Fourteenth Amendment in the period immediately following its ratification help to establish the public understanding of the text at the time of its adoption. . . . [For example, during] an 1871 debate on a bill to enforce the Fourteenth Amendment, Representative Henry Dawes listed the Constitution's first eight Amendments, including "the right to keep and bear arms," before explaining that after the Civil War, the country "gave the most grand of all these rights, privileges, and immunities, by one single amendment to the Constitution, to four millions of American citizens" who formerly were slaves. . . .

This evidence plainly shows that the ratifying public understood the Privileges or Immunities Clause to protect constitutionally enumerated rights, including the right to keep and bear arms. As the Court demonstrates, there can be no doubt that § 1 was understood to enforce the Second Amendment against the States. In my view, this is because the right to keep and bear arms was understood to be a privilege of American citizenship guaranteed by the Privileges or Immunities Clause.

Made in the USA
Lexington, KY
29 December 2011